Uncle Sam My Sailor and me

Experiences on the Lighter Side of a Long Military Life

Faye and Vern Nordman

BLUE FORGE PRESS

Port Orchard ✱ Washington

Uncle Sam, My Sailor, and Me
Copyright 2019
by Faye and Vern Nordman

First eBook Edition November 2019
Second eBook Edition August 2024
First Print Edition November 2019
Second Print Edition Auguest 2024

ISBN 979-8-89439-016-1

For information about film, reprint or other subsidiary rights, contact: blueforgegroup@gmail.com

This is a work of fiction. Names, characters, locations, and all other story elements are the product of the authors' imaginations and are used fictitiously. Any resemblance to actual persons, living or dead, or other elements in real life, is purely coincidental.

Blue Forge Press is the print division of the volunteer-run, federal 501(c)3 nonprofit, Blue Legacy (EIN 83-4307421), founded in 1989 and dedicated to supporting artisans marginalized due to race, age, disability, economics or other factors. We strive to empower storytellers from all walks of life with our four divisions: Blue Forge Press, Blue Forge Films, Blue Forge Gaming, and Blue Forge Sound. Find out more at www.BlueForgeGroup.org

Blue Forge Press
7419 Ebbert Drive Southeast
Port Orchard, Washington 98367
blueforgepress@gmail.com
360-550-2071 ph.txt

Dedication

To Susan, with many thanks.

Greetings

When my daughter was writing her first book, she joined a group of fledgling scribes who were also writing books. They met every other week and shared manuscripts, or parts of manuscripts, then discussed and critiqued each other's work. That was very nice; it kept them focused and on their toes, but the interesting thing to me was, that in such a small group of writers there were so many different subjects. My daughter was writing science fiction, another member was working on a novel with a religious theme, there was a mystery and a western, while others were writing about their 'experiences'.

So, the thought seeped into my tiny little brain that they were just kids. What experiences could they have had?

I have had 'Experiences.'

Maybe not earth-shattering experiences or ones that make the headlines, but definitely 'Experiences.'

I'm eighty-plus years old, not as old as some, but better than average. I was a 'Navy Brat' (the son of a career Navy man) and then I served for over thirty-five years in Uncle Sam's Military (Marines and Air Force) not as long as some, but longer than most. I have lived in twelve states and seven countries on three continents. Not bad. I was married to a wonderful lady for over fifty years and along the way we acquired five children, nine grandchildren and, so far, three great-grandchildren. I was a little kid in one war (World War II), a high schooler in another (Korea), served in yet another (Vietnam) and watched my country go through unimaginable changes from the Great Depression to Smart-Phones.

So, surely, somewhere, I must have had 'Experiences.'

I lost my Faye several years ago to cancer, but throughout her life she kept a journal and documented many of our experiences, especially our travels. So, to add to her reminisces I started rummaging around in the dusty, musty, cobweb covered corners of my alleged mind (not a trip I recommend) and, sure enough, I found 'Experiences'. Well, stuff that happened anyway, or at least I think they happened. So, I started writing them down and, combined with Faye's journals and letters, that's how this little offering came into being.

If you are looking for profound thoughts and an insight to great wisdom, this is not the book for you.

I'd like to think that our 'Experiences' are more of the lounge chair with a cold beer type, when you just want to relax on a warm sunny beach and enjoy a light read on a long summer day. I hope some of our experiences (all true, at least as near as I can remember) bring a smile to your lips—and maybe to your heart.

Enjoy.

Vern Nordman
November 2019

Uncle Sam My Sailor and me

Experiences on the Lighter Side of a Long Military Life

Faye and Vern Nordman

In the Beginning
—West Coast, East Coast—

I was born at a very early age of mixed parents, a Lady and a Sailor. My mother was a very proper New England Lady of Norman/English ancestry. There were at least a couple of our ancestors with William the Conqueror when he invaded England in 1066.

My great, great, great, great, great, great, great (I think 7 is right) grandfather came to the colonies in the 1630's and there are at least four towns in Massachusetts and Vermont that have our ancestors on their original town charters.

New England is also stuffed with our living relatives. My grandmother was the youngest of twelve children and grandpa was number eleven of fourteen.

Mom was a college graduate who lived at home with her parents and worked as an executive secretary in Boston, Massachusetts.

As I said, "Very proper."

On the other hand, my father was a sailor, an English/Canadian drifter with a Swedish name. When my brothers and I were kids we could seldom get Dad to talk about his family or his younger days. On the rare occasions that we could get him going I can remember him telling stories about drifting around the Pacific Northwest in the nineteen teens and early twenties: Dad working as a lumberjack, Dad working as a miner, even Dad working in the circus.

The only thing that we knew for sure was that in 1926 he joined the United States Navy and was a career Navy man from then on. Dad loved the Navy.

For us kids Dad's stories just brought on more questions. When Dad enlisted in the Navy, he said that he was born in St. Paul, Minnesota in November, 1904. But, listening to his stories, he had to be older than that or else he was cutting down tall timber when he was twelve or thirteen years old.

We also wondered how he came to be born in St. Paul with the name of Nordman when his parents and his two brothers and two sisters all lived in Saskatoon, Saskatchewan, Canada and their surname was Davis.

The questions were never answered.

Dad served for over twenty-five years in the United States Navy and retired as a Chief Machinist Mate. After Dad retired, he got a job in the Boston Navy Shipyard and worked for Uncle Sam for another fifteen years.

It's a good thing Dad joined the Navy because if he hadn't, I don't know how he and my mother would have met and then where would I be?

How did this rather unlikely couple get together? Well, it went something like this:

In the early nineteen-thirties Dad was in the Navy and stationed in southern California. One of his shipmates was a sailor from Massachusetts, named George Montague. At some point Dad's sister Catherine turned up (from Canada, I presume), met George and they were married.

Maybe it didn't happen quite that fast.

Not too long after George and Catherine were married, Dad's ship was sent on a cruise to the East Coast and the scuttlebutt was that one of the port calls was going to be Boston, Massachusetts. George was from the little town of Abbington which is just outside of Boston so he took leave and he and Catherine went back east by train so the new bride could meet his parents and, if all went well, they would be on hand to meet Dad's ship when it came into Boston.

Apparently, all went well and when Dad's ship arrived George and Catherine were on hand to greet the brother/brother-in-law and take him home to meet the folks. Among the folks was George's older sister Harriet, the very proper secretary who, of course, became my Mom.

I can't imagine that even in her wildest dreams my mother ever thought that she would become a Navy Wife.

Mom and Dad settled in Long Beach, California and it's a good thing that they did or all the information on my birth certificate would be wrong. I think that the hospital where I was born is now a parking lot.

That should tell you something right there. They didn't even put up a plaque.

For some reason I have no memories of those experiences.

When I was about three years old, Dad was

transferred from the West Coast to the East Coast. We packed up and moved from Long Beach, California to Norfolk, Virginia with a stop in Saskatoon to meet Dad's family.

I have a vague memory of snow and a story:

About the time that we arrived for our visit, my grandparents got electricity in their house for the first time. The electricity that was provided were single overhead drop lights in the living room and kitchen and one wall outlet with two plugs in each room. Apparently, my grandmother was very dubious about this electricity thing. She kept something plugged into all four outlets all the time so the electricity wouldn't leak out onto the floor.

When we got to Norfolk, we rented a little house, but my mother was not happy about being left home alone with two little kids (my brother Willard was born while we were in Norfolk) when Dad's ship was out to sea. I am told that when Dad's ship went out my mother would pack us up and we would go north to Massachusetts and live with my grandparents until the ship came back in. Then we would return to Norfolk and rent another house or an apartment until the ship went out to sea again.

I have some fuzzy memories of these events but only (I think) because I have the old photographs.

After a couple of years in Norfolk we packed up again when Dad got orders and was transferred to the big Naval Base at Newport, Rhode Island.

No 'Experiences' yet.

No, the first 'Experience' that I can really remember occurred on December 7, 1941. That's right, Pearl Harbor. I was six.

When the Japanese attacked Pearl Harbor Dad was an instructor at the Torpedo Station at Newport and we were living in a big, Navy, family housing complex called 'The Anchorage' which was just outside one of the gates to the base in Middletown, Rhode Island about two miles from downtown Newport.

On this Sunday, Mom and Dad had taken my brother Willard and I to the movies in downtown Newport to see Walt Disney's *Snow White and the Seven Dwarves*. We didn't have a car so we didn't go out much so this was a 'Big Deal' that I had looked forward to for days.

About the time that Snow White was hooking up with the seven little men in the forest (They let little kids see this stuff?) the movie stopped, the lights came up, some guy came out on the stage and said that all military personnel had to report to their duty stations.

Dad got up and left and Mom, my brother and I got on the bus and went home. I was really unhappy about not being able to see the rest of the movie. So, being six, I probably whined and cried and exhibited other unmanly behavior. I heard someone say that it was the 'Japs' who were responsible. I didn't know who the 'Japs' were but they were on my list from then on.

I don't remember World War II as a bad time at all; in fact, for a little kid living on a military installation, it was an exciting time. There were things happening all around the base and in our housing area. There was construction going on everywhere, which meant that there were things to climb on— heavy equipment and scaffolds—and dirt to dig in. Usually the workmen would just leave their stuff lying around overnight so for us kids' wheel-barrow races were very popular.

One thing to climb on was a big obstacle course

13

that the Navy built just outside the base gate downhill from where we lived. Wow! Talk about a playground. There were cargo nets to climb, big logs to run across and mud—lots of mud, glorious mud.

Of course, no one—not our parents, not the Navy—wanted kids to play on the obstacle course but, naturally, we did anyway. The sailors would chase us off, but as soon as they were gone, we were back on again.

We played with wooden guns that the sailors made for us and shot at 'Krauts' and 'Japs,' whatever they were, (I liked the 'Japs' part) in a kid-made, foxhole and trench network that ran for a hundred yards or more through a big field that was adjacent to the housing area and now looked like Northern France in World War I.

Somewhere along the line, and much to my mother's dismay, Dad finally got himself out of the classroom and into the war. From the time the war started Dad had been applying for a transfer to the fleet. He had been in the Navy for almost sixteen years when World War II began and he was determined that he wasn't going to be stuck as an instructor and miss it. He left to join the battleship 'South Dakota' somewhere out in the Pacific while we continued to live in the Anchorage.

The Navy did everything possible to make the families left behind feel like they were part of the Navy family and that we were contributing to the war effort. Among other things that went on were collection drives for all kinds of stuff.

On collection day all of us kids would get our little red wagons and we would go around the neighborhood collecting. We collected newspaper, we collected scrap metal and we collected 'fat.' We didn't know why, but it was fun and exciting.

On collection day the Navy would have a big truck parked at one end of the housing area and when we turned in our wagon load of whatever, we would get a treat, usually one of those candy cigarettes. We would walk around with our candy cigs hanging out of our mouths.

Cool, just like the real sailors.

Everything was rationed during the war. My mother was the queen of rationing. She had ration stamps for all kinds of stuff and she was always wheeling and dealing with the other Navy Wives. She could turn a pound of sugar into a pair of shoes in the blink of an eye.

I remember that during the war you couldn't get butter, all you could get was margarine, but it wasn't like the margarine that you see today. The wartime margarine came in a clear, one-pound plastic bag and it was a nasty-looking white glob of goo. It looked like lard; maybe it was lard. Also, in the bag there was a bead of yellow dye that you gently squeezed until it broke and then you kept gently (gently mind you!) kneading the bag until the nasty white lard thing turned to an acceptable blob of margarine yellow.

I used to like doing that but I usually wasn't allowed because I would squeeze too hard and break the bag. "Squeeze the bag," little kids got; "gentle and patience," not so much.

Turning the squishy lump from white to yellow was not an instantaneous process, but it could be, and often was, an instantaneous mess.

On Saturday afternoons Navy trucks would come through the housing area, load up all the kids and take us onto the base to the theater for the

Saturday afternoon movie. There would be a cartoon, the latest chapter of whatever serial was running and then the main feature, usually a western.

Exciting experiences for a little kid.

The Monster in the Cellar
—Massachusetts—

They say that being a Navy Wife is the toughest job in the Navy. You better believe it. It's the toughest job in any service. Probably the worst part of military life (from the spouse's point of view) is the constant moving. I know that that's the part my mother hated the most.

During World War II the Navy was tolerant of families who were living in base housing whose sponsors were off with the fleet and were no longer actually stationed there. But, as soon as the war was over, we were expected to pack-up and move on.

When the war ended Dad was still on the battleship South Dakota somewhere out in the Pacific which meant that the ship's home port was somewhere on the west coast or maybe Hawaii. While we were making plans to head west Dad was re-assigned to Norfolk, Virginia.

Mom really didn't want to go back to Norfolk. I mean, she *really* didn't want to go back to Norfolk. She didn't want to go west either. With three little kids (my brother, Loren, was born while we were at Newport) Mom didn't want to be constantly packing up and moving around every time that Dad got orders.

Mom wanted a house, her own house.

At this time Dad had over twenty years of service and was eligible for retirement, of course, Mom wanted him to retire.

But there was one small problem: Dad was a sailor's sailor who loved the Navy and he didn't want to retire. I guess you could say that things were a little tense around the household.

The compromise was: they would buy a house which would be a permanent place for Mom and us kids and Dad would stay in the Navy.

They bought a house in the town of Stoughton, Massachusetts, not far from Abbington where my mother had grown up. My mother, my two brothers, my grandmother (grandpa had passed away the previous year) and I moved in.

Dad was with us to get us settled, but after that I only saw him off and on for the next five years until he finally did retire.

Mom swore that she would never move again, and she didn't. She lived in that house until she passed away almost forty years later.

The house was of typical New England design and construction, wood with two stories and an attic, three bedrooms and a full bathroom upstairs and a living room, dining room, bedroom, kitchen and full bath downstairs. Although it was suffering from disuse, all things considered, the house was in pretty fair shape.

The elderly lady who lived there before us only used the downstairs dining room (that was her bedroom also) the kitchen and the downstairs bath. The rest of the house had been closed off for years. The grownups opened up the house and went to work. I was only ten and probably not much help.

Dad was one of those pretty handy guys who could build or fix just about anything. Soon everything (plumbing, electricity, etc.) was ship shape (Navy pun intended) and Mom and Grandma had the place clean.

I have a very vague recollection that there was one of those big, old, black, coal burning, cast-iron stoves in the kitchen. That monstrosity was quickly replaced with an electric range.

The kitchen also had an icebox, a real icebox. The iceman would show up every four or five days with a big block of ice. You put the ice in the thing and as the ice melted it would keep the contents cool, but it would also generate about fifty gallons of water which, of course, had to removed.

Guess who was elected for that job.

However, it wasn't long before the icebox was gone too and a real refrigerator was installed in its place.

It was while we were fixing and replacing things that I found out that there was a Monster living in the cellar. A real, metal, fire-breathing Monster.

The house did have central heating in the form of an old coal fired furnace, i.e., The Monster. The old lady who lived there before us didn't use the furnace. She had a small kerosene space heater for the two rooms that she occupied, so the furnace hadn't been turned on in years. Dad took out the space heater but It gets cold in New England in the winter so he had to make sure we had a working heating system before he disappeared over the horizon.

Dad took me with him and we went to check out the furnace. I will never forget the experience.

Climbing down a rickety old wooden staircase we descended into the bowels of the earth. When my eyes adjusted to the gloom, I could see that the cellar was completely unfinished with a loose dirt floor and plain stone walls. There were several, crudely knocked together, wooden benches and shelves scattered about with piles of old tools, tin cans, glass jars, bits of wood and lots of unidentifiable junk on, around, under and behind them.

Spider webs were everywhere. For illumination there was one electric wire that ran down the center beam of the unfinished ceiling which lighted the cellar with two twenty-five-watt drop lights. With these lights on you could barely see in the dim, gloomy dark. There were shadows all around and I KNEW that there were 'things' (besides the spiders) that lived and moved in the shadows.

Talk about spooky! This place could be the setting for any horror story you wanted to conjure up.

In the middle of the dirt floor toward the front of the house squatted The Monster. It was about six feet high, five feet wide, constructed of solid iron with two doors in front, one about even with the top of my head that Dad said was the fire box door and one lower down that he said was for the ashes. In between the doors there was a long narrow slot with a lever that Dad said was for shaking the grates so the ashes would fall to the bottom for removal.

The Monster was big and black and ugly and covered in dust and ash. I could tell right away that it didn't like me; I knew that I didn't like it.

The furnace had metal ducts sticking out of it all over and these ducts angled up and disappeared into holes among the beams of the unfinished ceiling.

Dad told me that the furnace burned coal and pointed out the coal bin that was just under one of the cellar windows at the front of the house. He also informed me that taking care of this Metal Monster would be one of my chores while he was gone.

I mean, we all had chores! I didn't know what an 'allowance' was until my kids sprang the term on me. I thought they were putting me on. But this chore was really above and beyond.

While Dad was explaining the workings of this Metal Monster to me he turned it on and was happily poking around, opening doors, pushing buttons and flipping switches when he came to the switch that operated the big fan that blew the hot air from the furnace up through the ducts to the vents in all the rooms upstairs. That fan probably hadn't been turned on since Columbus sailed over on the Mayflower.

Dad flipped the switch and with a roar the fan came to life. It was very powerful fan and when it came on it blew a thousand years of accumulated dust, dirt, ash, insects (both dead and alive), small rodents and some unidentifiable things, all over the house that Mom and Grandma had just spent a week cleaning.

You could have heard my mother's scream in Chicago.

Dad and I rushed up the stairs to see what the screaming was about, leaving the fan on and blowing away. Coming into the house through the kitchen was like walking into a fog bank.

Dad ran back down into the cellar to turn off the fan.

As the dust, dirt and other accumulated stuff

settled, onto everything, you could tell right away that Mom and Grandma were not happy.

For self-preservation Dad prudently stayed in the cellar until the atmosphere was once more as clean as the air.

Dad and I went to work cleaning the Metal Monster and getting it ready for operation. The worst part was cleaning the ducts that wandered all through the floors and walls of the house. Dad cleaned everything he could reach but for the narrower places he used me. He would just shove me into the hole and if I didn't get it clean with the rag I probably would get it clean with my head.

It was really dirty in some of those places and for a week I looked like a chimney sweep from the movie 'Mary Poppins.'

To help in the cleaning I offered up my two younger brothers who, being smaller, we could push farther into the ducts, but Dad said that they were too little. Well, wasn't that the point?

It wasn't long after this that Dad sailed away and we settled down to living on our own. It was summer, it's warm in Massachusetts in the summer, and I kind of forgot all about the Metal Monster in the cellar. Then autumn came, the air got cooler and the coal was delivered. Actually, the coal delivery was pretty neat. The coal truck backed right up onto our front lawn, the driver shoved a metal chute through the little cellar window at the front of the house and a million tons of coal cascaded into our cellar.

Grandma told me that I had to save newspapers (I already had a paper route) and chop wood so we would have kindling to get the coal going. I didn't have any idea what she was talking about, but shortly thereafter a truckload of wood appeared and I was introduced into the joys of chopping wood. The ax I used was old (we found it in the cellar), dull, kind of rusty and darned near as big as I was.

I didn't really chop the wood—I just, kind of, beat it to death.

It was now time to crank up the Metal Monster. Mom, Grandma and I went over the operation of the furnace and they told me what I had to do to start a fire and keep it going. I didn't have a clue. Grandma showed me how to lay a fire with paper and kindling and then add the coal.

Worked like a charm when she did it.

Grandma did suggest that I chop the wood a little smaller, something a bit less than log-cabin construction size. Picky! Picky!

Mom and Grandma went upstairs and left me to it. I thought that I should add more coal. Remember, the coal pile was up against the front wall of the cellar, the furnace was about twenty feet back in the middle of the cellar and to make it more interesting, the furnace was turned the wrong way. The door to the fire-box was on the side of furnace facing away from the coal-pile so I couldn't just scoop up some coal and turn and chuck it into the furnace.

No, I had to get my shovelful of coal and walk around to the other side of this Metal Monster. I left the fire-box door open so I could chuck the coal in. (I swear I did.) But, when I got there with my shovelful of coal the door was closed. I had to set down the shovel, open the door, pick up the coal, and then chuck it in—the fire went out.

The Metal Monster really had it in for me. I'll bet that when it was installed it was turned around the other way.

With slight variations that was my life for the

winter. Obviously, I wasn't solely responsible for the Metal Monster, we would all have frozen to death if that was true, but I was its slave. Mom and Grandma directed operations and I did most of the running up and down the stairs.

I had three main jobs:

1) Bank the fire at night. I was never very good at doing that so when we went to bed Mom or Grandma would go down into the cellar with me to make sure it was done properly so it would smolder through the night and not go out. That was good because I didn't like going down into that spooky cellar at night...alone.

2) Stoke up the fire in the morning. If the fire had gone out during the night the house would be cold, I would have to remake the fire, and everyone would be mad at me.

3) Take care of the ashes. More on this later.

I was usually sent down to check the Monster in the morning, at noon (my school was just across the street so I came home for lunch), after school (before I delivered my papers) and in the evening.

The Metal Monster ate coal by the ton and when I mentioned this to my grandmother and complained about walking around the cellar with shovels full of coal she gave me one of those 'How did this dunce ever get into my family?' looks and down into the cellar we went.

She rummaged around behind the old benches and she came up with a wheelbarrow. It was an old rusty wheelbarrow with a squeaky metal wheel but it was serviceable. Grandma said to fill it up with coal and wheel it around in front of the furnace. Neat!

And sometimes it even worked. I say sometimes because the next day I left the wheel barrow full of coal in front of the furnace when I went off to school (I swear I did) but when I came home for lunch the wheel barrow was empty.

If we had a television and if the X-Files had been invented the theme music would be on a continuous loop. Then there was the ash.

Coal burns hot and it burns for a long time but it does not burn up completely or cleanly. Stinky smoke goes out the chimney (and into the house) and ash, lots of ash, drops down through the grates to the bottom of the furnace.

The Metal Monster generated so much ash that I had to shovel it out every day. You can produce all the scientific evidence you want, but I know that more ash came out of the bottom of that Metal Monster than the amount of coal that went into the top. (Kind of like the ice-box with the ice and water thing.)

The Town of Stoughton came around and collected trash once a week and they would empty the ash barrels if they were out at the curb in front of the house.

Out behind the house we found two big wooden barrels and these were decreed to be ash barrels.

My job: ash out of Monster—ash into barrels— barrels out to curb—repeat.

I am not too bright.

I put the ash barrels in the cellar between the Monster and the short flight of stairs that went outside through folding cellar doors. The cellar doors were about three-quarters of the way up the driveway from the street.

When trash collection day came around I had almost a full barrel of ashes sitting in the cellar and a big problem. There was no way skinny little eleven-year-old me was going to get a barrel of ash, that probably weighed twice as much as I did, up those stairs. So, I had to take the empty barrel outside and then fill it from the full one, one small bucket full by one small bucket full at a time.

That took a while. I didn't count the number of trips that I made up and down the stairs.

I'm still not very smart because, although I now have a full barrel of ash outside the cellar, the barrel is sitting by the cellar door toward the back of the house and a long way from the street.

I finally managed to wrestle the barrel down the driveway and out to the curb.

For future reference I just left both barrels sitting by the curb (I have a photo) and filled them with my little bucket. That involved many trips from the Monster to the barrels. And, of course, each trip meant going outside in the wind and rain and snow but, it worked most of the time, except when the town snow plow came by and buried my barrels.

The Metal Monster loved that one. I swear that I heard it laugh.

Fortunately for me, my mother hated the Metal Monster as much as I did.

If you are going to use coal you should have a steam/radiator system. The coal heats water, turns it into steam and the steam goes to the radiators to heat the rooms upstairs. If you have a forced-air system, like we did, you will get heat but you will also get fumes, and dust and ash all over the house.

For some reason Mom didn't care much for that.

The next summer the Metal Monster was replaced by a beautiful, bright, shiny oil-fired furnace that required no maintenance at all.

I remember the day the workmen came to take

the Metal Monster away. I sat on one of the benches in the cellar cheering as every piece was dismantled.

It didn't go without a fight. Most of the nuts and bolts were so stuck together that they had to be knocked loose with a hammer and chisel. Some of the ducts had been there so long that they were practically fused into the walls and did not want to let go. A duct fell on one guy and another got a cut on his arm. But the workmen finally prevailed and the Monster lay in pieces in the dirt.

I asked what was going to be done with the pieces and the workmen said that they would probably just go to a junkyard. I thought that that would be a big mistake. In my opinion, just to be safe, (think of *Christine*) the pieces should have been melted down and the lump sunk in the deepest part of the ocean.

If the pieces were not going to be melted down then they should be scattered in different junkyards, preferably on different continents.

Dad's Patio
—Massachusetts—

When Dad finally did retire from the Navy, and was home all the time, life for us kids didn't change much except that he was fun to have around. But, fun for us kids meant that he must have been driving my mother nuts. The fun was that he always had a project (or two) going on around the house. He would start these projects, usually without consulting Mom, get them about ninety percent completed and then wander off to some other project.

One of the joys of being the eldest son was that I was always elected to be his Chief Accomplice.

For example:

The back door of the house went out onto a small, covered, wooden porch. You know the kind. There was one step from the house to the porch and another from the porch to a dirt/grass strip between the porch and the driveway. The porch was about six feet square with wooden posts in the front corners holding up the roof and wooden railings on the sides. Very typical.

Mom kept her car parked up at the end of the driveway by the back door. Out in the backyard Mom had her clothes lines and a small garden, so she was in and out the back door and over that porch a lot.

Dad decided, again without consulting Mom, that the porch was old so he was going to replace it with a concrete patio so Mom wouldn't have to walk on a shaky wooden porch (it wasn't) and then get her feet wet or muddy going to the clothes lines or the car. A nice thought, but as the idea grew in his mind, so did the patio.

Dad's patio was not going to be just any patio. HIS patio was not only going to cover the footprint of the existing little wooden porch but it would extend toward the front of the house all the way to the cellar door, about twenty-five feet, and the other way all the way to the back of the house, about another ten feet. The new patio was also going to be about four feet wider than the existing porch.

This was going to be one big patio.

One evening when I came home from work (this was the summer between my junior and senior year in high school and I was working downtown at the lumber yard) Dad was waiting for me by the back porch. He handed me a sledge hammer and told me to knock out one of the two posts supporting the porch roof.

Okay. I had learned long ago not to ask foolish questions, like, "Why?"

I whammed my post, Dad knocked out the other one and once again the Law of Gravity prevailed and the roof came crashing down. My mother flew to the back door to see what had happened and was greeted with a pile of rubble.

You could tell right away that she was not happy. Once Dad explained what it was that he was going to do, she was even more unhappy. I would say that on a scale of one to ten for happiness she was at a negative eighty-six.

She could see that for however long it was going to take for this project to be completed she was going to have to carry her laundry out the front door, around the house, up the driveway to the back of the house where the clothes lines were. And, make the same trip to work on her garden or get to the car.

Undeterred, we cleared away the trash and Dad staked out his patio. (I forget what he did with all the wood.)

When he had it all marked out there was one small problem: it would take a Hoover's Dam worth of cement to fill up this hole.

"No problem," said Dad. "We (he was using the term 'we' loosely) can fill up the hole with rocks and pour cement on top."

Where, I wondered, were we going to get enough rocks?

Not to worry! Dad had a plan. Dad always had a plan.

A neighbor, two doors down, had a huge pile of rocks in his back yard (where those came from, I never knew) that we were welcome to have if we hauled them away. My part of the 'we' was to load the rocks into the wheel-barrow, push the wheel-barrow over to our house and dump them into Dad's patio hole. So, for the rest of the summer I would come home from work, have supper and then push wheel-barrow loads of rock until it got dark.

I did fix Mom up—somewhat. My first loads of rocks went to filling the hole right by the back door. Then I laid plywood over the rocks so she didn't have to do the front door bit. She still didn't seem happy, but at least I had deflected the unhappiness from me. Let Dad fend for himself.

Dad's part of the 'we' was to buy me a new wheel-barrow. I don't know why. I thought the old one that I had used for coal back when we had the Metal Monster was working just fine. The metal wheel that was silent on the dirt floor of the cellar had a real musical quality on the sidewalk.

It took me most of the summer to haul enough rocks to sufficiently fill the hole and by that time Dad had wandered off to other projects so Mom hired a contractor to do the cement work.

When all was said and done, it was a very nice patio. It even had a hole in it for an umbrella clothes line so my mother had to only go a couple of steps out the back door on a nice cement surface to hang up the clothes.

When I went back to Stoughton for my fiftieth high school reunion I went by the house and the patio was still there.

Dad's Remote
—Massachusetts—

I was in high school when we got our first television set. It was a state of the art black and white model with about a ten-inch screen, one of those screens that was straight on the top and bottom and curved on both sides. It came with its own little stand that had long skinny legs and it had a 'rabbit ear' antenna.

Dad loved television, especially the variety shows (they say that vaudeville died and television was the box that they put it in) and the TV Guide was his Bible. He kept it by his chair and communed with it regularly. Not that there was a whole lot of choice in television stations or equipment in those days. The TV set itself only had thirteen numbers on the dial and one of those was a test pattern. But there weren't even enough stations to fill up those. As I recall there were

33

three stations out of Boston and two out of Providence, Rhode Island and none of them were on all day.

We set the TV up on its little table in a corner of the living room and Dad soon scrapped the rabbit ears and erected an outdoor directional antenna on a long metal pole that he bolted to the house just outside the living room window. The pole extended the antenna high above the roof of the house and it got pretty good reception once you had it pointed the right way. We lived in between Boston and Providence so, if you were watching a Boston station and wanted to switch to a Providence station you had to go outside and turn the antenna.

This was no problem for Dad because he had a remote.

You think remotes are new?

Ha!

Back in the early fifties Dad had a semi-automatic, gas operated remote.

It was called—'Me.'

It was very easy to operate. When Dad wanted to change channels, he would point at me and say, "Get channel four or five, or whatever," and the Remote would get up, walk nine feet over an inlaid wooden floor to the TV, grasp the dial in one hand and change channels.

If the channel change involved changing the antenna direction the Remote went outside (in the wind and the rain and the snow) and turned the antenna with Dad yelling directions from his chair until the Remote got it right.

Let There Be Light
—Massachusetts—

I graduated from high school without a plan. I never had a plan. My mother always said that I was like a leaf on the breeze. That might be one way to put it. I always felt that I was more like one of those round metal balls in an old pin-ball machine.

Mom wanted me to go to college. She had graduated from college back in the twenties when there weren't many ladies who could say that, but four more years of school was not high on my wish list. (It wasn't low on my list either.)

I took a summer/fall job with a Portable Floodlighting Company. What kind of company you ask? I will elucidate for your intellectual illumination.

Today it seems that every high school has lights on their playing fields, but back when I was in high school only the very rich schools would have a lighted field for night time competition or practice. In the larger urban areas, there would probably be one big stadium that would have lights and that field would be shared by all the schools in the district. In rural communities like the one I grew up in, we played our games in the afternoon.

However, if a school without lights did want to play a night game there was an alternative: Portable Floodlighting.

The company that I went to work for in the early 1950's had half a dozen trucks of various configuration and provided lights for just about everything you could think of from block dances to football games. The company even had six World War II surplus searchlights mounted on flatbed trailers (four searchlights on one trailer and two on another). These were used to attract people to store openings, political rallies or whatever. They were fun - especially the truck with the four lights on it.

These were big lights! If you remember the old-World War II movies with the bad guy's searchlights stabbing up into the sky to impale the good guy's bombers - those kinds of lights. The searchlights were permanently mounted on the flatbeds, each searchlight on its own base. We could tip them up to any angle and there was a motor in the base of each light so that the searchlights could turn independently, and, if desired, at different speeds. There were even filters that we could use to cover the face of the light that would change the color of the beam.

I was really disappointed when I found out that we didn't have one with a Batman emblem.

The reason for the searchlights, of course, was to attract attention to whatever was going on - gas station openings were very popular. The idea was that people out driving around would see the lights and try to track them down to see where they were coming from. It worked, too. Back in the day we would draw in hundreds of people.

Today everyone would probably just google it. They don't know what they're missing.

The only real problem with setting up out in a public area was keeping people off the truck. It seems that everyone wanted to climb up onto the flatbed for a closer look at the lights and it was hard to keep them off.

Well, I can't say as I tried to keep everyone off the truck. There was always time to give certain individuals of the young, nubile, female persuasion a closer look. I'm not completely stupid.

I only worked the searchlights a few times during the summer because I was primarily hired for football games. When fall came around I was on a different kind of truck and on the road just about every weekend. To light up a field for a football game you only needed two people, the crew boss/truck driver and the young, dumb, wet-behind-the-ears helper (that would be me).

The rig that we used was a regular eighteen-wheeler semi-trailer truck. Mounted on the center line inside the trailer were two large generators. There were hooks and racks on the sides of the trucks interior that held ten, forty-foot extension ladders and ten four by four-foot wooden frames that were each fitted with six 1000-watt floodlights.

Other equipment included rolls of electrical cable, iron stakes, sledge hammers and cut up pieces of old inner tubes for insulation.

Picture a football field. To set up for a game we

would first drive the truck around the perimeter of the field dropping off an extension ladder, a floodlight frame and four stakes at the 10, 30, 50, 30 and 10-yard lines on both sides of the field. We would then park the truck behind one of the end zones and start walking around the field.

We would go to each ladder and, with our handy-dandy, ultra-sophisticated sledge hammers, knock the four stakes into the ground forming a large square, stand the ladder up in the middle of the square and tie four pre-attached ropes from the top of the ladder to each stake. Then the ladder extension would be pulled up to its full height and four more pre-attached ropes would be tied off.

Each ladder had a rope and pulley attached at the top. The bank of floodlights would be tied off and hoisted to the top of the ladder. Each bank of lights had fifty-foot long electric cables attached which reached down to the ground.

When the ten ladders were up, five standing on each side of the field, we would roll cable from the truck to the ladders. The cable was pierced at twenty-yard intervals, so that the electrical wires hanging down from the floodlights could be spliced in. This was done by using a highly sophisticated four-inch bolt and a nut and covering it with a piece of inner tube for insulation.

Once all the connections were made, all you had to do was attach the cable to the generators, crank them up, throw the switch, and, viola, instant lights.

It only took about an hour and a half to set up a field and we could tear down and be off the field in an hour.

As I recall, the company charged $250 a ball game, the crew boss got fifty bucks for a weekend's work lighting a couple of games and the helper got twenty-five. Decent money in those days.

Every game was an adventure; every field and situation were different. The lights and ladders were set up just off of the playing field—between the spectators and the action. So, when people weren't trying to climb the ladders to get a better view, they were tripping over the ropes.

We usually sat by the truck to watch the game and when we saw a ladder swaying, I was sent over to shoo the spectators away from the ladder.

Fat chance!

There was one really big guy I used to work with. He was big enough that when he told people to get off the ladders, they got off the ladders. They sure weren't going to listen to me.

Sometimes the fans of the victorious team would think that it was a fine idea to tear down the ladders along with the goalposts and I remember one game where the losers wanted to blame the lights for their loss and the cops had to protect us while we took the equipment down and got out of Dodge.

It was great fun, but when the football season ended, I was unemployed. That was OKAY with me because I was off to see the world.

The Bucket Issue
—South Carolina—

*B*ack in the depths of time, back when the air was clean and sex was dirty, back when I was young and dumb (no comments please) I thought that it would be a good idea to join the United States Navy. Well, actually, it wasn't a new idea seeing as Dad was a career Navy man who had served for over twenty-five years and retired as a Chief Machinist Mate. When I set out to see the world it just seemed natural that I would head for the Navy.

I went to the local Navy Recruiting Office, presented my warm body and said, "I'm yours."

Somehow, I got the distinct impression that they were not too impressed by that statement, but being the good recruiters that they were, they smiled and said, "That's fine young man we'll just get all the paper work filled out and we will probably be calling you up in about fourteen months."

"Fourteen months?" I said, "I was kind of thinking of like - now."

The recruiter smiled and said, "Well son, the war is over (Korean War) and the manning requirements of the Navy are at 100% right now, but I'm sure something will open up in the next year or so. We can get you signed up and then you just go home and wait until we call."

Bummer, this was not going as I had planned at all and while I stood there dithering, I noticed someone over at a corner desk crooking his finger at me. I looked over and a gravelly voice that belonged to a burly United States Marine Corps Sergeant said:

"Come here, kid."

I walked over and got a good look at the body that the gravelly voice belonged to. This guy was right out of Central Casting. You want a Marine Sergeant, it was him. He was big. Even sitting down, he was big. He had a chest full of ribbons and he looked really tough with a face like an English Bulldog. I got the feeling that he could chew rocks and spit out nails.

He rumbled again, "Kid, I can have you out of town tomorrow."

Eight point two seconds later I had signed on the dotted line.

And that's how I came to join the United States Marine Corps.

The sergeant didn't quite get me out of town the next day, (I had to take a physical) it was the day after that I was on a train heading south toward that bastion of Southern Hospitality and Gracious Living, the United States Marine Corps Recruit Training Depot, Parris Island, South Carolina, better known as 'Boot Camp.'

Once there, and while it was being impressed on my young and tender mind and body what a completely useless piece of (possibly) human offal I was, I was allowed to participate in many secret and mysterious rituals of the United States Marine Corps.

Among the many experiences this young 'Boot' had was the 'Bucket Issue.'

The first few days at Parris Island were just a blur of running around like the proverbial chicken with its head cut off, filling out forms, taking tests, getting yelled at and very little sleep. I think it was about the third day when they finally gave us our utility uniforms.

When we put our uniforms on what a sorry looking lot we were. The Marine Corps obviously has a policy that recruit utility uniforms will only come in two sizes; too big or too small, mostly too big. Collectively we looked like a bunch of refugees from a Salvation Army rummage sale.

On day four our 'Chief Yeller' (that is, the Senior Drill Instructor. I always thought of the Drill Instructors as 'Yellers') appeared among us. Our Chief Yeller was a six-foot four-inch, rail thin, rawhide tough, buck sergeant from North Carolina named Hart, a misnomer if there ever was one—the man didn't have a heart.

He also had two Assistant Yellers, not that he needed them; one of him was more than enough to handle the seventy-five of us. Maybe he had to sleep sometime—but, I'm not sure of that.

Anyway, when one of the Yellers appears among you, you are supposed to yell 'Attention' and stand at attention in front of your 'rack' (for some strange reason, the Marine Corps calls beds 'racks'). Because there were so many of us, our racks were double bunked and conveniently placed about six and a half inches apart.

The Chief Yeller told us that we were going to go and draw our 'Bucket Issue.'

Ooo-kaay! I heard the words, but the meaning escaped me.

Then he spoke the word that we had come to know so well:

"Outside!"

The command, 'outside,' means that you are supposed to stop whatever it is that you are doing and leave whatever building you are in and 'Fall In' (form a military formation) on whatever street, sidewalk, parking lot, etc., is handy.

We were billeted in a 'squad bay' (a big open room) on the second deck (the Marine Corps calls floors 'decks') of a large barracks block shaped like a big letter H. At the command 'outside' seventy-five bodies went through the squad bay's single door and poured down the stairs.

Stairs are known as 'ladders' in the Corps. Now, I know what a ladder looks like and these were definitely stairs.

We ran out onto the road with every intention of 'falling in' but watching us try to fall in would be, to say the least, interesting. I don't think we had ever done it the same way twice. After much scrambling and bumbling around, and some very colorful language from the assembled Yellers, we were finally in some semblance of order. However, nothing satisfied the Yellers and we were ordered back up to the squad bay.

By the way, we were a platoon, there were four squads in our platoon, platoons live in squad bays; another Mystery of the Corps.

44

Of course, once we were back up in the squad bay we were ordered back outside and this process was repeated several times.

The Yellers ran us up and down the stairs until it was time for us to leave for wherever it was we were supposed to be to get our 'Buckets.'

We finally marched off. Well, at this stage of our training, to say that we were 'marching' would be using the term 'marching' much too loosely. 'Herding' would be more accurate. We were seventy-five misplaced civilians, in baggy uniforms, heading down the road.

At least we were all heading in the same direction.

We eventually arrived at our destination which was a large metal warehouse with double doors big enough to march the entire platoon through.

Were those doors open?

Of course not.

All seventy-five of us were sent one by one through a regular door.

One of the holy grails of the Marine Corps is that you always wear a 'cover' (Marines call hats 'covers') when you are outside. As soon as you cross the threshold from outside to inside the cover comes off.

We entered the warehouse in single file through the little door and just as the right hand went up to remove our covers a fully loaded metal bucket was planted firmly in our midsection. We were then allowed to run the rest of the way into the warehouse.

The interior of the warehouse was mostly an open space with a long counter backed by shelves running down one side. The floor of the open space was marked out in six-foot yellow squares. The Yellers yelled at us to get on a square.

"Just one on each square, idiots."

So, there we were, one recruit, clutching his bucket (and cover) on each square.

A very large supply sergeant (it seemed that all supply sergeants were very large) stood up on the counter in front of us and said, "We will now inventory your basic field issue."

So that's what it was; and I thought it was just a bucket.

The large sergeant spoke again, "Ground your buckets on the deck by your starboard boondocker."

Translation: Put the bucket down by your right foot.

"In your bucket, you will find one poncho."

Now, I knew what a poncho was—a big square piece of canvas, with a hole in the middle to put your head in; covers your whole body. These ponchos were conveniently located at the bottom of the bucket underneath everything else and they were folded up to about the size of a postage stamp. I never did figure out how they did that.

The large sergeant then gave us a run of instructions, and following his instructions at the speed he was giving them was impossible.

"Take your poncho out of your bucket."

"Hold your poncho up in your right hand."

"Your other right, idiot."

"Shake out your poncho."

"Inspect your poncho."

Sure enough, one of our brighter lights piped up with, "Sir, my poncho has a big round hole in the middle of it."

Now this kid was either a wise guy or just plain dumb. Forty Yellers descended on him like a pack of wolves around a wounded caribou.

Continuing as if he hadn't smelled blood (or fear) in the air the sergeant continued:

"Ground your poncho."

"In your bucket you will find one shelter half." Okay! This tarp must be it.

"Hold up your shelter half." This sucker is big. How did they get it in the bucket?

"Inspect your shelter half." For what?

"Ground your shelter half." And down on the floor it went.

"In your bucket you will find five tent pegs." Naturally they all had to be held up and inspected individually.

"In your bucket, you will find twelve tie-ties."

Say what?

A tie-tie, in Marine speak, is a foot-long piece of clothesline. They can be used to tie your shelter half down to the tent pegs or tie clothes to a clothesline or whatever. Clothespins were apparently beyond the range of Marine Corps technology.

The Navy calls tie-ties 'clothes stops.' Don't ask me. I thought language was supposed to make communicating easier.

All kinds of strange and wonderful things came out of my bucket; a web belt, a canteen (with a cup), a canteen cover, a metal mess kit with a metal knife, fork and spoon, a first aid kit, an ammunition pouch, a helmet, a helmet liner, even a scrub brush. When the bucket was finally empty my six-foot square was covered with 'stuff.'

The large supply sergeant spoke, "The bucket inventory is now complete. Put your equipment back into your buckets."

There was no way.

47

I mean, these buckets must have been packed by demented elves at some secret Marine ritual conducted around a blazing fire by the light of the full moon. There was no way mere mortals were going to get all that stuff back into those buckets.

The Yellers were in full howl. We were cramming stuff into buckets, into pockets. Maybe I can throw the poncho and shelter half over my shoulder. Maybe I can just clap the helmet onto my head. No, that would violate the 'cover rule.' The Yellers get terribly upset about that one.

About four heartbeats after we heard the order to pack the buckets we heard:

"Outside."

Out we went, holding our stuff anyway we could.

The Three Stooges would have been proud.

In retrospect sixty some odd years later, putting everything in the middle of the shelter half and hauling it out like Santa Claus might have put me on the fast track to general, but you just don't seem to think of those things when you are standing in a six by six square with a thousand Yellers screaming at you to pack your bucket and get outside.

The Yellers didn't even care how we fell in. As soon as we were on the street, off we marched, accompanied by the occasional sound of various pieces of highly sensitive Marine Corps equipment falling to the pavement.

Naturally we tried to save our stuff because we had been told that the penalty for loosing equipment was at least ten years on the rack (not the sleepy kind—the stretchy kind) with regular floggings thrown in. However, attempts to retrieve said equipment disrupted the ranks, which caused more stuff to fall, which, naturally, infuriated the Yellers.

When we were almost to our barracks, we were given the order to double time (think of it as group jogging in step). The sound of stuff hitting the ground was like hail on a tin roof.

Down the road we ran to the barracks. Up the stairs into the squad bay we went and there we were, everyone standing at attention in front of his rack, clutching his bucket and whatever gear he managed to hang on to.

One of the Assistant Yellers walked into the squad bay, held up a tent peg and said, "One of you idiots dropped a piece of gear."

A piece of gear?

'A' piece?

You must be kidding. The road behind us was so littered with gear it looked like Napoleon's retreat from Moscow. With all that stuff we could have opened our own surplus store and retired like kings.

The Chief Yeller marched into the squad bay and said, "Squad leader, first squad, get your idiots outside and retrieve Second Platoon's gear."

First squad started out the door still holding their buckets. Well, no one told them to put the darn things down. This drove the Yellers into a new frenzy. By the time first squad was herded back to their racks and their buckets grounded they were ruled too stupid to accomplish the task and second squad was sent.

While all this was happening the rest of us were standing at attention in front of our racks holding buckets and assorted stuff as best we could. Occasionally some piece of gear would hit the deck (fall to the floor) and the guilty party would be treated to a personalized yelling session.

Second squad returned with their arms full of

stuff which was dumped in a pile in the middle of the floor. The Chief Yeller said to the squad leader, "Did you recover all of Second platoon's equipment?"

Now there was a loaded question. With stuff scattered halfway across the base, from here to the warehouse, there was no way that you could be sure that you had it all. The squad leader hesitated, waffled and was fired on the spot.

"Assistant squad leader, second squad, you are now squad leader. Get your idiots back outside."

You can see how this squad leader business worked. The platoon was divided into four squads. Each squad had a leader and an assistant who were changed faster than friends on Facebook. Whoever was up next was all done scientifically, that is, alphabetically. The assistant became squad leader and whoever was next in alphabetical order became the assistant. When you reached the end of the alphabet— you started over. I was in fourth squad and they had already been through me twice. I think I lasted about ten minutes each time. A record that warranted a trophy, I think.

Second squad returned with more stuff which was added to the pile in the middle of the squad bay. By this time, of course, nobody knew what they had so the entire bucket issue had to be inventoried all over again. Hold up your poncho, etc. etc. But this time any missing items had to be retrieved from the Yellers' pile in the middle of the squad bay, with a maximum amount of yelling, of course.

In the end, we got all our stuff. A simple issue procedure that any normal, intelligent, rational human being or organization could have accomplished in half an hour had taken the Marine Corps half a day.

The squad bay was trashed.

We were trashed.

We stood at attention in front of our racks with piles of stuff at our feet.

What we were supposed to do with all this stuff was an experience yet to come.

This Is My Rifle
—South Carolina—

Reveille! Reveille!

There is nothing like being woken up from a sound sleep by the blast of a police whistle, followed by the crash of a metal trash can being kicked the length of your sleeping quarters, accompanied by some very loud and colorful language. But that was how we had come into the world every morning since we had been at the United States Marine Corps' Charm School, Parris Island, South Carolina.

We had now been at Boot Camp for two weeks and it seemed like we had a thousand years to go.

I would never make it. They were going to kill me here, I knew it.

You stumble out of your rack and make your way to the 'head,' (the Marine Corps calls bathrooms 'heads'), to share the washing and shaving experience with fifty-nine of your closest friends.

Two weeks ago, we had started with a platoon of seventy-five, now we were sixty. I knew that a couple of guys got hurt on one of the obstacle courses and went off to sick bay, but the rest just seemed to disappear—absorbed by the Entity.

The platoon would be off on another adventure of Marine Corps education and enlightenment and when we returned to the barracks a bunk would be empty. All the clothes and equipment would have been removed and the empty footlocker and mattress would be sitting on the empty bed.

A couple of us would be detailed to carry the bed, footlocker and mattress outside. A supply truck would appear, load up and take the stuff away. That was that. We never knew what happened to Fred, or Bob, or Charlie. They were just—gone.

Spooky. It was kind of like being in a bad old Science Fiction or Horror Movie. You really didn't want to think about it too much.

The Chief Yeller told us that today was going to be an 'Important Day' because today, unworthy as we were, we were going to be issued our—rifles. He told us that every Marine, no matter what his job, was a rifleman. (I found out later that that wasn't quite true, but it sounded good).

Our Chief Yeller had us at attention on the parade field for hours (it didn't just seem like hours - it was hours) impressing on our tender minds the 'Traditions of the Corps.' He gave us the whole load, from the Halls of Montezuma to the Shores of Tripoli, with World Wars I and II and Korea thrown in for good measure.

All right, enough already, I'm impressed. Let's get on with it, after all, it's only a gun.

Did I say that out loud?

I shouldn't have said that.

We quickly learned that one of the biggest of the Marine Corps no-noes was to call a rifle a gun. They even had a little ditty that went:

"This is my rifle. This is my gun. This is for fighting. This is for fun."

That's about the extent of Marine Corps humor.

Finally, the Chief Yeller ran out of gas and he marched us off heading for the Armory. (That's where they keep the guns.) We didn't know where the Armory was, but we soon realized that wherever it was it was a LONG way away from where we were.

We marched across the Second Battalion Parade Field which was a BIG parade field. We knew how big it was because in the last couple of weeks we had whiled away many a happy hour learning how to march on it.

I think, even today, I could still get out there and march, but not without potty breaks.

We crossed a major road and went across an even bigger parade field. Finally, we went down a long road with warehouses on both sides. The Armory, of course, was at the end of the road. I think it was about as far from our barracks as you could get and still be in South Carolina.

We soon found out that this was not like the Bucket Issue, this was serious stuff. We were going to be issued—a Rifle. And Rifles had Rules:

We would memorize and never forget the serial number of our rifle.

We would take care of our rifle.

We would love our rifle.

After checking the serial number on our rifles, a half-a-dozen times we signed for our rifles and went outside to fall in. Now, after two weeks, we were getting pretty good at this falling in business.

You fall in standing straight, feet slightly apart, hands clasped in the small of your back, eyes looking straight ahead. We knew that. We had certainly been yelled at enough that we should have learned it.

But now, when we are 'Falling In,' what do you do with this—'thing.' This rifle that we had just received?

Do you hold it in one hand?

Both hands?

Where?

How?

One of our brighter lights just laid his rifle on the ground next to him. For some reason the Yellers didn't go for that. In fact, they landed on him like a couple of turds from a tall cow.

I just, kind of, held mine out in front of me.

Of course, the Yellers let us bumble around until everyone was out of the Armory and in formation. Then one of the Yellers gave us lesson number one in the Manual of Arms, how to stand at attention with a rifle.

Pretty simple. You just stand at attention with the rifle grounded by your right foot.

Then came lesson number two, 'Trail Arms.'

Now at trail arms, you keep standing at attention, but with your right hand holding the muzzle, you raise the rifle a couple of inches off the ground and cock your wrist forward. You are now at attention with this—thing - hanging off the end of your right arm.

We started marching back toward the barracks with our rifles at trail arms.

Did I mention that the rifle weighed around ten

pounds?

Before we were halfway down the road the thought began to seep into my tiny, little brain that this rifle was getting heavy. By the time we got to the end of the road you could hear, tickety, tickety, tic, as rifle butts contacted the pavement.

The Yellers didn't like that at all and halted the platoon. While the offenders were being pointed out the error of their ways for letting their rifles hit the ground, the rest of us were still standing at trail arms.

My trail arm was going numb.

We crossed the big parade field and the road. Tic, Tic, Tic. More yelling.

By the time we were halfway across the Second Battalion Parade Field my right arm was one big ache from my fingers to my shoulder and I was sweating like the proverbial stuck hog.

We crossed the Second Battalion Parade Field and instead of marching us down the main road that led to the front of our barracks they marched us down the service road behind our barracks.

Now why would they do that, you ask?

Because, just before our barracks the service road crossed a little alley that had a little curb. As we went over the curb you could hear "tickety, tickety, tic" as the rifle butts hit the curb.

Then we heard the command, "To the rear march."

They marched us back down the service road for a little way before they turned us around and we again headed for home.

Across the alley and up over the curb.

Tic, Tic, Tic.

"To the rear march."

Back down the road we went again.

I am dying.

When they turned us around again my only thought was, "If anyone lets their rifle hit that curb, I will break mine over their head."

My right arm was killing me but I think I had my right wrist up even with my right ear, *my* rifle wasn't going to hit the ground.

We went across the alley, up over the curb and we heard—the sound of silence. (They really should write a song.)

It might be my imagination but it seemed to me that the Yellers were really disappointed when they told us to fall out and get into the squad bay.

During the next half hour or so that it took to get any feeling back into our right arms and hands, the Yellers told us where they wanted the rifles stowed. We had to make loops with two of our 'tie-ties' and hang the rifles from the outer edges of the top bunks. This didn't make a lot of sense (but what did?) and it was very hard to accomplish one handed.

For the next six weeks we did everything with our rifles. We ran with our rifles. We exercised with our rifles. We dragged our rifles over every obstacle course on Parris Island. We learned the Manual of Arms and we marched thousands of miles with our rifles.

We practiced the four basic firing positions; offhand (standing), kneeling, sitting and prone. The Corps calls this practice 'Snapping In.'

We took our rifles apart and put them back together again until we could do it in our sleep. We learned the name of every minute piece of our rifles. We cleaned our rifles and for any infraction of modern or ancient Marine Corps tradition, lore or practice, real or imagined, we slept with our rifles.

We did everything with our rifles except shoot the darn things. For that we had to wait until we went to the rifle range.

The Rifle Range
—South Carolina—

*A*lthough most of the time I spent in Boot Camp is just a blur, some events, like, the bucket and rifle issues stand out clearly. My time at the rifle range is another experience I will never forget.

Back in my time, back when you had to walk nine feet just to change the television channel, shooting was a really big deal in the Marine Corps. Maybe it still is, although I wouldn't be surprised if they used smart phones and virtual reality these days. In my time, we had real targets - bulls eye targets with the rings and a black dot about the size of a dime in the middle. There was none of this sissy human silhouette stuff with the target the size of a small SUV.

As I recall, there were three qualification levels for marksmanship: Expert, Sharpshooter and Marksman. I think the Corps even paid a couple of bucks extra a month to Marines who were good shooters. When you are only making about fifty bucks a month, a couple of bucks more is a big deal.

To show how serious the Corps was about shooting, when it came our time to qualify with the Marine Corps Basic Infantry Weapon, our beloved rifles, we moved from the main base and lived for a week out at the rifle range.

The big day finally came. The day we had been talking about for weeks. The Yellers came among us and told us to pack our field packs that we were going to carry, and watched while we put the rest of our stuff into our foot lockers that were going to go by truck ... of course.

Another mystery of the Corps, I never did figure out what difference it made what was packed in our packs and what was packed in the foot lockers seeing as everything was going to the same place.

Anyway, we loaded up our field packs, put all our other stuff in our footlockers, left our happy home of many, many weeks in the upper squad bay of the big 'H' barracks, fell in on the road and started marching toward the rifle range.

The weather was lousy - cold, with wind and rain. It seemed like the weather had been lousy ever since we had been at Parris Island, wind and rain mixed with rain and wind. Maybe the weather is always lousy on the South Carolina coast in the winter.

I have heard that Parris Island is hot and humid and miserable in the summer. So, we can conclude that the weather at Parris Island is either lousy or miserable.

I recommend just avoiding the whole thing.

Off we marched in the rain, covered by ponchos that wouldn't keep out a light mist. As we slogged along, we soon realized that whatever other sterling qualities our Yellers may have had, land navigation was not one of their strong points.

We marched all day and we never seemed to get to the rifle range. Sometimes we could hear the pop, pop of small arms firing off to our right, sometimes we could hear it off to our left. But we didn't actually get to the rifle range until late afternoon. I didn't think Parris Island was that big.

I should have left bread crumbs on the road to prove my theory that we were being marched in a giant circle around the rifle range.

When we finally did get to the range, we found a whole new world. There were no big wooden 'H' barracks here. While we were at the rifle range we would live in Quonset Huts. These were the old-fashioned pre-World War II curved metal kind with a wooden floor, a door at each end, and a couple of little windows on each side.

There was an oil-fired stove in the middle of the floor that chugged its little heart out and sometimes managed to warm up an area of about ten feet around it.

For our sleeping arrangements there were four metal bunk beds on each side that were shoved as far into the curve of the Quonset as you could get them.

There were five Quonsets allocated to each platoon, one for each squad and one for the Yellers. When we were back at the main base ("Mainside" in Marine speak) a platoon lived in a squad bay, but out here at the rifle range a squad lived in a Squad Quonset.

After a lot of bumbling around in the wind and the rain we finally found the truck that had our footlockers, retrieved said footlockers and moved into our Quonset as best we could. And, seeing as we were all soaked, we soon had clotheslines strung everywhere around the inside of our new home and they were draped with soggy uniforms and ponchos.

The place looked like laundry day in the Lower East Side and smelled like it was inhabited by a pack of shaggy, wet dogs.

The Quonsets were cold and damp and with the rain pounding down outside it sounded as if we were in a fifty-five-gallon drum with a bunch of Orcs throwing marbles at us.

There was a wide wooden boardwalk that ran in front of the row of Quonsets that housed our platoon and ended at the head. (Which was actually just another Quonset.)

With the continuous rain, this boardwalk was always covered with a layer of mud and was as slippery as snake snot.

Whenever we fell in, we would do it on the boardwalk in front of the Yellers Quonset (the one closest to the head).

The Yellers had a little porch on their Quonset where they could stand out of the rain and yell at us while we stood in the rain...of course.

After a damp and cold night in our little Quonset (the first of many), listening to the rain pounding down on our tin roof, we got up the next morning all fired up and ready to go shoot something, anything.

Not so fast.

It seemed that we had new masters now, the Range Instructors, and they were not going to let us shoot on their precious range until we had mastered all the shooting positions—offhand (standing), sitting, kneeling and prone. Well, gee, we had been 'snapping in' ever since we got our darn rifles six weeks ago.

No good. The Range Instructors were going to make sure we did it their way and off we marched to the coldest, wettest, windiest, most exposed hillside they could find and there we practiced snapping in.

We were having such a great time out there in the wind and the rain pretending to shoot, and getting yelled at, that we didn't even go back to the camp area for noon chow, it was brought out to us.

A real treat, cold 'C' rations and rainwater, one of my favorites.

After a couple of days of snapping in we finally got to a real range and we were allowed to shoot real bullets at real targets.

I did not have any experience with guns before I joined the Marines. I grew up in a small suburban town and there were no guns in our house. But, once we started banging away, I loved it. I wasn't half bad either, at least I could usually hit what I was looking at. That is once I figured out this left-handed business.

I am one of those weird people who do some things with one hand and some things with the other. I write and bat right-handed, but I throw and bowl left-handed. When they got me out on the range and handed me a pistol, I took it in my right hand, but from the first day that they gave me a rifle, I had been snapping-in left-handed.

I soon found out that my rifle was a bit awkward for someone shooting left-handed.

Imagine yourself holding a rifle in a shooting position. The rifle is loaded with an eight-round clip that pushes in from the top and when the clip is empty it automatically ejects—to the right away from the right-handed shooter. For a righty to reload you just take your finger off the trigger, pick up a fresh clip, hold the slide back with the heel of your right hand, push the fresh clip in with your right thumb, release the slide and you are good to go.

For a lefty, your right hand is wrapped up in the sling and is busy holding the end of the rifle where the bullets go out. To inset a new clip the left-handed shooter has to pick up the clip with the left hand, reach over the rifle from the left, try to hold the slide back with your left thumb (strong slide) and use whatever fingers you have left to push in the clip, trying not to pinch a finger in the process when the slide releases.

Dawn came on Qualification Day, the day we were going to shoot for record. These would be the scores that would determine whether we were Experts, Sharpshooters, Marksmen or nothing.

Well, dawn might have come somewhere in the world, but not on the rifle range at Parris Island, South Carolina. The sky was black, the wind was blowing a gale, it was cold and the rain was pounding down making our Quonset sound like a pop-corn machine in an echo chamber.

We stood in miserable formation on the boardwalk in front of the Yellers hut watching the Yellers and the Range Instructors who were in conference on their little dry porch.

They disappeared inside, we stood in the wind and the rain.

A little while later a jeep pulled up and a guy went into the Yeller's hut. I think he was the Company Commander.

We stood in the rain.

Then a military sedan pulled up. This one had a driver with some officer in the back. I didn't know who that could be, the Commandant of the Marine Corps, maybe. He went inside.

One of the assistant Yellers stuck his head out of the door and told us to get out of the rain and back into our Quonsets. That was nice of him. At least we got out of the rain. Not long after that we got the word that qualification had been postponed until the afternoon.

That afternoon the weather was no better and qualification was postponed again until the next day. Wow! Changing the training schedule, that must have taken an act of congress. We wondered what, if anything, the Yellers would pull out of their hats to keep us busy.

I swear this is true.

An assistant Yeller appeared among us in our Quonset and said, "With all this rain, what are you going to do if we have any flooding?"

We had no answer for that one. Somehow, thinking about flooding had never entered our minds. I don't know why.

He said: "If we know a flood is coming all items of equipment will be safer if they are at the highest point available." You can't argue with logic like that.

"I think this squad needs a little flood drill. In the event of a flood all equipment will be moved to the top racks."

And then he said," Flood."

We picked up our footlockers and put them on the top bunks. These were followed by all the shoes and anything else that was loose on the deck. Then we put our rifles up on top and finally we climbed up.

There we were, thirteen rookie Marines of Fourth Squad, Second Platoon, Second Battalion, perched on the top of our bunkbeds with all our gear.

Then the Yeller asked, "Have you idiots any air

raid drills?"

You can see where this is going.

We had an air raid drill and everything, including us, went under the bunks. Then it was FLOOD! AIR RAID! all afternoon.

We were all experienced enough by now not to ask what we would do if we had an air raid during a flood.

By the time evening chow rolled around the footlockers were weighing about five hundred pounds each. It is amazing what kind of a physical workout you can get by just using a few common household items.

The next morning the weather was even worse. The sky was many shades of dark, the wind was howling, the temperature felt like it was right around freezing and the air was full of lumpy rain. But, having postponed qualification yesterday, today we were going to shoot for record, no matter what.

The experience was, to say the least, interesting. Along with trying to remember all the things the Yellers and the Range Instructors taught us about shooting, we also had to play the weather.

Shooting offhand you had to lean into the wind and rain just to keep from being blown over. Just as you were ready to squeeze the trigger the wind would whip around from another quarter, knock you back on your heels and the round that you had just fired would land somewhere out around Bermuda.

In the sitting and kneeling positions, we were in freezing cold water up to our chins.

When we went to the prone position you needed a snorkel and looking out through the rifle's sights the targets were a shimmering patch of white somewhere out in the distance that looked like they were under water.

Maybe they were under water.

We would have been better off using harpoons.

Needless to say, our range qualification was a disaster. After all that preparation and anticipation, no one qualified as Expert or Sharpshooter and only eight of us qualified as Marksmen, the lowest award given.

I only made it by one point which was pure luck. Somebody must have put a couple of rounds into one of my targets, but I wasn't going to argue.

We trudged back to the Quonsets with our spirits lower than the proverbial well-diggers butt.

The next day, a bright and sunny day, of course, we loaded up and marched back to Mainside, moved into a different big 'H' barracks, (that we had to clean) and waited for the last days of Boot Camp to pass.

Orders
—South Carolina—

While it was happening, it seemed that I would be at Parris Island forever but time did slip by rather rapidly. It was mostly just a blur of activity, but the day right near the end when the assignments came down really stands out.

Naturally, the subject of where we were going to be assigned after boot camp was our main topic of conversation. Where were we going to go? What were we going to do? Of course, we all wanted to go to Advanced Combat Training (ACT) and then to a combat unit in the Fleet Marine Force. Of course, we did. We were mostly eighteen, nineteen, twenty-year old kids with half formed brains, and those tiny brains had been thoroughly washed, dried and permanently pressed over the last twelve weeks. We were ready to be John Wayne. Hell, we were John Wayne.

Two days before graduation the Chief Yeller came into the squad bay, put us at ease, pulled a chair into the middle of the room and sat down. He told us to gather around, and we did, sitting on the floor in a semi-circle in front of him like first-graders in front of the teacher waiting for a story.

He started reading out the assignments.

It seemed that some of the guys were going to ACT and the Fleet Marines but the Marine Corps is a large organization with many specialties, everything from aircraft mechanics to cooks. I remember that a couple of guys were going to go radio school and one was going to be a clerk-typist. And then he came to me.

He said, "Idiot."

Hey! We had known each other for twelve weeks; we were on a first name basis.

"Idiot, ET School, Great Lakes, Illinois."

No. Wait. That can't be right. It's supposed to say: Advanced Combat Training, Camp Lejeune, North Carolina.

I didn't have a clue what 'ET' was, so I said, "Ah, pardon me your honor, sir, but what is ET School?"

"That's Electronic Technicians School, idiot."

My heart sank. "Ah yes, your majesty, sir, but what do electronic technicians do?"

"Electronic technicians service, repair and maintain all the sophisticated electronic equipment that is used in the United States Marine Corps."

I was afraid of that.

I am sure that the people involved in the business of personnel assignments are fine, intelligent, dedicated individuals that use nothing but state of the art dart and Ouija boards to fit the right

72

man (and woman) to the right job. What they didn't seem to understand was that putting me into close proximity with anything electronic or mechanical was not a particularly good idea. (To this day my kids won't let me anywhere near their computers.)

While it's true that I have the manual dexterity of the average rhinoceros, the chances of me actually repairing anything with more moving parts than an anvil are slim to none.

But Mother Corps said Electronic Technicians School and Electronic Technicians School at Great Lakes, Illinois was where I was going to go. But it was all in the family, about twenty-seven years earlier, when my Dad was in the Navy, he had gone to school at Great Lakes and, of course, he could fix or repair just about anything.

The apple (me) fell pretty far from that tree.

Our Chief Yeller finished reading out the assignments and then he pulled another piece of paper from the stack. He looked at it and then he looked at me and got a kind of bemused look on his face like he couldn't really believe what he was going to say next. He kind of shook his head and said, "This order came down from Battalion along with the assignments. You, Idiot, have the highest overall rating in the platoon in all phases of training over the past twelve weeks and have been designated Second Platoon's Honor Graduate."

Life is certainly full of surprises.

With that we finally graduated and I was off to the Naval Training Center, Great Lakes, Illinois.

Travel Chits and Me
—South Carolina to Illinois—

Back in my day, the military didn't give you money for travel. I guess they thought that we couldn't be trusted not to spend whatever money they gave us on beer and wild women. Now that I think about it, in my younger days half my money WAS spent on beer and women. The rest, I guess, I just wasted.

What the military gave you when you were sent from Base A to Base B were travel chits. In my case, train chits from South Carolina to Illinois with stops in between and more chits for meals that could only be used in railroad cafeterias.

On my way to Illinois, I went up to Massachusetts to see my folks. Well, not really, I had only been gone three months. I really went home to impress the girls with my shiny new uniform.   They weren't impressed.

I hit the rails for the Navy Training Center at Great Lakes, Illinois. I think you could safely say that my journey from Boston to Great Lakes was an experience. I went into Boston and got on a train heading for New York. (There was a train station in my hometown of Stoughton but, somehow, I was never able to use it.)

My travel chit said Boston, New York, Chicago so what could go wrong? I had to ask.

The train pulled out of Boston and I settled into my seat, a very nice seat—all plush and comfy, and looked around. This was a very nice train, first class. I thought that this Marine Corps travel was pretty good. Soon a conductor came through collecting tickets and I thought that he gave me kind of a funny look but I went ahead and pulled out my Official Government Travel Chit.

He said, "Your ticket please."

I said, "This is my ticket."

He was not amused. Looking back, I guess he thought I was some kind of a wise guy. He wanted a ticket—a real ticket and I didn't have a ticket.

So, there I am a brand-new Marine standing there in my brand-new uniform trying to explain to this very snooty conductor that I had a travel chit. Of course, seeing as this was a super-dooper train he had probably never seen a government travel chit.

Hey, I was so green I could have been mowed. Nobody told me that before you got on the train you were supposed to go to the station ticket office and trade the government travel chit in for a real ticket.

Well could they take care of it here—take my chit and give me a ticket? Not a chance. I guess my chit would never have gotten me on their posh train in the first place.

They kicked me off the train.

They kicked me off the train in the middle of the night.

They kicked me off the train in the middle of the night at some little station, whose name I can't remember, in the middle of Connecticut. The station was locked up tighter than a bank vault without a soul in sight. I spent a long miserable night cuddled up to my sea bag on a bench out on the station platform.

When dawn came, I was still alone and hungry waiting for someone to show up who could convert my Official Government Travel Chit into a real ticket. Finally, about nine someone did show up, opened the station and took my train chit.

I guess not too many trains stopped at this particular station because I waited all day until one showed up that would take me to New York. That's when I found out what kind of trains government travel chits were really good for.

The passenger car I got on was probably used by Custer and John Wayne when they headed west to the frontier.

It would give a cattle car a good name. It had hard seats, the windows were either open or closed (whatever they were—they stayed that way) and the toilet hadn't been cleaned since the First Battle of Bull Run.

I was also getting really hungry because I had spent all my money trying to impress the girls back home and all I had left were the government issued meal chits but, there was no cafeteria at my little station in Connecticut.

When I finally got to New York I thought the train station there was Heaven, Eden and Utopia all rolled into one because it had a cafeteria that would take my meal chit and I finally got something to eat.

I found the ticket window and got a ticket to Chicago (I had learned that much anyway) but I had no idea where I was supposed to go or what train I was supposed to take.

Fortunately, I fell in with a bunch of Sailors, Marines and Soldiers who were also headed toward Chicago and It's a good thing that I did because as green as I was who knows where I would have ended up, Timbuktu probably.

We piled onto the train and it was the same type that I had just ridden from Connecticut only this time it was so crowded that it was standing room only. Two guys in a seat and people standing in the aisles, sea bags, barracks bags and duffle bags all over the place.

I was holding my sea bag in my lap.

It is about seven or eight hundred miles from New York to Chicago and I swear the train that we were on stopped at every town, village and hamlet between the two. It took days, weeks, to get to Chicago. When they invented the term 'Milk Train' they had this train in mind.

Now, I'm a growing boy and I was getting hungry again. I could eat in the cafeterias in the stations that we stopped at along the way, if the station had one. The problem was, I never knew how long the train was going to be stopped. Sometimes the train was in and out of the station in a minute and at other times it seemed like we sat there for a half an hour.

Some of the guys would take a chance and race off the train and try to grab a sandwich hoping they would make it back before the train pulled out. But if you weren't first in line at the cafeteria counter that probably wasn't going to work.

To this day I don't know what happened to a sailor named Joe. One minute he was standing next to me, we stopped at a station and when I looked again, he was just a sea bag in the aisle heading toward Chicago.

Another consideration when contemplating running off the train for food was that I had a seat, well part of a seat, and it was a window seat no less. I was certain that if I left my seat, I would lose it. I stayed put in my seat and stayed hungry.

I spent the last of my meal chits when we got to Chicago and the last of my train chits for the North Shore Line that went up to the Naval Training Center at Great Lakes.

I was now officially broke.

When we finally got to the Naval Base at Great Lakes it was again the middle of the night. The sailors went one way and I was given a cot in the Marine Corps transit barracks which I gratefully fell into.

But not for long.

When the dawn came, I thought that I was back in boot camp at Parris Island. There was a large Gunnery Sergeant shaking my rack and yelling at me to get dressed and report to his office—immediately. He even left a Corporal with me to hustle me along. My head was spinning. I had no idea what was going on.

When I was hustled into the Gunny's office, he started yelling at me that I was two days AWOL (Absent Without Leave) and who did I think I was reporting in late to Great Lakes.

He then hustled me into the Commander of the Marine Detachments office.

In boot camp they had told us that one of the worst things you could do in the United States Marine Corps was be AWOL. So, there I was, on my first day at my first duty station in the United States Marine Corps standing at attention in front of the commander's desk trying to explain about train chits, super-dooper trains, meal chits, milk trains and Connecticut and that's why I was two days AWOL.

I knew it was the firing squad for sure.

I stood there in front of the Commander's desk confused and scared to death. I was AWOL. I was in deep doo-doo. I was petrified.

The commander of the Marine detachment was a very stern looking old Lieutenant Colonel who looked like he hadn't laughed since the Romans sacked Carthage in the Punic Wars. He looked at me like I was a galley slave in his number three galley.

Looking back on the whole thing I guess he was probably trying hard to keep a straight face. Without cracking a smile, he said that he would consider my case and threw me out of his office. That was a bit of a relief, at least I wasn't going on the rack immediately.

But there was still the Gunny. The Gunny started on my left ear and chewed his way right through my head until he reached my right ear. Then he turned around and started back the other way. When he ran down, he put me to work cleaning the head popping in every few minutes to yell at me.

Fortunately for me that was the end of it and no official action was taken. I guess it wasn't the first time that a dumb boot had showed up late.

That was one thing that I really liked about the Marine Corps, you could screw-up but once you took whatever punishment was handed out the slate was clean.

Details! Details!
—Illinois—

S
o, what do you do with a boot Marine who is waiting for a school to start?

The first thing the Gunny did was move me out of the transit barracks and into a student barracks. I guess a bunch of Marines had just graduated from some school or another because the squad bay that I moved into was empty, just me. The place could hold about twenty people and all the racks (single. not double bunked) were there, but the squad bay was hollow, it echoed, and it was very lonely. And I had to keep the whole place clean by myself.

But, fortunately, not for long. Other Marines who were scheduled for various schools started filtering in and the squad bay slowly filled up.

That's when I found out that my Electronics Technician class was not going to start for a couple of months.

Made me wonder why they were so uptight about me being a couple of days late reporting in.

The next thing the Gunny did was to put me to work. The military calls it 'being on detail.' When you are on detail you report to the Gunny every morning and he sends you off to do any job on the base that the Powers-That-Be wanted done.

Until my class started, I was on permanent detail. In the following weeks I learned all kinds of useful skills.

I learned about horticulture. Well, I mowed lawns, all kinds of lawns, from the headquarters buildings vast expanse of green to lawns over in the senior officers' housing area.

Once when I was mowing an officer's lawn his wife came out and wanted me to weed her flower bed. That didn't last too long. She quickly discovered that I couldn't tell the difference between a geranium and a weed, even when the geranium was in full bloom and had a sign on it.

I learned about Civil Engineering. Well, I swept streets. Recently I have been told that street sweeping trucks have been invented. But I guess that they were beyond the Navy's budget or technology. They gave me a push broom and a tin trash barrel mounted on wheels and I pushed and swept my way up and down the streets of Great Lakes.

Also, in the Civil Engineering line, I rode around the base on garbage trucks stopping now and again to empty trash barrels.

I improved my knowledge of the culinary arts. Well, I worked in chow-halls, peeling potatoes, washing dishes, etc.

I think that I loaded and unloaded enough trucks to qualify for membership in the local

Teamsters Union. Thank goodness for all those flood and air raid drills or I would have died.

I also painted...lots and lots of painting. I painted the outside of buildings, I painted the inside of buildings and I painted rocks—seriously, rocks. The walk way up to one of the administrative buildings was lined with 1,286 softball sized rocks (if I remember correctly) personally counted and painted by me.

And, especially, (I guess because I was a Marine on a Navy Base), I was detailed to guard things.

There were a group of warehouses stuck way off in one corner of the base. They gave me a rifle and I walked around warehouses all night. I was never quite sure what it was that I was guarding against. Was someone going to steal a warehouse? And, if they did, what was I supposed to do about it? They didn't give me any bullets, which was too bad because there were some really big, mean racoons out there. I mean, these racoons were the size of Volkswagens.

As long as the racoons didn't bother me, I was content to stay out of their way and let them do whatever they wanted. If they wanted to steal a warehouse, they were welcome to it.

We won't even talk about the family of skunks that took up residence under one of the warehouses, which is probably why the Arc of the Covenant remains lost to this day. I'm sure that it was in there.

The worst part of the skunk episode was that when the guys came to work in the morning and found that there were skunks under their warehouse, they blamed me.

But, all things pass, and eventually it was time for me to demonstrate my monumental ineptness as an Electronics Technician.

E.T. School and Me
—Illinois—

*F*inally, my Electronics Technicians School class started and I was soon 'idiot' again.

There were sixteen of us in the class and I knew most of the guys because we had been pulling details together for these past many weeks.

The first couple of weeks of school wasn't too bad as it was book stuff—electric theory, how electric motors worked and such things. I'm pretty good with book stuff.

My troubles began when we had to actually fix something.

As the school progressed the instructors would show us a piece of equipment, explain what it did and how it worked and then take us to one that they had disabled in some way. We would have to troubleshoot said equipment with various pieces of test gear, find the fault and repair it.

I was hopeless. My brain would tell me what I had to do, but somehow that message never got translated to my hands. Half the time I couldn't find the problem because I wasn't using the test equipment correctly, or I was reading the gages wrong, or I wasn't using the right piece of test gear.

If I did manage to find the fault, no matter how long I worked on it, whatever it was that was broken was still broken. In addition, not only was the original problem not corrected, but two or three other parts of the machine, motor, wiferdill or mifingator were now malfunctioning also.

The test equipment that I was using was probably broken, too, and I'm sure that I was the one who had broken it...somehow.

One of my more vivid memories was when they taught us how to use a soldering iron. The instructor would take the pieces that had to be put together and create a seamless join.

It is not easy to make a lump out of solder, but I managed. I created Modern Art, an unidentifiable lump of something that would probably command huge prices in the right market.

There was a twitch in the instructor's eye that I am certain was not there at the beginning of class.

I knew that my days in ET school were numbered, but somewhere along the way back when I was pulling details, I had taken a bunch of tests and I was informed that I had scored an appointment to the United States Naval Academy Prep School.

I really had no desire to go to the Naval Academy but I didn't want to be an Electronics Technician either, so I had taken the tests.

So, before I could be bounced out of ET school,

I was shipped off to the Naval Academy Prep School at the Navy Training Center, Bainbridge, Maryland and to the best thing that ever happened to me.

That's where I met my sailor.

Hurricane
—Maryland—

I managed to find my way from the Navy Training Base at Great Lakes, Illinois to the United States Naval Training Center at Bainbridge, Maryland. I couldn't seem to get away from Navy bases. I specifically remember trying to join the Navy and I ended up going into the Marines, so what gives?

I also remember graduating from high school and not wanting to go to college now I was enrolled in a prep school that would last a year followed by another four years at the Naval Academy.

The flippers were sure slapping my little round metal ball around.

I had just arrived at Bainbridge and was getting squared away in my new digs, (which were very nice, they were two-man cubicles with two desks, bookshelves and built in lockers) when the word came down that a hurricane was headed our way and would probably hit the next day. Well, I thought, that should be interesting.

The next day, as the rain started to fall and the wind started to rise, we were told that the 'Powers That Be' had volunteered the prep school to assist the local authorities in doing...whatever.

That was generous of them; nobody asked me.

Sure enough, about mid-afternoon we were ordered into our foul weather gear, such as it was, (mine consisted of regular Marine Corps utilities, a field jacket, my handy-dandy, very thin and all but useless poncho and boots that were nowhere near waterproof).

Right about evening chow time trucks appeared to take us to Wherever, so we missed evening chow.

Not a good sign.

We loaded up into the trucks which were regular Navy issue, open beds with wooden racks on the sides, benches along each side and a leaky canvas cover over the top.

We were carted off to a local high school.

When we arrived at the high school, we found a hundred or so people milling around in the gym. I was really disappointed. I thought that at these affairs there were dozens of lovely young ladies serving coffee and donuts and dazzling smiles.

I guess they didn't get the memo.

After a couple of hours of the usual confusion and bumbling about that accompanies these types of things, we were split into groups and sent off on various tasks.

The group that I got put into was slated for traffic control. We were loaded back into the truck and off we went. It was now quite dark (dark, like the inside of a cow) the rain was coming down in sheets and the wind was blowing hard. We drove up dark roads and drove down darker roads. I had no idea where we were. Of course, I couldn't see anything from inside the back of the truck, but it seemed like we were really out in the boondocks.

Every so often the truck would stop and people would be ordered out. This went on through many stops and we dropped off one or two guys each time.

Finally, it was my turn. I was the last one. I climbed down out of the truck right into the middle of nowhere. As best as I could tell through the darkness and the wind and rain I was at a 'T' junction on a rural road. A very rural road.

My instructions, from a guy who stayed warm and dry inside the cab, were that I could allow traffic to proceed on the stem of the 'T,' the road that we had just come down, and traffic could turn to the left but, I should warn them that there might be water on the road and I was not allowed to let traffic turn to the right due to possible flooding.

Okay! I got it.

The truck turned around and headed back down the road the way we had just come and as the motor noise and the tail lights faded away I began to feel pretty lonely, and hungry, and wet, and cold.

The rain kept coming down and the wind kept blowing. I looked around, but, as dark and rainy as it was, I really couldn't see anything. As far as I could tell there was not a house, barn, shed, a building of any kind, or a light, in any direction.

I did have a flashlight, a little brown, two-battery, government issue flashlight. The beam, such as it was, bravely stabbed out into the darkness for a distance of about three feet.

From what I could see, or thought I could see, the area around me looked like it was totally flat, covered with tall grass and I thought I could hear running water. When I moved around a bit, I found that the area wasn't completely flat; there was a small knoll maybe ten or fifteen feet high on my corner of the 'T' with a single little tree growing on top, the only tree in sight.

I stood in the wind and rain and waited to direct traffic.

No traffic came, but after a while, water came. I noticed water creeping up onto the other side of the road, (the long side of the 'T') then it slowly crept across the road. The water crept over onto the corner of the 'T' on my side of the road and slowly, slowly the water kept coming.

I felt like I was trapped inside a really bad science fiction movie.

When the water got to my boots, I could see that it was soon going to cover my 'post.' I thought "Now what do I do?" I had been in the Marine Corps a little while now but I still remembered all the dire things that the Drill Instructors at Parris Island said would happen to you if you ever abandoned your post. There would be whips, chains, a firing squad, thumb screws...the rack.

But the water was still rising. What should I do?

I figured that I had three choices: I could stand here manning my post and drown (I really didn't fancy that one), I could head back up the road, but I didn't know what was back there and going back up the road would mean that I would be "abandoning my post," or I could take a chance on my little hill.

I picked the hill and slowly backed a little way up the knoll. I wondered if they would shoot me for abandoning my post. I reasoned that I wasn't really abandoning my post, it was right there in front of me and it wasn't a very high knoll; I wasn't that far away.

The water continued to rise and I took more steps back up the hill until I was standing with my back against the tree.

The water came up to my boots again. What to do now?

So, I climbed up into the tree.

The water kept on rising up the trunk so I kept climbing. It wasn't a very big tree, either. The water rose a couple of feet up the trunk and then seemed to stop.

There I was, all alone in the dark (and the wind and rain) sitting in my little tree and, as far as I could tell, surrounded by water.

Unfortunately for me the tree leaked and I sat shivering in the wind and the rain, all night.

No cars came for me to direct, which, I guess, was a really good thing, they would have needed pontoons. If they needed directions, I figured that I could swim down to my post and fulfill my function.

My little flashlight died and the dark was even darker.

A little before dawn it seemed that the water was starting to recede and as it got a bit lighter the wind and rain slacked off and I could see a little more of my surroundings.

No wonder I thought that I had heard the sound of running water earlier, it looked like I was on the edge of a small delta. On the other side of the road there was a tideland marsh with several little streams running through it and the TIDE was going out.

There was no sign of human habitation in any direction.

As the water receded, I climbed down from my little tree and followed the water line back down the little hill to my corner of the 'T' and resumed my post like any other drowned rat.

Still no traffic came, but at least the rain stopped.

I would be willing to bet that there never was any traffic on that road.... ever.

A couple of hours later, well it seemed like a couple of hours, (among the many things that I didn't have was a watch), I began to have feelings of abandonment.

The great "they" had forgotten me. I was doomed to stay out here on this forlorn "T" junction until I became part of the local folklore; the poncho covered skeleton standing by the side of the road waiting to direct traffic and dreaming of food and a hot shower.

Finally, I thought I heard the sound of a motor off in the distance and, wonder of wonders, my truck reappeared and I climbed into the back.

Funny thing, I was the only one in the truck.

I hadn't really been forgotten, had I?
As the truck turned around and headed up the road, I looked out of the back and I had my last look of my "T" junction and growing smaller in the distance was my hill...and my little tree.

My Sailor
Maryland

*T*here were about a hundred and seventy-five of us in the Naval Academy Prep School. Outside of the fact that we were all active duty enlisted men, mostly Navy and Marine Corps but we did have a few Air Force and Army, and lived a military life with inspections, details and marching everywhere we went, it was pretty much like any other school, I guess.

We lived in the barracks but we went to school in a big, old stone pile called Tome Memorial Hall, which was a large, two-story building with a columned entrance and a bell tower on top. I never knew what it was originally or how it came to be on the Bainbridge Naval Training Center.

Our classes were geared toward the Naval Academy, Physics, Algebra, Geometry, English and History. I was keeping my head up—barely. I had trouble with Algebra and Geometry. English had been hard for me in high school and spelling was (and is) a complete mystery.

Where was a personal computer with a good word-processing program and spell-check when I needed it? Oh, yeah. Not invented yet!

Along with the fact that my future academic career at the Naval Academy didn't look very promising, I discovered that I wasn't a very good sailor either.

I could probably get seasick in a bathtub.

On the plus side the prep school had a sports program that included football, basketball, cross-country and swimming. I had never played sports when I was in high school because I always had an after-school job, so I figured that I would go out for everything.

Football was first and I turned up all bright and shiny, with zero experience. I didn't even know how to put the pads on, but the staff was desperate (only a couple dozen guys turned out) so I was in.

The coaching staff didn't quite know what to do with me. I weighed about 175 pounds, so I wasn't exactly little, but then I wasn't exactly big either. I was in pretty good shape and I could run but I didn't know enough to play any of the skill positions.

They made me an interior lineman, a guard and gave me a quick tutorial on what to do. On this play push the guy in front of you that way, on that play push the guy this way and when the other team has the ball go tackle the ball carrier.

Okay! Got it.

We played a nine-game schedule against college freshman and junior college teams and I lasted two.

Our first game was against Baltimore Junior

College and I didn't do too badly. The guy I played against and I were pretty evenly matched and I blocked him most of the time and even made a couple of tackles. (There was no platoon system, offense and defense, in those days—you played the whole game.)

It was a good game but we lost 6-0.

The next week we went up against Potomac State College and we were *way* out of our league. They were big and they were fast. On the first play I got down into position and I couldn't see anything. The guy I was playing against blotted out the sun. (I found out later that he out-weighed me by 119 pounds.)

It was a long afternoon. On the first play he swatted me aside like a mosquito. After the first quarter he didn't really have to hit me; I would have been happy to go where ever he pointed. When I tried to block him, I would have had more luck trying to move Mount Everest.

But the worst was yet to come. Late in the game as I was picking myself up from another swat, somebody hit me from behind—just threw an illegal block into the back of my legs. I don't know why because I was nowhere near the action. Anyway, I went down hard and I had to be carried off the field.

Fortunately, even though my right knee was torn up pretty bad, nothing was broken. I was on crutches and in a walking cast for a month and hobbled around pretty good for several weeks after that.

That was the end of my athletic career.

By the way, we lost that game 83-0.

But I plodded on.

Then everything changed.

On a sunny spring afternoon, I was sitting in the base cafeteria with some of my classmates celebrating my promotion to corporal (why I got promoted I will never know) when we noticed a very attractive lady sailor (WAVE) sitting at a table all by herself.

Being the scholars that we were we quickly figured out that, 1) she was indeed a very pretty young lady and, 2) none of us knew her.

I suddenly heard a voice, that sounded surprisingly like mine, say I was going to go over and introduce myself, and I did.

You can't imagine how out of character it was for me to do that. I was usually as tongue-tied and awkward around the ladies as a male can get, but I did it.

She smiled, that wonderful smile that lit up my life for over fifty years, and invited me to sit down. I sat down and, to my surprise I discovered that I could talk. We not only talked, we laughed! I found out that her name was Faye and that she was from Seattle and that she was in Dental Technicians School and that she had the duty so she had to go.

I walked her over to the dental clinic and got a date for the weekend.

That first date we went to the movies, but I soon introduced her into our group of about a dozen guys and gals whose main claim to fame was our Saturday night beach parties. Well, we didn't actually have a beach, but we did have a river so we had riverbank parties. I guess that it's the same thing—a bonfire, swimming and inner-tubing, hotdogs and beer. Nothing exciting, but Faye loved it.

One evening we had a ham. I don't remember where that came from, but late in the evening I had a slice of ham in my hand and I was trying to figure out how to heat it up. Faye took my ham, picked up an empty beer can, punched a hole in the bottom, shoved a stick through both ends, draped my ham over the can and set it over the fire.

I was in love. My mother always said that the way to a man's heart was through his stomach.

Ah, yup. No arguments there.

The next few weeks were wonderful. Faye and I would meet on the base for coffee or just to walk and talk. We told each other our life stories and I would love it when we would lie on a blanket by the campfire down by the river and she would spin me tales about growing up in the still pretty much undeveloped country of tall timber, meadows, creeks and streams just north of Seattle, Washington.

Faye's World
—Washington—

From Faye's Journal

Once upon a time, when the world and I were a little younger, the area just north of Seattle was still pretty wild country. From the outskirts of Seattle, a forest of cedar, spruce, hemlock and pine rolled over hills, ravines, rivers and streams all the way to Canada.

There was only one paved road that ran north from Seattle, 15th Avenue, and it was only about twenty miles long.

Like beads on a string little communities, farms and homesteads sprang up along its length. At the very end of the paved road there was a little community that called itself Lago Vista (I never knew why) and that is where I grew up.

I lived in a house that my Daddy and my

granddad had built, or started building, many years ago when Mama and Daddy were first married. Originally it was just a cabin—one room and a lean-to kitchen—but over the years the kitchen was finished and a bedroom was added.

There was no piped-in city water this far from Seattle but we did have a well and there was a small creek that ran across our property out behind the gardens. The toilet facilities consisted of an outhouse out back. I guess that on a real estate brochure you would describe it as—two rooms, kitchen and a path.

When my brother and I came along our bedrooms were added in the attic.

My room was pillared by the red brick chimney on one side and a casement window that I could open or close upon the world, with a sill that was just the right height for leaning on and day dreaming, on the other.

I re-arranged my furniture twice a year. Summer would see the bed under the window, better to catch a cool breeze and watch Orion stalking across the sky. In the winter I put the bed over by the chimney and if the night was cold, I would carefully lift a portion of the quilts and place my feet on the warm bricks.

Countless are the times I would fall asleep or was awakened, tucked snuggly under the eaves, to the sound of rain pattering on the shingles.

Our house was next door to my grandmother (I always called her Gram, grandpa passed away before I was born) and although we did not have a real farm, we did have a huge garden out behind the two houses that grew everything from corn to carrots. We also raised rabbits and chickens.

There were other houses on our street (dirt

road) so there were a few kids to play with, but most of the time I was quite happy to be by myself.

Daddy and the other town boosters tried hard to make a town grow. They built a Community Center, organized dances, box suppers, pageants and plays but, in the end, Lago Vista never caught on and it became part of a larger near-by community called Lake Forest Park.

The heart of Lago Vista was "the spring" and Benny Horn's Pioneer Grocery Store and Lumber Yard.

The spring was in a natural clearing located just off of the paved road, about where the pavement ended. In the middle of this clear space a spring bubbled up into a basin of pure white sand. The spring water was deliciously sweet and so cold that it could make your teeth ache.

A young alder grew beside the spring and someone had pounded a nail into its trunk and provided a tin cup for passersby.

There was no chemically treated chlorinated city water in Lago Vista so, if you wanted fresh water and didn't have your own well, it was the spring. On Saturdays the spring became the social gathering place for everyone from miles around as cars, carts and wagons lined up to fill water barrels. Even people who lived closer-in toward Seattle and had the convenience of the city water supply would come out to the spring. Nothing tasted as sweet and good as water from that spring.

As more folks moved to the area, the spring was threatened by its own popularity. All those people tramping about its banks and hauling barrels in and out to be filled didn't do it much good. The Community Club and the county got together and boxed the spring with cement with a little ramp for barrels.

Before or after filling water barrels folks would go to Benny Horn's Pioneer Grocery to gas up at the glass topped pumps, settle their bills and buy groceries. They would especially go to hear the latest gossip that they might have missed at the spring or to share a few additional tidbits that they themselves might have picked up to pass on.

At the Pioneer Grocery just about everyone shopped "on the book." A sales book with your family's surname printed on the spine was kept in a drawer under the till. After payday the grocery bill would be settled, paid on or sometimes carried over. People didn't like to do that but times were tough, this was the thirties, and work was scarce. Benny Horn was one of the good guys who helped carry a lot of families through the Great Depression.

I loved the Pioneer Grocery. When Mama settled the bill, she sometimes had a few pennies or even a nickel left over for me. What anticipation and agony of decision! Under the counter were boxes and gleaming glass jars filled with candy. All kinds of candy of every size, color and shape imaginable. You could get two, three or even four of them for a penny. Should I get two big jawbreakers or four of the wax shapes filled with sweet syrup? The jawbreakers would last a long time and kept changing color. I enjoyed popping them in and out of my mouth to see what color they were. The sweet syrup was soon gone from the wax shapes but the wax would last and could be chewed like gum.

When I finally decided, my candy would be put into a small paper sack. A bag with a nickels worth of candy was a powerful thing. It could be hoarded to offer as daily treats for a whole week, shared in a grand gesture of largess or some pieces could be traded for other objects or favors.

Candy was a kid's currency.

When I was sent to the store, I had to walk under the power lines. Just before the Pioneer Grocery the huge metal lattice frames that carried the electrical power lines crossed my world. Like soldiers the towers and lines marched downhill from North city, spanned the canyon at McAleer Creek, and went up and over the hills heading north, passing out of knowledge.

I did not know or even wonder where they went.

There was another grocery store nearby called Leland's. Mrs. Leland was the kind of person that was born old. She never smiled and she made me very uncomfortable. There was no dawdling or window shopping at Leland's. Mrs. Leland would give children a cold stare and say, "If you're not here to buy something go play somewhere else."

Sometimes when Mama sent me to the store she would say, "And you can have two pennies for yourself."

If I was sent to Leland's Grocery, I tried to remember to wipe my feet so I wouldn't be sent back to the mat. I tried to stand quietly at the counter and ask, "Please, Mama wants to know if you have a spool of quilting thread?" instead of going to the rack and looking.

There were jars of candy at Leland's Grocery too, but I usually saved my pennies for the Pioneer Store because half the fun of buying candy was the looking and Mrs. Leland always wanted me to make up my mind in a hurry.

At the Pioneer Grocery I would skip in and

announce, "Mama would like a quart of milk and a pound of butter and I can have two pennies." Mr. Horn would laugh and say, "Okay, you choose what you want and I will get the other things." He would also cheerfully cash returned bottles for the deposit money. With some big quart bottles worth five cents each, they were a source of income not to be ignored. The eyes of all children, including mine, constantly scanned the roadside for discarded treasure.

Once in a while Gram would take me on a "special treat" and we would take the bus into Seattle, have lunch at Ivar's Acres of Clams (I would always have "Halibut Cheeks") and ride the ferry over to Bremerton and back. I remember riding on the "Silver Slug," the Kalakala, the art deco ferry that plied the route between Seattle and Bremerton. The only other times that I remember going to "the big city" was at Christmas when we went downtown to look at all the holiday displays in the department store windows.

That was my world. I went to school in a one room schoolhouse that was just down the street and had grades one through six. I knew practically nothing of the outside world beyond the woods and rolling hills that surrounded me.

Faye's Fish Tales
—Washington—

From Faye's Journal

J have a fuzzy memory of a fishing experience that
I had when I was very little.

My mother and Gram were going to have some
ladies over for a 'Stich and Bitch' and to get me out of
the way they said I could go fishing in the little creek
that ran across our property out behind the gardens.
Off I went with my little fishing pole that Daddy had
made for me.

I found a soft, grassy place on the bank to sit,
put a worm on my hook and dropped it into the water.
I should explain that Little Creek was only about three
or four yards across and maybe two or three feet deep.
Soon I had a tug on the line and when I pulled it in the

worm was gone. I put another worm on the hook and when I felt a tug again, I was so excited I jerked my pole straight up.

A dark speckled thing with four legs and a tail was almost touching my nose. I screamed (I had a really good scream that could be heard for miles) at the monster dangling from the end of my pole.

The monster wiggled and I shrieked.

I jumped up and started to run home but, I didn't drop my fishing pole. I ran and ran and every time I looked over my shoulder the wiggling monster was right behind me. So, I ran faster, gripped my pole tighter and shrieked louder. It seemed to me that no matter how fast I ran the monster kept chasing me. It never occurred to me to let go of my fishing pole.

Just as I came pounding up to the back of the house Mama, Gram and the ladies came pouring out of the kitchen door, probably thinking that I was being murdered.

If I was expecting help, love, tenderness or sympathy I was sorely disappointed. The ladies about fell down laughing. Gram came over, took my fishing pole and gently unhooked my poor salamander.

Mama and Gram said that I should put him back in the creek.

No way.

But they insisted and they did walk with me as I returned my monster to the water.

That was my earliest fishing experience at Little Creek. Our house was also near McAleer Creek. In those days McAleer Creek tumbled, sallied and flowed unhindered through the dark woods and shady thickets between Lake Ballinger to the north and Lake Washington to the east. It was dubbed the "Big Creek" for good reason - it was big. It was fifteen or twenty yards across and really deep in spots, but it was a wonderous place to explore. Clear and cold the water was home to trout, crawdads, fresh water mussels and, when in season, the salmon ran bank to bank as they hurried upstream to the gravelly reaches a little further north.

I was not allowed to go by myself to the Big Creek; it was off limits, and deemed too dangerous. So, of course, being a dutiful daughter, I snuck away to the Big Creek every chance I could.

Grown-ups, what do they know?

I called my favorite spot on the creek "The Log Hole." It was a place where the creek made a slight bend wide enough break the leafy canopy and let sunlight dress the banks in dappled profusion. It was here that a huge fallen log, about eight feet in diameter, lay gently slanted into the water. Up slope, one end of the log seemed rooted in a dense thicket, the other end lay in the water and caused McAleer Creek to swirl and eddy into a quiet pool—my Log Hole.

One of my earliest memories of Big Creek, took place when I was about five. I had taken the fishing pole that Daddy had made for me, dug a few worms out of the compost pit and headed for my Log Hole. It was wonderous. The salmon were running and as far as I could see up and down the creek the surface of the water was just a thrashing, churning mass.

If anyone ever tells you that spawning salmon will not bite on a hook don't you believe them! I put a worm on my hook, threw it into the creek and immediately the king of all salmon chomped onto it and headed up stream taking me with him. Because I wasn't about to let go of my fishing pole, he pulled me right off the bank and into the water.

After towing me about a hundred yards upstream he turned around and headed back downstream, running over me in the process. A hundred yards downstream he turned and plowed back up again. I don't know how many times he changed direction but, every time he did, he ran over me. After one of these maneuvers, I found that I had my arms wrapped around the fish and we were lying on a gravel bank out of the water. He was way bigger than I was but, fortunately, I was lying on top of him and no matter how much he thrashed about I was not going to let him get away.

Somehow, through all this, I still had my fishing pole.

Now that he was mine the problem was how to get him home. He must have out-weighed me by twenty pounds, and I wasn't quite sure where I was. Though I couldn't see it I figured that I was upstream from the Log Hole. I also couldn't see any kind of a path up from the creek through the thickets and the woods.

But he was my fish and I was going to get him home.

I started dragging him through the woods toward what I hoped was home. Lucky for me, I hadn't gone very far when I hit the old logging trail that came out of the woods behind Gram's house. I started dragging my fish up the dirt road.

I was just about into Gram's yard when she spotted me, hollered to my mother and they both came running.

Both the fish and I were a sorry sight. I was still soaking wet, my clothes were torn, I had lost a shoe and I was one giant bruise from my head to my toes. My poor fish, or rather, what was left of him, was in even worse shape.

But, when all was said and done, it ended well. The grown-ups were mad at me for going down to the Big Creek by myself but proud of me for hanging on to my fish so no dire punishments were forthcoming.

Mama and Gram salvaged what they could from my fish and we had him for dinner.

I think that after that they kind of gave up on trying to keep me away from the Big Creek.

One day I got my fishing line caught in the branches overhead and giving an extra hard tug I tumbled myself into the water. Angry at my carelessness and thankful that no one was there to laugh at me I got myself into a sitting position and my mouth opened in astonishment—the big log was hollow. I could look up its length and see sunlight. I quickly scrambled up the wooden tunnel and found that the brush didn't cover the other end. Instead there was a thicket of salal, huckleberries and salmonberries encircling a tiny lawn that was not much wider than my arms could span. Oh, it was a magical place, a hidden place and - forever more - my secret place.

Faye's Showtime
—Washington—

From Faye's Journal

Once in a while, when we had a flash of inspiration, my friends and I would put on plays, both indoors and outdoors. The performances were always in the evenings after our fathers came home from work so that they could enjoy the show and, we hoped, appreciate our hard work. Deciding what to do and how to do it, what could be used for costumes and props and practicing would take all afternoon.

If the weather was nice, we would hang old blankets on the clothes line for stage curtains and put on a variety show with singing and dancing acts, tumbling and magic tricks. One time when the weather was rainy, we found a big cardboard box, made it into a stage and put on a puppet show. Once we even put on a circus.

Sometimes (maybe most of the time) the show wouldn't come off just as we had planned it. For example, that time we decided to have a circus my friend Sharon wanted to be a lion tamer because she had a big yellow cat. She also had a costume with yellow tights and a brown tutu (left over from when she had been a honey bee in a dance recital). And, best of all, her mother had made a small tutu for one of her dolls from the scraps. The doll sized tutu would make a perfect lion's mane for the cat.

We thought the mane looked great, but the cat didn't like it. We practiced without the mane.

Showtime and time for the lion taming act! Sharon clapped the elastic band of the little brown tutu over the cat's head, turned and bowed to the audience. With the howl of a banshee the cat clawed at its mane, and then hissing and spitting leaped on top of Sharon's head which cause Sharon to add an impromptu dance routine to the performance. Finally, the cat jumped off Sharon's head and streaked for the nearest tree. Up the tree and into the highest branches it went, yowling all the way.

We didn't think it was very funny but our dads laughed as they got a ladder and rescued our "lion."

What was that show-biz phrase? Never work with children or animals? Never let children work with animals, either.

Faye's Berry Picking
—Washington—

From Faye's Journal

Speaking of circuses, every fall, when the huckleberries were ripe, the whole family, Mama, Daddy, Aunts, Uncles, cousins, everyone, would spend a few days camping in the mountains. We would have tents, fire pits, tarps over everything—our entourage was quite reminiscent of the circus trains hauling the Big Top to town. I loved it.

The main reason for this excursion was, of course, the huckleberries. Not the tart, pink coastal huckleberries but the big, blue, sweet huckleberries that grow up in the Cascade Mountains. Every morning we were off with our pails and buckets and we picked huckleberries—a LOT of huckleberries.

Well, the family picked a lot of huckleberries. I

was only four or five on this particular expedition of note and probably not much help, but I was a pretty good grazer. More berries made their way into my mouth than made their way into the can. Also, I was pretty non-discriminate in my berry selection: huckleberries, blackberries, salmonberries, blueberries. Any berry, if I didn't eat it, might make it into the can. Mama never said anything; she just kept my pickings separate and when she canned, she labeled them "Faye's Many Berry Jelly."

On this particular day I was given my bucket and was trailing along with the family happily picking and eating away when at some point I became a little separated from the rest of the group. I was a little higher up on the hill and I saw a huckleberry bush that looked like it was shaking. I didn't think about why it should be shaking, I just started picking (and eating).

The bush kept shaking.

Curiosity finally got the best of me and I stuck my head into the bush to see what was going on and came face to face with a bear. I let out a shriek. The bear let out a growl.

That got everyone's attention. Daddy said that when he heard the commotion and looked up, there I was running down the hill squalling at the top of my lungs and there was a pretty good-sized black bear bellowing at the top of his lungs and high tailing it up and over the top of the hill.

Once the family determined that I was not wounded they went back to berry picking. You better believe, I stayed close to Daddy for the rest of the day.

Faye's Wash Day
1930s–1940s
—Washington—

From Faye's Journal

Most of the time the washing machine lived on the back porch, its round tub, domed lid and wringer hidden under a cover that Mama had made from oilcloth. Beside the washer were two sturdy homemade tables, two galvanized #5 washtubs and a big copper boiler.

A big, black, wood fired cast iron stove dominated the kitchen—the kind of stove that had warming ovens on top. Opposite the stove was the sink with a cold-water faucet above it. Not a fancy shiny faucet that you see in today's kitchens, but an outdoor tap that you could screw a hose into. That faucet was a real modern work saver. It was sure easier than dipping what water you needed from the well or the water barrels that you had hauled from the spring.

If Monday's weather promised to be fair, or at least dry (this is Washington), Mama would keep the fire in the stove hot after breakfast, bring in the copper boiler, set it on the stove and fill it with the hose. While the water heated, Mama set a week's worth of bread dough to rising—perhaps a dozen loaves and two or three dozen dinner rolls. Then she put a large pot of soup to simmering on a back burner.

When you had to heat the stove, you didn't want to waste the wood so soup was a good choice for wash day. It needed little attention, had a long cooking time and used up leftovers that didn't keep very long in either the icebox or the cooler.

Then the tables, galvanized tubs and the washer were brought into the kitchen and set up. All the dirty laundry was sorted into piles, from Sunday dress shirts to darkest work clothes. Cold water filled the two rinse tubs and bluing was added to the first rinse. Boiling water was then siphoned into the washing machine. White things went in first with a cup of soap to start.

As I recall, the soap Mama used was a brand called White King because it came with a free dish inside each box. But I've seen Mama take shavings from a bar of lye soap, add water and melt them on the stove when there wasn't enough money for store bought washing powder.

A large lever on the side of the washer started the agitator churning back and forth. After washing for about fifteen minutes the agitator was stopped, the wringer positioned over the first tub and another smaller lever started the rollers on the wringer.

Wringers could be rather dangerous. The laundry had to be guided into the rollers and then, on the other side, guided into the rinse tub. If you weren't careful, fingers and hands could get caught in the rollers and get badly mashed, even broken. I heard of a man who nearly choked to death when his necktie got caught in the wash.

Of course, there was the time Aunt Ella got a booby caught in the wringer. But then, Aunt Ella seldom wore a bra and had the weirdest boobs you have ever seen. Each resembled a tennis ball in the toe of a gym sock. I remember she burned one, too. One cold morning she needed more eggs and dashed out to the henhouse. Upon her return, she stood by the stove hugging herself to get warm and the boob just popped out of her housecoat and landed on a burner.

I digress.

With tongs to keep yourself from getting scalded, hot sheets and towels were fed into the rollers. I did enjoy helping to take and put clothes through the wringer. But what really made the magic was the bottle of bluing that was always added to the rinse water. Oh, the joy of being allowed to add the bluing. First there were the whorls, whirls, wisps and swirls of changing patterns to watch until no longer discernable. Then you stuck your hand in and swished the water to a uniform color. The color was the second-best thing. A wondrous, unsullied blue that held a promise of Greek Myths and Mediterranean Islands until the hot sheets and towels came lapping down like steaming rivers of ribbon candy.

The clothes were then rinsed and sent through another wringer into the second tub, rinsed some more and then sent through the wringer for the third time and then into the laundry basket. Any clothes that needed starching were set aside, another load put into the washer and the basket of wet laundry was carried outside and hung on the clothesline to dry.

As needed, and in between times, the soup was given a stir and the bread dough got punched down, kneaded, shaped into loaves and rolls, put into greased pans to rise again, baked and tipped out to cool.

There was also a pan of flower and water starch on the stove. When the last load of wash was hung on the clothesline the rinse tubs were emptied and some fresh water poured into one of them. The cooked starch was added and the reserved clothes, swished about, wrung and hung. Rinse tubs and tables were put away back on the porch. The washing machine had a little tap or petcock at the bottom for draining the tub. The wash water went into buckets that were emptied into the sink.

As you can imagine, Mama's kitchen floor was no longer spotless. The washer was pushed back onto the porch (the legs of the washer had casters) and, using the last bucket of wash water, the kitchen floor was washed and then waxed when it was dry.

Now, while mama had a bite of lunch, made the beds and kept an eye on the weather, the radio was turned on so Mama could listen to the "soaps." Each program lasted fifteen minutes and there were three or four that she hated to miss. I think her favorite was "Stella Dallas." I headed out the back door when Mama turned up the volume and the announcer asked, "Can a poor girl from the country (hills?) find wealth and happiness in the big city?"

When dry, the laundry was taken from the line, carried in, folded and put away. Everything that needed ironing was sprinkled with water, snugly rolled and bundled for the morrow's chore. And, finally, the weeks baking was wrapped and put away.

So that was wash day and why we always had soup and bread on Mondays.

I've sent out for pizza with far less excuse for being tired.

The Reluctant Midshipman
—Maryland—

*B*eing with Faye was wonderful but we knew that it couldn't last.

I was sure that Faye was the gal for me and she seemed to feel the same way about me, but our trains were on different tracks. I was a student in the Naval Academy Prep School, and as soon as I graduated, in a few weeks, I would be discharged from the Marine Corps and sworn in as a Midshipman at the Naval Academy, for four years.

One thing that you can't have as a midshipman is a wife. They told me that you couldn't have a horse or a moustache either, but I figured I could live with that. I just thought I'd mention it.

My sailor was in the Navy in Dental Technicians School and when she graduated, also in a few weeks, she would be transferred to a Navy dental clinic somewhere in the world—probably far, far away from Annapolis.

The Navy has a lot of dental clinics scattered around the world.

My sailor wasn't happy about me going away for four years and I wasn't happy about her being re-assigned somewhere away from me, but what to do?

While we were dithering time ran out and despite my miserable performance in Algebra, Geometry and English I graduated from the prep school, was discharged from the Marine Corps and was sworn in as a Midshipman at the United States Naval Academy.

I guess you could say I was not your ideal midshipman. My heart was definitely elsewhere.

The Navy base at Bainbridge was not that far away, so when Faye could get liberty, she came over to Annapolis and I kind of slipped over the wall to meet her, not once, but several times.

Did I get caught?

Of course, I got caught.

I always got caught.

Needless to say, the Powers-That-Be at the Naval Academy were not happy with me and we soon parted company. I like to think of it as one of those "You can't fire me. I quit" situations.

While all this was going on Faye finished school and was assigned to the dental clinic at the big Naval Base at Newport, Rhode Island.

Yup! The same base where I had lived as a little kid during World war II.

When I resigned from the Naval Academy, I became a civilian, so I went up to Newport, and, finally, formally, and officially asked Faye to marry me.

We walked the streets of Newport contemplating our future. I was planning to get a job right there in Newport and stay there until Faye finished her enlistment. But my Sailor was a lot smarter than me. She figured that I had Government Issue blood running in my veins and I wouldn't be really happy outside of the military.

We decided to cast our lot with the Air Force.

I'm not sure why we picked the Air Force instead of the Marines or the Navy, but as the years unfolded it was absolutely the right choice. The Air Force gave us an interesting job, worldwide travel and the opportunity to meet and become lifelong friends with some wonderful people, many of whom are now, sadly, slipping away.

The Re-enlistee
—New York—

I went into the Air Force Recruiting Center in Boston and they seemed happy to see me. When they found out that I was a prior service person it seemed that they couldn't do enough for me and all the formalities were quickly taken care of.

One thing that they were really sorry about was that they couldn't give me my former rank back, I would have to drop one grade. So, I enlisted in the Air Force as an Airman Third Class, one stripe (a Private First Class in the Marines) which was better than I expected. I thought that I would have to start all over again at the bottom as a private (Basic Airman).

I left what few possessions I had with Faye, climbed on a bus and headed for Air Force Basic Training at Sampson Air Force Base in up-state New York.

When I got there, I almost fell down laughing. Trying to compare Air Force Basic Training at Sampson with the Marine Corps Boot Camp at Parris Island was like comparing Rivendell with Mordor (for you Tolkien fans).

Don't get me wrong, having already experienced Mordor, I'll take Rivendell.

The difference was apparent as soon as I got off the bus. Instead of being herded along by a gaggle of Yellers, I leisurely walked into the Reception Center and presented my orders to a clerk.

She informed me that as a prior service person I wouldn't be going through regular Air Force Basic Training. I would join a re-enlistee flight that would be made up entirely of prior service personnel. (The Air Force calls platoons "flights." I had to learn a new language.)

I guess that the Air Force Powers-That-Be figured that re-enlistees already knew all the purely military stuff so we were only at Sampson for three weeks to get indoctrinated into Air Force ways, get our uniforms, and, most importantly, find out what AFSC (Air Force Specialty Code) we were going to have— what our job in the Air Force was going to be.

I was directed down the hall to a small conference room. There were already four of five guys present and over the next hour or so the rest of our re-enlistee flight trickled in.

Once we were assembled, I began the most bizarre three weeks that I ever experienced in the military.

There were twenty in my re-enlistee flight (I think the regular basic training flights had seventy or seventy-five) and these guys were the greatest collection of characters that I have ever run into.

These were the characters who were portrayed by Phil Silvers, Andy Griffin, Bill Murry, Jim Nabors or Martin and Lewis on TV and in the movies.

All of them had been in the military during the Korean War, two in the Air Force and the rest in the Army, and two of them had also been in the Army during World War II.

Think of them as Professional Privates—Willy and Joe, Goldbricks, Goof-offs, Sergeant Bilko, Sad Sacks, Beetle Baileys. There wasn't a rule or regulation made that these guys couldn't get around—or wouldn't try to get around just for the hell of it.

I was the youngest re-enlistee by far and the only ex-Marine. I just went along for the ride.

The airman assigned as our Flight Commander stepped into the room. He was a short, dumpy Airman First Class and he started off on the wrong foot. He was going to impress on us the ways of the Force. He was treating us as if we were kid civilians just entering the military for the first time.

Funny, I can remember everything about this clown, except his name.

He was doomed.

After he spent about a half hour or so trying to impress us with his exalted status, he told us that seeing as it was late afternoon, we had only two places to go: the mess hall and the barracks. (Sorry, language again, the United States Air Force does not have mess halls, it has "dining halls.")

Our Flight Commander decided that we would go to the dining hall first. Now, we had just gotten off the bus and we all had our travel bags, so why didn't we go to the barracks first where we could wash up and drop our stuff?

"No," he said, "dining hall first."

My fellow re-enlistees still thought that we should go find the barracks first.

We went outside, formed up and he gave us the command "forward march."

Nobody moved. Actually, I started to go but stopped myself when no one else moved.

We went to the barracks. We sorted out our bunks, dumped our bags, washed up and then kind of straggled over to the dining hall. We were supposed to be marching to the dining hall and our commander was supposed to be marching us but it looked to me as though we were kind of all walking along together.

The next morning's reveille was another pleasant surprise. No police whistle. No crashing trash cans. No colorful language. At 0400 the lights just came on.

We got up at 0400 because at 0500 we were supposed to be out on a parade field with all the basic training flights for morning muster.

In all my years in the military that has to be one of the dumbest things I have ever seen.

I should point out that at this time the Air Force was only a few years old and was having an identity crisis. After being a part of the Army for over forty years the Air Force was now a separate service and was trying hard to shed Army customs and practices and develop procedures of its own.

This idea of the morning muster must have been carried over from the old Army. I mean the OLD Army. The John Wayne on the Western Frontier Army.

The plan was that all the flights, and there must have been at least twenty with seventy plus people in each flight, would march onto this big, unpaved field. The field was across the street from some kind of headquarters building that had a big porch wrapped around it.

It was still dark. Very dark, like the inside of a bowling ball dark.

The field had no lights and whatever grass that maybe had been there at one time had worn off long ago which made it nice and soupy when it rained.

Once all the flights were done blundering into each other in the dark and got lined up in some kind of order someone standing on the porch, way over there across the road, would call the roll and each flight would report, "Flight Umpty-ump all present and accounted for, sir."

Who knew? Who could possibly know? We could barely see the guy on the porch standing under his little light bulb. I know that he couldn't see us.

Once this fiasco was over our commander marched us back to the barracks.

The re-enlistees were not happy about having to get up at four in the morning to go through this useless exercise and they made their unhappiness known. Our commander made what was probably a self-preservation decision. He said that from now on we would march ourselves over to morning muster.

Later in the day the member of our group who had been appointed our "Section Leader," a big ex-Army guy from Brooklyn who, I heard, left the Army as a private (but I think he had been a corporal twice and sergeant once) said to me, "Kid, you got a loud voice. Tomorrow morning you go out there and report us in."

The next morning, while the rest of the re-enlistees slept in, I wandered out on the parade field and kind of found a spot in the swirling masses. When they called the roll, I reported flight 2502 (or whatever it was—can't remember) all present.

No one ever said anything so I guess they never figured out that it was just me and that the rest of the flight was not really present, but presently sleeping.

Over the next few days we took physicals, a lot of tests and were issued our uniforms. In those days the Air Force work uniform was a one-piece coverall—like a mechanics coverall only blue. Then we got down to the main reason that we were at Sampson, to see what career field we would pursue in the Air Force, our AFSC.

The Air Force is a giant cooperation and it takes everything from accountants to veterinarians to run it. They might even have a Zamboni driver out there somewhere. For every airplane and pilot there are dozens of people on the ground in all kinds of support rolls.

The flesh peddlers who were running the assignments section looked at me and saw an ex-Marine and they were thinking security.

No! No! Anything but that.

I could see myself lugging a rifle around a large aircraft, in the middle of a large airfield, in the middle of the night, in the middle of the winter, in the middle of a snow storm, somewhere in the middle of the barren north.

My test scores were pretty high, so before I had to mention the racoons and skunks, they let me off of the security hook. They looked through their books and said, "How about Photographic Interpretation?"

Say what? I understood the two words, but when they were put together—what did a "Photographic Interpreter" do?

It turned out that they weren't quite sure either, but it had something to do with aerial photography, they were pretty sure that it didn't involve fixing anything and there was a six-month school to train you to do whatever it was that a Photographic Interpreter did.

You know old pin ball me. I signed up.

One thing that drove my decision was, that I somehow had it in my tiny little brain that the Photographic Interpretation School was right there at Sampson. Upstate New York was not exactly next door to Newport, Rhode Island where my sailor was, but it's not all that far away, either.

Imagine my shock when I found out that the school was not at Sampson Air Force Base in upstate New York, but at Sheppard Air Force Base, which was (and still is) in Wichita Falls, Texas.

Texas?! Bummer! Too late now.

As a general rule, re-enlistee flights were not involved in the normal routine of the training regimen. They didn't do the obstacle courses or go to the firing ranges. And, especially, they didn't pull any details, like working in the dining halls—KP (kitchen police).

That is until the gang of goof-balls that I was with came along.

I never knew half of what these guys were up to. When we went to get our uniforms, they lifted anything that wasn't nailed down. When we went for shots, they would see what kind of alcohol was lying around that they could get away with.

We were always late for where ever it was that we were supposed to be.

In short, we were becoming a major irritant in the lower regions of the Powers-That-Be. They retaliated by putting us on KP. Weekend KP.

We showed up at the dining hall on time, all

133

twenty of us and we did what we were told. These guys were not stupid.

When two of our members were told to peel potatoes, they peeled potatoes—about one every five minutes. When they were told to speed it up, they peeled the potatoes down to about the size of a grape.

I was on the dish washing crew. Each dish, pot and pan that we washed was spotless when we were finished with it. I guess the downside was that at the pace we were going we would be still working at it today.

It was the same in all other areas of the dining hall.

The guys who were cleaning the floors and tables kept working by the door so they could pop outside for a smoke when no one was looking.

We got kicked off KP.

In the annals of Military History no one ever got kicked *off* KP.

When I got back to the barracks, I found that my merry group had lifted enough cheeses, salamis, fresh fruits, and such, to open a small deli.

We only had a week left. The P-T-Bs were still unhappy with us so on the next Sunday, our last day at Sampson, they put us on garbage collection detail.

We lost a truck.

Well, we didn't really "lose" a truck, we just kind of mislaid it for a few hours.

When we showed up at the motor pool to pick up our trucks and start our trash collection detail there were ten garbage trucks lined up waiting for us and two of us were assigned to each truck.

Sampson was a big base but don't look for it on your map, it is long gone. Don't blame us. I'm sure we had absolutely, positively nothing to do with it. Really.

Each truck was given a street map that showed our pick-up area and off we went.

My partner was the oldest one in our group. He had been in the Army in World War II, said he was a clerk, got out after the war, had a few jobs, got married, got divorced and went back into the Army during the Korean War. After Korea he got out again and now, he was giving the Air Force a try.

We took our time and chatted as we drove around picking up our metal barrels and dumping them into the truck. We figured that we probably shouldn't get back to the motor pool until late afternoon because if we got back too early, they would just find something else for us to do. We figured that a 1500 return would be about right.

We also figured that they didn't expect us to go hungry while we were on detail, so we parked our truck by the dining hall and had a leisurely (a very leisurely) lunch.

When we drove back into the motor pool eight trucks were already there, we made number nine. After parking the truck, we joined the others. It seems that they were not going to let us go until everyone was back.

We waited. And, waited. But our last truck didn't show.

Of course, there were no cell phones in those days so we couldn't make a "Where the hell are you?" call. Finally, two trucks were sent out to see if they could find our wayward garbage men.

It seemed that as soon as the searchers were out of sight truck number ten drove in.

Where were you?

Pickin' up trash of course.

Now we had to wait for the two searchers.

Eventually they returned and we were released and headed back to the barracks. When we got there the two guys from truck ten pulled a couple of cases of cold beer out from under one of the bunks and told the rest of us to help ourselves.

While we were enjoying a cool one, they told us their story.

It seems that their garbage collection route took them into a warehouse area that was way out on the base perimeter and the only thing between them and the outside world was an eight-foot high chain-link fence. On the other side of the fence there was a field, and across the field they could see a road and on the side of the road, a tavern. (Queue the haloes of light and the angelic choir.)

Also, on the other side of the fence, there was a big tree whose branches grew over the fence. So, naturally, they parked the truck by the tree, climbed up on the truck, went over the fence into the tree, climbed down the tree, walked across the field to the tavern and had a couple of brewskis.

When they were ready to return to the base, they thought about the rest of us and while they were trying to figure out how they were going to get a couple of cases of beer across the field and over the fence a bunch of locals that they had been chatting with jumped in to help.

A pick-up truck appeared and a half a dozen guys loaded our two wayward trash collectors and the beer into it, drove across the field and helped them over the fence.

Our boys stopped by the barracks and stashed the beer before they turned the truck in.

What a group.

The next day we left Sampson and I never ran

into any of those guys again. I am positive that if they had stayed together as a group, I would have surely heard about them either running a prison or a small country somewhere.

Intelligence
—Massachusetts—

I headed for Texas, with a stop to see Faye in Newport and the folks in Stoughton. Faye and I decided that we would get married whenever we could get leave together. My folks were all for it—they loved my sailor. Me? They weren't too sure about.

I got off the bus in the old home town and I was standing on the sidewalk in my bright shiny new Air Force uniform with my one little stripe on my sleeve, my big duffle bag at my feet (in the Marines I had a "sea bag" now my seas were duffels) dithering as to whether I should call the folks for a ride home or just walk, when a guy I knew came wandering by.

He was an older gentleman and about as Irish as the Blarney Stone. I'll try to write with an Irish accent.

"Ah! Red, me boy," he said. (I did have hair

once, and it was red). "And what are ye' dooin' for yourself these days?"

Now, remember, I am standing here in my bright, new, shiny uniform.

"Well Joe, I just enlisted in the Air Force."

"Ah, that's good," he said, "I didn't like to see you hangen' aboot' the town."

Just when in the last few years I had been "hangen' aboot' the town," I don't know.

And then he said, "And where would you be off to now?"

I didn't want to get into an explanation of photo interpretation school, seeing as I didn't really understand it myself, but I remembered that they had told me that it was a part of the Intelligence career field. So, I just said, "Well, Joe, I'm going to spend a couple of days with the folks and then I'm off to Texas to Intelligence school."

Joe thought about that for a moment and, then he said, "And, the Lord knows ye need it."

Nothing like family and friends to tell it like it is.

Getting Hitched
—Massachusetts—

I found that really liked Photo Interpretation. Basically, you look at aerial photography, identify stuff and write reports.

To be able to write these reports, as the old song says, we learned a little bit about a lot of things.

We learned all about transportation systems—roads, railroads, shipping, bridges, marshalling yards and how to recognize their key features from the air.

We learned about industries, both big and little, how to tell an electrical power generating plant from a coke, iron and steel mill.

We learned how to identify military equipment of all kinds and from all nationalities.

There was a big block of instruction on metrics so we could determine the actual size of all this stuff from aerial photography.

We learned how to put aerial photographs to

gather to make mosaics, how to interpret RADAR images and how to use maps and aerial photography to make RADAR predictions when there was no actual RADAR imagery available.

And, of course, we were introduced to Photo Interpretation humor. For example: we would be looking at photography that had been taken on a cloudy day and one or more of us would be sent down to supply to get some "cloud eradicator" to remove the clouds from the prints so we could see what was under them, or the object that we were interested in would be right at the edge of the print and we would be sent out to find a "print stretcher."

I fell for it every time.

However, the most important thing that I learned was that the entire school system at Sheppard Air Force Base closed down for ten days over the Christmas Holidays. When I reported this back to the East Coast, Faye found out that she could get a few days leave over Christmas and as Sherlock would say, "the game was afoot."

Of course, being a junior enlisted man back in those days I couldn't just go and get married. I had to have my commander's permission and to get it I had to jump through more hoops than Bozo the Clown's dog.

First, I had to fill out a lot of forms—you could run a city with less paperwork. Then I had a series of interviews. One was with a "Financial Planner" who turned out to be a baby-faced Second Lieutenant who informed me that I didn't make very much money.

As you know by now, I'm not the sharpest pencil in the box, but actually, I kinda had figured that one out for myself.

Then I had to hunt down a chaplain. This guy

was as old as dirt and as sour as an old lemon. In a long rambling discussion, he predicted nothing but gloom and doom, disaster at every turn if I went ahead with this. I was, obviously, too young and dumb to know what I was doing.

I wish he had given me something I could argue against.

There might have been other interviews but I can't remember.

Eventually it was all done, I had all the required paperwork and I was scheduled for an interview with the Commander. I never met him. He delegated that duty down to one of his junior officers and this guy did his best to discourage me too.

I was beginning to think that there was some sort of a conspiracy at work here.

Maybe not.

Meanwhile, my sailor was going through the same administrative nonsense back at Newport.

We planned to be married in Stoughton, Massachusetts over the Christmas holiday, and with Mom and Dad doing the heavy lifting it all came together. Faye and Mom took care of all the wedding arrangements. Mom was the church secretary, so whatever she wanted to happen, as far as the church went, happened.

Dad took care of whatever legal paperwork was necessary.

I assumed that when one marries there was a certain amount of paperwork one has to accomplish and I would also assume that the prospective groom should be present to accomplish these things.

I guess not.

Against the wily, old Navy Chief, the local bureaucrats didn't stand a chance and by the time I got home it was clear that my role in the whole affair was to get fitted for my Tux, stand on the "X" and speak when spoken to. I didn't even have to sign anything. I didn't ask. And, on Christmas Eve, 1955, Faye and I were married.

The church was beautiful, my sailor was lovely, all our friends and relatives were there and outside there was a howling blizzard battering the eaves.

We were on our way.

Well, I was on my way—three days later I was on a train heading back to Texas.

Promotion
—Texas—

When I finished Photo Interpretation School, I hoped to get an assignment somewhere close to my new bride at Newport. When I filled out my Dream Sheet (the flesh peddlers always make you think that you have a choice of assignment and I always fall for it) I said send me East—New England, the Northeast even the East Coast.

I wanted to go East—they sent me East.

Germany.

Uh! Not quite what I had in mind.

Just before I left the photo interpretation school, I found out that the Air Force Air Training Command had an incentive policy that went like this: If your test scores throughout school were 95% or higher and if you had six months' time in your present grade when you graduated you would be promoted one rank.

I had the test scores and the day we graduated—to the day—I had six months' time in grade as an Airman Third Class so I got promoted to Airman Second Class.

Am I lucky, or what?

I had thirty days leave before I had to report to Manhattan Beach, New York for transportation to Germany and I didn't want to hang around Texas waiting for my promotion orders to get published so I asked a buddy of mine in the orderly room to send me a copy when they came in. He did and I was able to sew my new stripe on while I was on leave.

Faye found us a nice furnished place in one of those big, old Newport mansions that had been converted into apartments.

Faye had to work and we would ride the bus down to the base every morning and I would walk her over to the Dental Clinic and bum a cup of coffee and maybe a donut while she went to work. Then I would hang out in the cafeteria or the gym or the library until lunch. We would have lunch together, then she would go back to work and I would hang out some more. But we still had our evenings and weekends. That was our honeymoon. A wonderful time, just the two of us.

All too soon my month's leave was over and I was off to Germany. Well I was off to New York to wait for transportation to Germany. Back in those dinosaur days air transport was still brand new and only accounted for about 10% of all overseas travel, the rest went by boat. Old boats. Old, smelly, uncomfortable, slow boats. I am a lousy sailor so I wasn't looking forward to that.

The replacement depot was a madhouse. People were coming and going all the time. You had to keep checking the bulletin boards as overseas shipments could be posted any time of the day or night and it was considered very bad form to miss a shipment.

Of course, for we lowly enlisted swine there were always details. One morning me and two other guys were given a truck that was loaded with lawn mowers, hedge clippers and other such implements of horticultural destruction and we were sent to the far side of the base to mow some general or admiral's lawn. We even had box lunches.

It was a sunny and pleasant day so we took our time and made the job last until late afternoon. When we finally returned to the billeting area, we found that we had been declared lost and were the objects of a frantic search.

"Where were you guys?"

"Over the other side of the base mowing lawns, where you sent us."

"You were on a shipment for this afternoon, you missed a shipment."

"Well don't look at us; how were we supposed to know?"

The shipment that we had missed was a Vomit Vessel that was pulling out that evening and we had already been replaced. That didn't make me unhappy.

Well they were going to make sure that we went out on the next shipment and they did. The next day my transportation to Europe was a beautiful, comfortable, four engine Lockheed Constellation that flew me right into Paris, France.

Darn the luck.

My new assignment was in a Tactical Reconnaissance Squadron at Sembach, Air Base, West Germany. I settled in to make my year and a half go by until I could get back to my sailor.

I had only been there a couple of weeks when I

was called up to the orderly room and confronted by the Administrative Officer and the First Sergeant. They seemed unhappy with me and they wanted to know why I was wearing two stripes. It seems that my records had finally arrived and there was no copy of my promotion.

To say that my tale of being promoted on finishing school was met with skepticism would be an understatement.

Fortunately, I had my dog-eared, folded-up copy of my promotion orders that my buddy had sent me when I was on leave and I was off the hook. I have always wondered what would have happened if I didn't have that one copy.

Two Rooms and a Bath Down the Hall
—West Germany—

As many of you will remember, back in the Stone Age there were no smart phones, tablets, computers and that sort of thing. There were telephones, but long-distance calls and especially overseas calls were very expensive so most information travelled by mail, Snail Mail, as the kids call it today.

I mention that because I got a letter from my sailor informing me that sometime during our honeymoon month in Newport, she had gotten pregnant. I don't know how that could have happened. Probably the water.

Now back in the dark ages (that many people,

who should know better, seem to want to go back too) married ladies were tolerated (barely) in the Navy, but pregnant ladies, married or not, were not welcome, so that summer Faye was discharged from the Navy.

We, however, were delighted. The Navy lost a good sailor, but we were now Us. Faye jumped on a boat and headed for Germany.

By the time I got the word that she was coming she was just about on her way and I had to scramble to find us a place to live. Of course, there was no government family housing available for the lowly likes of us, so I had to find something out on the German economy. In this quest I had four things working against me: I had very little money, I didn't have a car, I didn't speak the language (well I could say yes and no, please and thank you and order a beer) and I didn't know my way around the neighborhood.

One of the pilots in the squadron had a Junker car that he was getting rid of and he let me have it cheap. It was a Mercedes, but not one that Mercedes would ever claim. It was a black, four-door sedan with a sun roof (that I never opened because I was afraid that I wouldn't be able to close it again) that was built just after the war out of spit, bailing wire and used ration cans. But it did run—most of the time.

Immediately noticing what a pathetic life form I was, the base housing office took me under their wing. They had a list of houses and apartments that were available in the local area—a short list, but it was something. And, most important of all, there was a German national who worked there who was willing to drive around with me and talk to prospective landlords.

He was great. A jolly, roly-poly older gentleman who was determined to find me something that I could afford. Seeing as I hadn't solved the money problem, that wasn't easy.

What a guy. I would have been lost without him.

We found a two-bedroom apartment in the little village of Otterberg. Otterberg is a few miles north of the large industrial city of Kaiserslautern in the German state of Rhineland—Palatinate and was about five miles from my base at Sembach.

The village was noted for a church and monastery that went back to the twelfth century. I think the apartment that we found must have gone back at least that far, too.

The house was typical for the area, a two-story stone building that was divided into five apartments, two up, two down and an attic. We lived in one of the second-floor flats. Our apartment consisted of two large rooms (a living room and a bedroom) and the use of a bathroom down the hall.

Our landlords, who were an older German couple that we called Oma and Opa (grandma and grandpa) lived in the other second floor apartment. Two German families had the downstairs apartments and an Army sergeant and his wife and baby lived upstairs in the attic.

The bathroom down the hall was really two rooms, a toilet in one and a huge bathtub and a sink in the other.

The toilet was one of those older ones with a wooden water box mounted on the wall above it. When you wanted to flush you pulled the chain.

The bathtub was huge and it was made of metal not porcelain. Hot water was a do-it-yourself affair. There was a very large boiler in the corner of the room with a firebox in the bottom that would take either coal or wood. A bath required advance planning. You had to get a fire going and heat the water in the boiler for a long time because to fill this tub, you needed a *lot* of water.

You could swim laps in this tub.

When Faye got in, she disappeared from sight. In fact, Opa and I ended up building wooden steps so she could get in and out.

We loved every minute of living in Otterberg. We were as poor as the proverbial church mice but as happy as two clams in a mudbank. Our little flat was furnished in what I would call "Early Neanderthal." In the living room/kitchen we had a couple of easy chairs and a kitchen table with three chairs—borrowed from our landlord, and our shelves were stacked bricks with boards in between.

The kitchen was at one end of the living room, a sink (with hot and cold taps that both produced cold water unless you had the boiler in the bathroom going) a little refrigerator and a small stove. Faye had her kitchen utensils stored in a couple of orange crates.

Our heat was provided by a small kerosene heater, so the living room was toasty—the bedroom, not so much. But we had those big German quilts to snuggle under.

I found out that you could buy kerosene from the Army for five cents a gallon, but you had to furnish the container. So, I scrounged up a fifty-five-gallon drum, a truck and a couple of warm bodies. We went over to the Army compound, filled the barrel, wrestled it home and mounted it on a wooden frame in the dirt cellar of our building—right next to Opa's still for making schnapps. It's a wonder we didn't all blow up.

There were only a couple other American

families in the village so we got to know them, and the locals, very well.

About four months later, after the mandatory dark, cold and stormy midnight ride over icy, rural, German roads, our first kid, John, was born in the United States Army Hospital at Landsthul about fifteen miles away.

Survival Rations
—West Germany—

Several years ago, Faye put together a cookbook of family recipes and some of her sage advice. I am sure that she had our time in Otterberg in mind when she put in a chapter on survival rations. For example:

Cream of Mushroom Soup

In the Beginning, God created Cream of Mushroom Soup. He did so because Uncle Sam was mortal and sometimes messed up Air Force paychecks and, more often, because said paycheck didn't quite make it to the end of the month. Mushroom Soup used to cost a nickel a can.

1. Open one can of Cream of Mushroom Soup with the manual can opener that Uncle Austin thought was a jocular wedding gift.

2. Empty the contents of the can into a small

saucepan.

3. Add one can of water.

4. Heat, stirring frequently, until piping hot.

5. Share with spouse.

6. At lunch, pretend you are slimming.

7. At supper, repeat instructions one thru five.

8. Enjoy, it's the nearest thing to living on love.

To vary this diet, learn to play pinochle. You might be invited to play cards, and if you are, you're sure to be offered coffee—maybe even peanuts.

Of course, time and experience has taught that a box of oatmeal also goes a long way. When you divide the initial cost by the number of servings, oatmeal is good value for the money. It does add variety to the soup diet. If you have the opportunity to pop into a cafeteria for a free glass of water and are able to snitch a few packets of sugar, oatmeal can be quite tasty.

The Tipsy Troubadours
—West Germany—

A month after John was born it was Christmas. We had a little Christmas tree, actually it was just a branch that we found on one of our walks in the woods, but it looked tree-ish. Faye had decorated it with things that she had made: paper loops, paper ornaments, popcorn strings, stuff like that.

When she was down at the local market, she saw a set of six little tin Christmas tree ornaments and bought them for one West German mark (twenty-five cents) and they were the only store-bought items on the tree.

And then, out of the blue, two large boxes arrived from the colonies, one from the west coast and one from the east coast. We went from rags to riches in a heartbeat. Between them the folks thought of everything. There was food: cookies, brownies, gingerbread men, a fruitcake and my mom even stuck in a bottle of real maple syrup from one of the Montague farms in Vermont.

There were clothes for the baby, Christmas decorations including fresh cut holly from the big bush in front of the house in Seattle and our six little store-bought ornaments were joined by many more.

Of course, there were presents of much appreciated wooly shirts and sweaters, but the best gift was a short-wave radio that Faye's dad sent. That radio became our primary source of evening entertainment especially since we never knew what we were going to pick up. Depending on the atmospheric conditions, we received signals from all over the world and half the fun was trying to figure out where they were coming from and what language we were listening to.

One night we heard two police cars talking to each other—in Kansas.

On Christmas Eve, our first wedding anniversary, Faye said that we should share what little we had with anyone who was stuck on base over the holidays. I jumped into the car, headed over to the barracks and rounded up four of our friends who were just sitting around. We pooled our pennies (paper pennies—we were still using occupation script) and any German pfennigs we had, bought a couple of six-packs and some snacks and headed home.

It turned out to be a great afternoon. We talked, laughed and especially played with the radio. For some reason along about evening we started singing—mostly Christmas Carols.

Soon, there was a knock on the door. It was Opa, our landlord from across the hall, who wanted to know if everything was okay.

I didn't think our singing was that bad.

Anyway, once he saw that we weren't really killing each other, he went back across the hall and returned with Oma, a strudel and a jug of his homemade schnapps. Having sampled some of his squeezings before I can tell you that this stuff was lethal. You could use it to strip paint.

Our voices improved immensely after the jug had gone around a few times so we naturally thought that we should go Christmas Caroling. We bundled-up (baby John included) and hit the cobblestone streets of Otterberg.

It was a beautiful winter evening—clear, calm, cold and as the song says, "The stars were brightly shining."

This happy crew marched down the Hauptstrasse (main street) stopping along the way render one carol or another. As we made our merry way through the town, windows were opened and heads popped out followed by whispered comments, smiles and waves.

The best part was when people began to join us. Most of the new arrivals were German and they brought with them bottles of one thing or another—beer, wine, whisky and schnapps, which were passed around.

God, I love the Germans.

We were about two dozen strong and singing in an unintelligible mixture of English and German when we found ourselves in front of the Burgermeister's (mayors) house. We gave him our best version of Silent Night (or a reasonable facsimile). He stepped out onto a second-floor balcony, surveyed the scene, gave us a wait a minute sign and soon came out to join us with his wife and two other couples (I think they were his sons and daughters-in-law) and, of course, a couple of bottles.

Around the village we went, with our mayor in the lead, singing lustily, gathering people as we progressed and it seemed that everyone who joined us brought at least one bottle with them. By this time not all the songs were Christmas Carols as quite a few drinking songs were added to the repertoire.

I would guess that we were forty or fifty strong by the time we ended up back at the Burgermeister's house and the party broke up with smiles, laughter and best wishes for the season all around.

The guys bunked down in our living room, stayed over Christmas and we all went back to work on Boxing Day. A great holiday that had three outcomes:

One, it started our family tradition of the annual open house. For the next fifty years wherever Faye and I were living we had an open house. Everyone came to our place on Christmas Eve.

Two, a few days after Christmas there came a knock on the door and when Faye opened it, she found herself looking up at a very large German policeman. He didn't speak very much English but he got across the idea that he was making inquiries for the Burgermeister concerning the Christmas Eve singing. (See? The redhead always gets caught.) Faye invited him in, gave him a cup of coffee and in broken English and German they had quite a chat.

Faye was very good at picking up languages; me, not so much. In all my years of being stationed in Europe and working with various NATO countries I only became halfway fluent in three languages: English, Canadian and American.

When I got home from work and Faye told me

160

the tale, we wondered what had prompted the visit.

A week later I found out when I was called into my Commander's office. He told me that he had a letter from the Wing Director of Operations and the Wing Commander (his boss and his bosses' boss) with all sorts of official scrolls and letters in German attached.

The gist of all this correspondence was to congratulate me for fostering and promoting German/American relations and to keep up the good work.

My commander was pleased but naturally curious as to what it was all about. When I told him the whole story of the "Tipsy Troubadours" and our rather inebriated caroling tour around the village I thought he was going to hurt himself laughing. He thought that it would probably be best if we kept the whole story just between the two of us and he would see to it that all the correspondence went into the records as a public relations attaboy.

Smart man, probably ended up a general or something.

The third thing that came out of our first Christmas concerns those six little ornaments that Faye bought on the market for a mark. They were our treasures, carefully packed away after each holiday and always the first items to decorate the next years tree.

Some years later one fell and broke but we still had the five. After Faye passed away, I gave one to each of the kids and as far as I know they still have them, their very own, four-cent, family heirloom.

Dinkins Mill
—South Carolina—

When my tour in Germany was about to end, I headed over to the assignments section to fill out my "Dream Sheet," you know, the piece of paper that gives you a choice of three bases for your next assignment. I am certain that no one ever looks at them. But, I'm a sucker, I always filled them out.

Faye and the baby had left Germany a few months before and were currently living in the old house that Faye had grown up in just north of Seattle, Washington so I put in for three bases in Washington State: one south of Seattle, one north of Seattle and one east of Seattle.

Hell of a plan. What could go wrong?

They say that the assignments people always take into consideration your wants and desires, but you can't prove it by me. When my assignment came through it was for—South Carolina.

South Carolina? Having survived Parris Island, Mordor and Mount Doom, South Carolina wasn't even my last choice.

The assignments people are real jokers, surely, there must be at least one Air Force Base in the United States between Seattle, Washington and South Carolina.

Faye and the baby had to come back across the country by train (in those days commercial flying was in its infancy and way out of our price range). We met up at my folk's home in Massachusetts and after a brief visit, we loaded our stuff into a beat-up old Ford that Dad found for me for a couple hundred bucks.

Actually, there wasn't much to load, just about all we owned was the clothes on our backs. We headed south to the middle of South Carolina.

The first obstacle in going to a new base was finding a place to live. There is base housing, but it is allocated strictly by rank of which I had very little. At this time, I was an Airman First Class, and as far as base housing went, I was so low on the totem pole I couldn't see the bottom of the Raven's butt. But we did luck out and found a mobile home that we could afford to rent in a little trailer park called Dinkins Mill, about ten miles from the base.

The trailer wasn't much, but it was furnished and had the essentials of a stove, refrigerator, etc. but no air-conditioning. Additionally, it had a slab of concrete adjacent to the front door that had been roofed over and screened-in to make a little cabana, we slept out there a lot.

Did I mention that it was hot in the middle of South Carolina? Only now it was also humid. Yay.

Dinkins Mill had been created many years ago

by constructing a small wooden dam across Dinkins Creek and building a little mill below the dam (the mill was long gone, but the dam was still there) and backing up a small lake (called Dinkins Mill Pond) into the surrounding swamp.

When they decided to make the trailer park they just skinned off the swamp vegetation on one side of the pond, bulldozed a loop road, poured about twenty concrete slabs for trailers, dug a septic system and ran in power and water hook ups. Very basic, but it did have advantages: It was cheap and there were about a dozen other people who worked at the base living there so rides to work and shopping could be shared.

There were fish (perch and brim mostly) in the deep hole in the creek below the dam; there was also a corn field next to the park and a potato patch across the street. I mention these because on the many times that Uncle Sam's paycheck didn't quite stretch to the end of the month my ever-resourceful sailor would snitch a couple of ears of corn from the field, dig up a few potatoes, jig a few fish from below the dam and we would have fish chowder until payday rolled around.

But this experience is about snakes.

When we arrived, it was late fall (November) and there wasn't a snake in sight. I never even thought about snakes.

Let's see, living on a reclaimed portion of a swamp, next to a swamp pond butting up against more swamp, in the middle of South Carolina—nope, never gave snakes a thought.

When spring came around and the days started warming up some of the wives said that they thought that they had seen a snake. When we got home from work—in the cool of the evening—we dutifully looked, but alas, no snakes.

I still didn't think much about it until the day we came home from work to find all the ladies in one trailer forming a protective ring around their assembled offspring demanding to know what we were going to do about the snakes. We went out and looked, but we still didn't see any snakes and we couldn't understand why our loving spouses were very unhappy with us.

The snickering probably didn't help.

The next day was Saturday. I was sitting in the kitchen watching our one-year old divide his breakfast equally between his mouth and the floor when there was a shout from outside. It was my next door (trailer) neighbor. I heard his trailer door slam and I heard footsteps going down the trailer, I heard footsteps coming back up the trailer, another door slam and then two very loud booms.

Well, that brought everyone boiling out of their respective tin cans. We found him in the middle of the road with shotgun in hand standing over the carcass of a fair-sized bull snake that he had just blown all over central South Carolina.

Well, I thought, that explains the snake sightings. Not so fast. There was shout and one of the guys said he thought he saw another snake. The war was on!

Everyone (about a dozen of us) went to arm themselves with whatever weapons of serpentine mass destruction were on hand. We weren't the best armed force ever assembled (probably a good thing, too). As I recall we had two shotguns, two pistols, a 22-caliber rifle and one guy had a really wicked looking machete.

We were also not the most organized or disciplined armed force ever put together. The term "circular firing squad" comes to mind.

As we beat through the bush, weapons were randomly discharged and stray rounds began flying. The ladies yelled at us to watch it, but we were beyond rationality. So, the ladies prudently gathered up the young and hunkered down in the trailer thought to be farthest from the action.

For some reason, I had a rake and was acting as a kind of beater for this armed mob of crazed vigilantes. This put me on the wrong end of the weapons being employed, but on we went. When someone would spot a snake, or something that looked like a snake, the "Swamp Militia" would converge on the spot. With much shouting and jumping around weapons would be fired, knives and other sharp objects would slash through the weeds and clubs of all kinds would rain down on the brush.

Anything that moved, animal or vegetable, was in mortal danger. How we kept from killing each other, I will never know.

At the end of the day there were thirty-three dead snakes stretched out on the road. At least that was the official count. Most of the bodies were so badly mangled or just blown apart, that one may have counted for two, or more. And, several carcasses were of dubious ancestry.

Five were declared officially poisonous: two rattlesnakes, two water moccasins and a copperhead. I didn't know what a copperhead looked like, so I took their word for it.

The Battle of Dinkins Mill was over. The snakes were vanquished and there were no casualties among the victors. The non-combatants came out of the bunker while the macho-men declared victory, fired up the Barbie and broke out the beer.

Government Thinking
—South Carolina—

After our number two kid was born (must have been the water) my sailor had series of health problems and spent a lot of time in and out of the hospital. I soon ran out of leave time and money for baby-sitters to take care of both a two-year old and a baby. But my Mom came through again and volunteered to take care of the little ones while Faye went into hospital.

So, we moved out of our little trailer at Dinkins Mill, put what little we had in storage, Faye and the kids went up to Massachusetts and I moved on base.

While the family was gone, I lived in one of the old two-story wooden barracks. This building was old, it must have been there when Sherman came marching up from Georgia. The barracks had open bays on the first and second floors with two rooms at the end of each bay for the bay chief and barracks chief with the latrines at the other end of the open bays.

Seeing as I was now a staff sergeant, I had the dubious honor of being the barracks chief, so I had one of the little rooms. Not bad and it was better than sleeping, or trying to sleep, out in one of the bays.

The airmen living in the barracks weren't recruits, just young single guys and as Kipling said, "Single men in barracks don't grow into plaster saints." Booze was not allowed in the barracks, but there was plenty of it outside the barracks. So, we had the occasional incident, but all of these I managed to deal with without it coming to the attention of, shall we say, "higher authority."

For the most part they were good kids though we did have one thief. If there is anything that one cannot tolerate in a barracks it's a thief. His barracks mates caught him and brought him to me. I saw no need to notify the base cops, or anyone else, and we pointed out to him the error of his ways ourselves. A little, shall we say, rough counselling, has straightened out many a wayward young man.

My biggest problem as barracks chief was trying to keep everything in this ancient building working. My room was right on end of the building and the wind whistled through it as though there were no windows at all. If there was even a slight breeze the windows in the open bays would shake, rattle and crash as though the orcs from Mordor were trying to break in.

The plumbing was something else. Every once in a while, we would get rusty water coming out of the pipes, sometimes (actually many times) there would be no hot water and there were two toilets in the first deck latrine that never worked properly.

We were not able to control the heat as it was

piped in and we got what we got. Sometimes we didn't get. And, to make our summers more miserable, the building did not have air-conditioning.

Through this I became an expert in submitting work orders for repair of this and that to the base Civil Engineers.

Sometimes someone from the Engineers even showed up to fix something. Not often, but sometimes.

I mention all this because about a year later, after Faye had recovered and we were again living off base, I was driving past my old barracks that had now been abandoned and I saw a bunch of what looked like construction vehicles sitting in the barracks parking lot. I thought, surely, they are not going to do a major repair on this ancient relic. So, curiosity getting the better of me, I pulled into the parking lot to see what was going on.

After having a chat with the workmen, they reassured me that no they weren't there to fix anything they were there to tear the building down. I thought that that was just a dandy idea and wished them well, but as I started to drive away, I saw a base Civil Engineer truck parked on the other side of the building and I wondered what the heck that was all about. So, I stopped again and went in.

I found two plumbers in the latrine getting ready to work on the two recalcitrant toilets. A nice idea; a little late, but a nice idea.

I told them that no one lived in the building. That no one had lived in that building for months. That the building was going to be torn down.

They weren't interested.

I told them that there was a crew out in the parking lot right now getting ready to tear the building down.

They still weren't interested.

In fact, they became rather irate and told me in no uncertain terms that they had a work order to fix the toilet and they were going to fix the toilet. They even pulled out the work order and waved it at me.

I asked if I could see the work order and one of them handed it to me. I almost fell over because It was one of my work requests, submitted over a year ago.

I pointed this out to the two plumbers and they still weren't interested.

I could see that resistance was futile so I gave up and drove away shaking my head at the thought that while one government agency was fixing the plumbing at one end of the building another government agency was at the other end of the building getting ready to tear the darn thing down.

Faye's Madonna
—South Carolina—

Faye was an artist, a very good artist, and at every base we were ever stationed at sooner or later she would be involved in the local art association or art league or whatever artsy thing was going on. She was also, when the situation demanded, a very tough, no nonsense, little lady.

When Christmas rolled around each squadron was expected to put up a Christmas display along the boulevard that ran from the main gate to the central base area. This, of course, became a competition between the squadrons to see who could put up the best display and after finishing second or third the last couple of years our squadron commander was determined that this year our squadron display was going to win first place.

The pressure was on, and as they say, fecal matter only rolls downhill. The commander leaned on the executive officer, the executive officer leaned on the administration officer and the first sergeant and so on. A committee was formed to select the design and plan for the construction of this year's display. At their first meeting the only thing that they could agree on was that they were in deep doo-doo and that they needed help.

They decided that their only hope was to try and bring in the Secret Weapon—Faye.

The committee came to me and asked if she would be willing to help. I'm not the brightest bulb in the chandelier, but I knew better than to volunteer my sailor for anything. I said that I would ask if she would attend their next meeting.

She was skeptical that group of military muscle heads could produce anything artistic, but she agreed to come to the meeting and at least listen to their proposals.

Faye and I sat in the back of the conference room listening to these guys wander all over the map. It was clear that all they knew was that they needed a Christmas display but it was also clear that outside of updating last years, display they had no other ideas.

It seemed that most of the committee favored upgrading last year's entry which apparently had just been handed down and polished up year after year. It was pointed out that that design hadn't won in the past. So, they then figured that they need something new, but they had no idea what.

They went around and round not getting anywhere. Faye was sitting beside me and I could feel the temperature rising. Suddenly, she was not sitting next to me anymore. I looked up and there she was, all five-foot nothing of her, standing at the front of the room and in a voice that I had never heard come out of

174

her before (I think she was channeling Ra) she asked if she could have their attention, or maybe she just told this gang of officers and rough tough old sergeants to sit down and shut up.

They sat. They shut.

Then she told them that if they wanted her help this was how it was going to be, she would design and decorate a display and under her direction they would build it and no crap from anyone. Got it?

They got it. They looked like a room full of bobble-heads and their tails were wagging like little puppy dogs.

First, she wanted to know where they would work. They mumbled and fidgeted and admitted that they hadn't really thought about that. She stood there tapping her foot. Well??

They suddenly realized that she wanted an answer—like, now. Galvanized into action they all started talking at once proposing and dismissing various buildings in the squadron area. They finally settled on the supply building.

Faye said, "Fine, where's the supply building?"

Oh! It's right here, just a couple of buildings away.

Faye said, "Fine." And she started marching toward the door.

These guys were in shock, I guess that they had never run to an artist with a full creative head of steam up. Out the door we went and over to the supply building. Luckily someone had a key to open the door or she might have marched right through it.

I could just see the wheels turning in her head and I was pretty sure at this point that she knew pretty much what she wanted to make and what it was going to take to make it.

She told them that she wanted one end of the building cleaned out and that they would meet Saturday morning. okay?

The bobble heads were in full bobble.

When I came home from work the next day, Friday, the kitchen table, the coffee table and half the living room was covered with large sheets of paper with drawings, sketches, lists and I don't know what all. I should mention that at this time we had two boys, John was just four and David was two, and I don't know how she kept them out of the stuff.

My orders were to make dinner and take care of the kids.

Saturday morning, she marched into the supply building. Fortunately, the guys had one end all cleaned out. She was ready with lists of everything she needed for both material and warm bodies. Who are the carpenters? She gave them some lists. Who are the painters? More lists. Do we have any metal workers? We did. Good. Do we have any wood carvers? It turns out that we did—and some very good ones too. And the whole squadron mobilized and went to work.

She took over one corner of the supply building as her command post, had a drafting table brought in and covered the walls with sketches. Soon four or five separate groups were working on different aspects of the display. Faye was everywhere, kind of like Patton driving the Third Army across central Europe.

Of course, we all still had our regular jobs to do and Faye had two little kids to take care of, but every minute that anyone could spare was spent on the project which was now highly classified lest any other squadron should find out what we were up to.

My job remained the same—take care of the kids.

The finished product was spectacular. What Faye designed was a golden, seven-foot tall statue, a standing Madonna holding the child. We had some really talented craftsmen in the squadron and when Faye finished painting it, it was beautiful.

The statue was placed in a fifteen-foot tall, four-foot deep, triangular shadow box that stood on a three-foot high stand. Faye painted the inside of the shadow box with a pastoral background that blended up into sky and stars. The Madonna was placed in a forest scene and around her feet were, models of flowers and small animals that the guys had made and Faye had painted.

The models blended into Faye's paintings on the back and inside of the shadow box. The display also had lights and music.

Faye and her crew put it up along the roadway on the first Sunday of December and it caused an instant traffic jam. The road was a boulevard with two lanes each way and a median in the middle. The right-hand in-bound lane was soon filled with parked cars as people stopped and got out to get a better look. Others were slowing down to look and some were parking in the out-bound lane also.

That's pretty much the way it was for the month that the display was up much to the unhappiness of the base cops who had to station air policemen out there every day to keep the traffic moving.

Faye's display was so over-the-top that some of the other squadrons tried to get banned from the competition but our commander wasn't having any of that.

Needless to say, we won first place, our commander was happy, the committee breathed a sigh of relief and Faye was the hero of the Squadron.

The Lowly Second Lieutenant

—Nebraska—

There I was, a brand-new Second Lieutenant in the United States Air Force.

Yup! After over eight years as an enlisted man I went to Officer Candidate School and was commissioned a Second Lieutenant.

My mother was pleased that I was now an officer, Dad—not so much. During Dad's many years in the Navy he didn't have much use for officers. He said that they just got in the way. In his opinion the officers should just sit in the Ward Room and drink coffee and let the Chiefs run the Navy, the way God meant it to be.

My sailor was also dubious about the status

change. She had no desire to be involved in the back-biting politics of the Officers Wives Club. Maybe not, but everywhere we went she worked her butt off for the local wives' club. She did posters, flyers, table decorations and anything else in the artsy field that was required.

Whenever there was a fund raiser, she would always donate a painting or two.

When I was commissioned The Powers-That-Be said that I didn't even have to go to school. They decided that with my previous schooling (the Photo Interpretation School back at Sheppard) and five years' experience, I could go right to work as a photo interpreter.

By the way, as a brand-new Second Lieutenant I figured that I needed the status of a new car, so I bought a brand-new Ford Falcon—a two-door with bucket seats. Just what a married man with two growing boys, needs.

Obviously, getting a commission didn't give me any brains.

Anyway, we were off to our new assignment, Headquarters, Strategic Air Command (SAC). What an assignment for a lowly Second Lieutenant. Headquarters SAC had so many senior officers bouncing around the building that Lieutenant Colonels made the coffee and they used Majors for door stops.

In my new status as an officer and a gentleman (I never did get that second part down) I had no idea where I would be working or exactly what I was going to be doing.

I soon found out that the SAC Headquarters building has more levels below ground that it has floors above ground and I kept being moved down,

down, down.

I ended up in the lower regions assigned as the night shift officer—in charge of a group of cartographers and photo interpreters working in a sub-sub-basement making secret maps.

My job was so secret that I was not permitted to know what I was doing and believe me, I knew nothing about cartography.

I quickly learned that the map makers working for me were a bunch of jokers.

Their favorite trick was trying to spiff up the maps we were making by putting little boats in the rivers, trains on the railroad tracks and airplanes on the air fields.

For self-preservation I learned all I could about cartography and I became the chief editor. I caught most of my jokers' little cuties but how was I going to punish them? They were already working nights in dungeon buried under the SAC Headquarters building.

Then of course there was the problem of finding a place to live. As usual, when we arrived on base there was no housing available for us. A year ago, when I was a Staff Sergeant, I had a little status in the non-commissioned officer ranks and was slowly working my way up the list to where I at least had a shot at base housing, but as a Second Lieutenant at Headquarters SAC I was back at the bottom of the officers list.

We looked at a few houses and apartments for rent in the area and ended up buying our first house in a housing development called Twin City Plaza. The house wasn't much, just a two-bedroom, one bath, 900 square foot rectangle on a slab of concrete, but we liked it.

Twin City Plaza was a fun place to live. The

entire neighborhood consisted of young families just like us so there were lots of kids. Nobody had any money but we all seemed to keep busy with family activities and impromptu neighborhood parties.

The worst part of working nights, from my point of view, was that I missed out on a lot of time with the boys. I was sleeping when they went to school and I would be gone when they came home.

We tried to make up for this on the weekends by loading up our little car with camping gear (camping: verb. Spending lots of money and traveling hundreds of miles so you can live outside like Daniel Boone) and driving off into the hinterlands of the boondocks of the country side and getting ourselves thoroughly lost.

We did this by letting the boys pick the direction whenever we came to an intersection. The boys called the direction choosing right, left or straight. A good game with apparently a lot of rules, but only the boys knew what they were.

In our wanderings we found lots of neat "stuff"; small towns, roadside attractions, and I bet we hit every campground within a hundred miles.

Of course, there was no GPS in those days. At the end of the day finding out where we were, finding our way home or even finding a campground was challenging.

We managed to maintain this quiet existence for almost three years when two events occurred.

One, we learned that my sailor was pregnant. That was a surprise. Our youngest was six and we hadn't taken any precautions over the years, so I guess we just thought that the factory was out of business.

Must have been the water.

The second event concerned the war in

Vietnam. Vietnam was just starting to stir as far as our active military involvement was concerned and the flesh peddlers down at the personnel center were probably sitting around, having coffee and talking about who they could mess with today when my name must have come up.

"What about old Vern?"

"Yeah! Let's send him TDY (Temporary Duty) somewhere."

"Where?"

"What about Vietnam?"

"Good idea."

Come on guys, my wife's pregnant and we have two rambunctious boys banging around the house, my sailor could use a little help. They told me not to worry, I would only be in Vietnam for thirty days.

The lying dogs.

Well, the initial TDY was only for thirty days but at the end of the thirty days I was extended for another thirty days.

I had been shanghaied.

Three times they extended my TDY, 123 days all together. I didn't get home until a month before our number three, Mike, was born.

By the time I got home Faye was so big that she couldn't reach the peddles on the car (manual transmission) so she had taped blocks of wood to them.

But all went well, my sailor was a real soldier. Does that make sense?

She wasn't even too upset with the personnel folks. She only made one voodoo doll.

I hoped it worked.

Beer for Breakfast
—Vietnam—

While I was in Saigon on temporary duty (TDY) there were some strange rules concerning how much you were paid for every day that you were TDY. If you lived on base and used base billeting and ate your meals in the base dining hall the Air Force would pay a buck seventy-five a day. But if you got a letter from the billeting office stating that free government quarters and meals were not available you could live out on the civilian economy and the Air Force would pay sixteen dollars a day.

Sixteen bucks a day was more than my base pay and base billeting was very generous in handing out non-availability letters.

Another Lieutenant and I decided to take a chance on living out in the wilds of Saigon. It wasn't easy. The Powers-That-Be gave us twenty-four hours to get settled before they wanted us to show up for work.

The U. S. military ran regular bus routes from the base into town so we joined a couple dozen other new guys and climbed onto an Air Force bus and headed out. Our bus turned out to be a regular school bus only painted gray with wire grills covering the windows so the bad guys couldn't ride by on a Vespa and chuck a hand grenade in to keep you company.

Saigon is a big city and we knew nothing about it except that every now and then bombs went off so it was probably not a good idea to live anywhere near where bombs went off. Of course, bombs went off everywhere so that wasn't really much help.

We also figured that we didn't want to live anywhere near any kind of military facility (see above) and that we wanted to be on, or at least near, one of the bus lines.

Looking back, I can't imagine that we were that dumb. Imagine yourself taking a bus into your nearest large city (a city that was known to have terrorists, that you had never been in before and you didn't speak the language) and finding a safe place to live in twenty-four hours.

Our driver took us downtown to the hotel district. We found that the hotels came in two varieties. There were modern hotels with western facilities and air conditioning. They were very nice—but pricey. A few guys opted for one of those.

Then there were older hotels that were not so modern and didn't have air conditioning (some of them didn't even have screens on the windows and Vietnam is very buggy).

A quick check on a couple of them revealed that they were more than just hotels. Many of the rooms rented by the hour. For some reason we even had a couple of guys who went for that.

We stayed on the bus and were becoming more and more discouraged when we found a suitable place that had decent rooms, modern plumbing and air conditioning. The downside was that it was run by the Army which violated the military rule but by this time we were in no position to quibble. I also wondered that seeing as this place was run by the Army how this would affect our non-availability letters but I didn't ask any dumb questions.

We settled in and went to work sitting at a light table and looking at aerial photography twelve hours a day.

The worst part of living where we were was the commute. Our hotel was on the outskirts of Saigon on the far side of town from our base. We were on the bus for two to three hours every day going to and from work.

We kept our eyes open for something that might be closer to work and after a few weeks we heard about a new hotel over on the base side of town that was in the final stages of construction and was just opening up. We checked it out and found out that even though the building wasn't completely finished they were renting out the rooms that were done.

We worked nights, seven to seven, so we were lucky to find that this hotel had a quiet, air-conditioned, basement room with its own western style bathroom tucked away in the back of the building that was very good for daytime sleeping.

As I said there was still construction going on in various areas of the hotel. When you entered the hotel through the front door there was a door immediately to the right and that room always seemed to have workmen in it so I asked our Vietnamese manager what was going on. He told me that it was going to be a bar:

"Number one bar in all Saigon."

We didn't think much of that because the back of the "number one bar in all Saigon" would have a common wall with our room.

A couple of weeks went by and one morning when we came home the door to the bar was closed and locked. We asked the manager what was up.

"Bar finished. Number one bar in all Saigon."

Great. Open up and we'll have a beer.

"No! No! No can do. No have keys. Bar open one o'clock."

We went off to bed, but the next morning when we came in there was our smiling manager waiting for us.

"Have keys." And, with a flourish, he opened the door.

We said, great and in we went and after he proudly showed off his number one bar (which looked like any other bar) we said how about a couple of beers?

"No! No! Beer all lock up. No have keys."

He had the key to let us into the bar but not the keys to sell us anything. The beer was locked up in what looked like a huge double refrigerator. The refrigerator was wrapped up with a chain that was big enough to moor the Queen Mary with the biggest padlock I had ever seen.

"No! No! Bar open one o'clock."

The next morning the door to the bar was open and there was a young man behind the bar, probably one of the managers sons.

Great! How about a couple of beers?

"Yes! Can do! Have key." And he produced an enormous key to open the enormous padlock. Then, with great ceremony, he unwrapped the anchor chain, opened the refrigerator doors and gave us our beer.

Very nice and off we went to get some sleep.

When we got off work in the morning, we had been stopping at the Officer's Club on the base for breakfast but I noticed that there was a grill in our hotel bar so we decided to give that a try and see what we could get to eat.

The door to the bar was open, our smiling young fella was behind the bar and the anchor chain was removed from the big refrigerator. As he handed us our beer I pointed to the grill and said, "How about some breakfast."

"No! No! No have food. Food all lock up. Bar open one o'clock."

That did not compute. The refrigerator was open, that's where he got the beer. Ah, life is not that simple. Our bartender pointed to a smaller refrigerator that was next to the big fridge, that I hadn't noticed before, and this one also had a chain around it with a padlock. That's where the food was and he didn't have the key.

We finally talked him into selling us a couple of bags of potato chips, had a couple of more beers and went to bed.

As you can guess by now, the next morning we sat up at the bar with a beer, ham and eggs and toast. Things were looking up. I asked about the juke box.

"No! No! Juke box not on."

I walked over and saw that it was just unplugged so I plugged it in and we had a little music with our breakfast.

The next morning, we figured that we had really

189

cracked the code because when we walked in, we found two hookers sitting at the bar. We sent them on their way but before they got to the door, they bumped into a couple of soldiers who had stuck their heads in and asked if they could get a beer.

The bartender said, "Yes! Yes! Can do. Food! Music!"

The soldiers swept up the two girls and headed to the back of the bar where the juke box and the little dance floor was and the party started. We went to bed but our room was on the same level as the bar and with the common wall it got a little loud.

When got back to the hotel the next morning there were half a dozen soldiers in the bar along with four or five hookers and there was a pretty good party already underway.

As we walked in there was our smiling manager and he said, "Yes! Yes! Number one bar in Saigon. Bar open eight o'clock."

We had won many battles along the way; the bar was open when we came home from work and we could get a beer and breakfast, but we lost the war. There were so many loud and raucous early morning parties in the hotel bar that we couldn't get any sleep and we had to move.

Rock 'Um, Sock 'Um Robots

—Iowa—

*T*he toy of the Christmas season was Rock 'Um, Sock 'Um Robots and the boys, who were seven and five, wanted one. Of course, they had asked Santa and Santa was going to come through. A Rock 'Um, Sock 'Um Robot was safely tucked away in our bedroom closet.

It is hard for little kids, and some not so little kids (not to be sexist, but the females in my family are the worst present pokers on the planet) to get to sleep on Christmas Eve but we found a formula that seemed to work most of the time. We would get the boys tubbed and scrubbed and into their pajamas and then just let them stay up during our annual Christmas Eve party.

They usually didn't last long. By eight or so we would find them asleep under the coffee table or behind a chair. They were always smart enough to crump somewhere where they wouldn't be stepped on. When we picked them up and carried them off to bed, they never even twitched.

Once the boys were tucked away some of the younger airmen wanted to see what Santa was going to bring so we hauled the stuff out of the closet and arranged it under the tree. This brought Ooos and Ahs from the younger crowd, especially for the Rock 'Um, Sock 'Um Robots. Two of the guys couldn't resist and started to play with it—and they broke it.

They were devastated. They were so broken up I thought one of them was going to cry. They had ruined the boys' Christmas.

Well, we were in a pickle.

Walmart and Target and such 24/7 things hadn't been invented yet so I couldn't just run out and buy another one. Plus, it was Christmas Eve and I couldn't imagine that anything would be open.

My two airmen headed for the door. They said that they would find one if it took all night and off they went.

While the party went on Faye and I considered our options—none of which seemed very good. We didn't think an IOU from Santa would go over very well and we couldn't just unwrap one of the presents under the tree and put it out as a Santa present. That last option depended on the boys not noticing that a present was missing, fat chance of that.

We were still dithering a couple of hours later when our two young airmen burst through the door and wonder of wonders they had a brand spanking new Rock 'Um, Sock 'Um Robots.

Of course, we all wanted to know where in the world they found one at this time of night on Christmas Eve and they had quite a tale.

They left our house without a clue as to where they would find toys but they figured that their best chance would be back over the river in Omaha. Lights, any lights, grocery store, drug store, any store or even a gas station that looked open was checked out. There weren't many and only a few of them had any toys.

As the evening went on, they said that they found themselves were way over in West Omaha and they were about to give up and just get something, anything when they came across a little mom and pop drug store that was still open. They went in and way up on a top shelf this little drug store had some toys— including a Rock 'Um, Sock 'Um Robot.

Christmas was saved. I don't know what was wrong with the one the guys broke but the second one turned out to be darned near indestructible. The boys bashed away at each other for weeks until the next fad, which if I remember right was Bop-A-Bear, came along.

Saigon II
—Vietnam—

*J*ust a couple of months after getting back from my long "Temporary Duty" in Vietnam I was assigned right back to Vietnam for a year. This was when Uncle Sam decided that we were going to support the crooked South Vietnamese government and kick the North Vietnamese out of the country. Not the brightest decision my country has ever made.

I found myself right back at Tan-Son-Nhut Air Base (TSN) just outside of Saigon (now Ho Chi Minh City). Not only that, I was assigned to the same outfit that I had just left four months before. The unit had a new name, but it was the same one.

I flew into TSN about midafternoon on a typically hot muggy Vietnam day. When the door of the airplane opened and the scent of fish sauce blew in, I knew right where I was. Seeing as it was late in the day, I figured I had two choices: I could check in at the squadron or I could find a place to live.

I didn't fall of the turnip truck yesterday, I headed for base billeting. This time my relationship with the billeting folks would be different because I was not here on temporary assignment so there would be no non-availability slips. I was here on permanent assignment so unless I wanted to live off base and pay for it myself, I would take whatever quarters billeting dished out.

Saigon is hot—very hot. Double South Carolina hot. It is also really muggy—like a sauna. So much so that even the mosquitos wrapped little towels around their waists as they flew around looking for their victims. And there were a LOT of mosquitos—big, mean ones. One bite and you were a shriveled husk. You know you are in trouble when they use chicken wire for mosquito screens.

It also rains a lot in Vietnam, so finding a place to live in a nice snug air-conditioned building would be very desirable.

Forget it! I was now a First Lieutenant, but all the rooms in the BOQ (Bachelors Officers Quarters) were already occupied by people way senior to me.

I got a tent. And, it wasn't even my own tent. It was a big army tent called a GP Medium (General Purpose Medium), big enough to house ten people and all their gear. There were already nine other people in residence so I got the last cot available—the one closest to the entrance so all the dust and dirt could blow in onto my gear, when it wasn't raining. Not that it mattered, it was so hot that everyone kept the sides of the tent rolled up anyway so the dust could cover veterans and newbies alike.

I dumped my gear and went to take a look

around. Things did not look good.

My tent was the last in a row of eight tents, the tent farthest from the latrine and closest to the flight line. Jet engines are very noisy. There was also a helicopter pad nearby. Helicopters are very, very noisy.

I knew that men and material were pouring into Vietnam and, looking at the chaos around me, it seemed to me that not much thought had been given as to where the people who were coming into the country were going to go, what they were going to do, where they were going to live, or how they were going handle all the supplies.

Stuff was piled everywhere. Boxes and boxes of who knew what, spare parts were just lying out in the open, and there were pallets of still more stuff that had not yet been unpacked.

There was also activity—lots of activity. There were dozens of people running around moving boxes and equipment from here to there and back again. The best way that I can describe it is if you took a stick, found an anthill, poked the stick in the anthill and stirred it around a bit and then watched what the ants did. It would be that kind of activity.

I decided to go and find the Officer's Club, get a beer and maybe some conversation and see if things were as disorganized and confused as they seemed.

I did, and chatting with people over a tepid beer that was only slightly cooler than the air outside I discovered that things were just as disorganized and confused as they seemed. I went back to my tent and spent a long, sleepless night listening to the occasional roar of an airplane taking off or landing and hoping that my little job would turn out to be something productive. Little did I know what was in store for me.

Who's in Charge
—Thailand—

Bright and early on my first morning back in Vietnam, I reported into my new squadron at Tan Son Nhut Air Base just outside of Saigon. I no sooner got my foot in the door when I was called into the Commander's office. For once my conscience was clear. I knew that I hadn't been here long enough to do anything too bad. The Commander informed me that the Squadron was forming a detachment at another base and that I would be going there.

Okay by me, I didn't know where Detachment 1 was but I figured that anything would be better than TSN and the tent they had given me down by the flight line.

The next morning, after another sleepless night, I drug my bags over to the Aerial Port (it wasn't much of a drag, my tent was practically on top of it) and I was loaded into a C-130 Hercules cargo plane with all the other spare parts. I was the only passenger. We took-off and after a few stops at bases around Vietnam to drop off bits of this and that we flew to Thailand.

Thailand? I didn't know we were doing anything in Thailand.

Come to find out that our operations from Thailand supporting the war in Vietnam wasn't the best kept secret in the world, but the Powers-That-Be were trying to keep it from becoming general knowledge. In fact, during the Vietnam War we operated from six bases in Thailand and from these bases we were flying direct support, strike, reconnaissance and airlift missions in both North and South Vietnam.

I landed at Udorn Royal Thai Air Base about noon on a warm sunny day. I was not only the only passenger, I was the only cargo of any kind. The C-130 barely stopped rolling long enough to drop me off and as soon as I was clear, it took off again.

There I was, standing all alone on a vast expanse of concrete. I couldn't see another living soul, vehicle or even an airplane. Nothing was moving. It was still and quiet. The change from the mad house of Tan-Son-Nhut to this completely laid-back, quiet, peaceful atmosphere couldn't be more pronounced.

I liked it! It was like going from downtown Manhattan to rural Iowa.

There was a shack at the edge of the tarmac and I picked up my bags and headed for it. Sure enough, it was what passed for the terminal and aerial port here in the wilds of Northeastern Thailand. There was even a warm body, a human body, inside. I then proceeded to have what was probably not the most enlightening conversation of my life. It went something like this:

Young Airman, "Hi, Lieutenant."

Me, "I'm just checking in can you tell me how to get to CBPO (Consolidated Base Personnel Office)."

The young fella gave me a blank stare and said, "Ah gee, Lieutenant, I don't think we have one of those."

Interesting. OKAY, try something else, "Can you tell me how to get to Detachment 1 of the 13th Reconnaissance Technical Squadron?"

Another blank stare. This kid was good at blank stares. "Ah gee, Lieutenant I never heard of that."

"Okay," I said, "Do you have a vehicle?"

Young Airman, "Yes sir."

Good. We got past the blank stare. "How about running me over to billeting?"

If he said that they didn't have a billeting office I didn't know what I was going to do.

Billeting got me a cot in a fourteen-man wooden hooch that was sectioned off into individual cubicles whose sides didn't quite go all the way to the celling but provided some privacy. The single-story building had overhead fans, screens and drop-down sides for protection when it rained. There was a raised wooden walkway to the latrine. Not the Ritz, but it sure beat my tent.

I dumped my stuff and went looking for Detachment 1. I didn't find it but I did walk by the Headquarters building, such as it was. If it wasn't for the sign, I would have thought it was just another hooch.

Inside the headquarters building and sitting at a very neat, clean desk, was that staple of all headquarters buildings—the Crisp Clerk.

Crisp Clerk, "Can I help you, Lieutenant?"

Me, "Yeah! I'm just checking in. Can you direct me to CBPO?"

"Udorn doesn't have a CBPO, sir."

"Well, I'm assigned to Detachment 1 of the 13th Reconnaissance Technical Squadron so if you could tell me where they are located, I'll get squared away over there."

A puzzled frown came over the Crisp Clerk's face (Crisp Clerks don't do blank stares—but it's the same thing).

He said, "If you will excuse me a minute, sir, I'll have a word with the Administrative Officer."

He disappeared into an office and a few minutes later reappeared with a very young-looking Captain.

Administrative Officer, "What unit did you say you were assigned to, Lieutenant?"

"Detachment 1 of the 13th Reconnaissance Technical Squadron, sir."

He frowned and disappeared into his office leaving me and CC looking at each other. I'm beginning to wonder if I'm even at the right base.

A few minutes later he reappeared and said, "Detachment 1 will be here at Udorn, but it hasn't been activated yet."

Great! I'm a man without a country. Now what?

That evening I met a few of the guys who lived in the hooch. A couple of them said that they were reconnaissance pilots, that were here on temporary assignment from Okinawa and that they had brought their photo lab and photo interpreters with them. None of these guys knew anything about Det. 1 and why would you need another photo facility here at Udorn when there already was one?

Why indeed?

The next morning, they took me with them over to their operating area which was on the other side of the main runway and what was going on started to become a little clearer. Maybe the pilots didn't have the big picture, but the troops did.

In a nutshell, the reconnaissance support facilities currently at Udorn were being operated as The Green Python Reconnaissance Task Force by people on temporary assignment from Okinawa. When they went back to their home station, in a couple of weeks, they were leaving all of their photo processing, printing and interpretation equipment behind at Udorn and that would be the nucleus of Detachment 1.

Then came the not-so good news. I asked if the commander for Det. 1 had arrived. Nope, not that they knew of.

How about the operations officer? Nope.

Had any other officers turned up? Nope, I was the first, but some of the enlisted men had trickled in and Okinawa folks had just put them to work.

I was the only officer assigned to Det. 1. Not good. Definitely not good.

But, all in all, things were a lot clearer than they were yesterday. This was a fully functional operational unit and the people who were running it would be around for at least a couple of more weeks before they rotated back to Okinawa. Plenty of time for my fearless leader—whoever he was—to show up.

Ha!

While I was getting the fifty-cent tour of the facilities they hit me with a couple of messages that had come in addressed to Detachment 1. The first message was from Headquarters, Tactical Air Command back in the states. It seems that the Major who had been designated as the Commander for Det. 1 had come down with malaria and was in the hospital in Florida, ETA (Estimated Time of Arrival) at Udorn unknown. No replacement had been selected.

Great.

The second message was from Headquarters Pacific Air Forces in Hawaii. The Captain who had been selected to be Det. 1's Operations Officer had been diverted to another assignment. No replacement had been selected.

Great. Just great.

I had no sooner finished reading those two messages when I got a phone call from my masters down in Saigon. Did I know that the designated Commander for Det. 1 was in the hospital and that the Operations Officer had been diverted?

"Yes, sir, I have the messages."

Well, until they got things straightened out and they found replacements for those two they were cutting orders appointing me as the interim commander.

Great. Just #!!@! great.

The lying dogs never did send an operations officer and it was three months before the major got well and finally showed up.

I knew that for self-preservation, if nothing else, I had better learn everything about this operation before everyone from Okinawa disappeared over the horizon. I hunted up the guy who was running the outfit and started following him around like a little puppy dog.

Fortunately, for me, I had been around the Air Force for a few years so this wasn't my first rodeo.

The reconnaissance operation went like this: Every day the reconnaissance pilots (they flew RF-

101s, had eighteen aircraft and flew about twenty-two sorties a day) flew over hostile territory, so, every day thousands of feet of aerial photography were delivered to the photo lab/photo interpretation sections. This enormous dump of potential intelligence information was developed, interpreted, reported, printed, duplicate film copies were made and the entire load was then sorted, cataloged, registered (it was all classified Secret), and packaged to be picked up by courier aircraft at 0300 every morning for distribution to units all over Southeast Asia and beyond.

They did this every day, seven days a week without missing a beat. A well-oiled, smoothly functioning machine. Very impressive.

Now all I had to do was keep things going until my fearless leader showed up.

The Personnel Game
—Thailand—

*I*t was easy to see that my job as the interim Commander of Detachment 1 of the 13th Reconnaissance Technical Squadron would be to keep up the good work until the real commander showed up. But, (there is always a but) to accomplish what they were doing the boys from Okinawa had about ninety people. At a quick count of noses, I figured that when they faded away, I would be left with only around forty.

The troops from Okinawa were leaving, I was staying, the reconnaissance aircraft were staying and they were going to keep flying and taking pictures and all of my people hadn't arrived to handle the workload.

I could see doom approaching. I pointed this out to my masters down in Saigon.

Yes! Yes! They were aware that there would be a

temporary shortage of personnel until people in the pipe-line actually arrived and to just be patient eventually all would be well.

I said that was fine but it didn't help me out tomorrow and I finally convinced them that I needed warm bodies—like—now. They said they would see about getting me some temporary people to tide me over.

Gee! Thanks! Keen observers of the obvious those boys.

The folks from Okinawa left on schedule and my merry little band and I started running like rats in a wheel. We got the job done, but it was only by working twenty-seven hour days.

Of course, some people assigned to Det. 1 did start to trickle in and along with them some more temporary folks showed up, not necessarily from Okinawa, but from bases all over the world, to fill in until the permeant roster was full.

I soon found that getting temporary people to fill out the roster was fine as far as it went, but it had two major flaws:

1) Most of the temporary people were only assigned for a short time, usually thirty days, so that by the time we got them up to speed they were scheduled to leave.

2) I had no control over who turned up so I couldn't count on getting the right people for the various job specialties that we had. I would be short of photo interpreters and I would get photo lab personnel.

My masters down in Saigon seemed to have no sympathy to my plight, but I had a plan.

Back when I was sent on temporary duty to Saigon and the Powers-That-Be shanghaied me, they just extended my TDY. I needed people, but I am only a First Lieutenant. I didn't have the juice to just extend people. So, my tiny little brain concocted a plan to Shanghai the people I needed until all my permanently assigned people arrived.

It worked like this:

Airman Jones was assigned temporary duty to Detachment 1 from Base X back in the states. A couple of days before Airman Jones was scheduled to return to his home station, I would ask his supervisors if they wanted to keep him.

Silly question. Unless Jones was a complete idiot or an ax murderer, of course they wanted to keep him.

Maybe even then.

Then I would ask Jones if he would volunteer to extend his temporary duty. It made me feel better if he said yes but it didn't really matter, Jones was staying if I had to nail his feet to the floor.

I would then send a message to Jones's home base stating that the fate of the Western World was directly depended on Jones staying at Det. 1 for another thirty days. (I'm not greedy)

A brief word about communications in Southeast Asia during the Vietnam War.

They were terrible.

Since satellites, computers and cell phones were yet to be invented, telephone calls were made by landline over lines that wandered all over Southeast Asia and were over fifty years old. Getting a connection from one side of the base to the other was iffy, calls in theater (Southeast Asia) were difficult and calls out of the theater were darn near impossible.

So, for the most part, we communicated by message. Every base had a Communications Center.

You gave them your message and they sent it out. But, like everyone else in this goofy war, they had obsolete equipment, inadequate facilities and too few people.

To try to keep the message traffic moving there was a precedence system, from "Routine" to "Flash" depending on the urgency of the subject. By content, Routine should have covered about 90% of all messages and Flash would only be used if the godless commies were landing on the White House lawn.

Naturally, every one abused the system and sent messages at a higher precedence than they should have, which meant that the communications channels were hopelessly clogged and a Routine message could take hours or days before it was even sent from its base of origin and even more days before it got to its destination.

I am a straight arrow; all my personnel messages requesting an extension for Jones and his buddies went out Routine.

By the time my message requesting Jones's extension found its way to his home base, the Powers-That-Be at said home base acted on it and the answer found its way back to me I had probably kept poor Jones slaving away in the mines for an extra four or five days.

Of course, the answer to my request to extend Jones could only be yes or no. If yes, I have no problem and Jones's temporary duty was extended. If the answer was no, I had three choices:

1) I could put Jones on an airplane and send him home. Fat chance.

2) I could compose another message to try to get home base to change their mind.

210

3) I could crumple up the message refusing my request to extend Jones and throw it in the waste basket.

I picked three every time.

By the time Jones's home base figured out that I hadn't answered their message or that Jones hadn't turned up on their doorstep I had probably kept him for another four or five days.

Eventually the "Where's Jones" message would arrive from his home station with references to previous messages and I would reply to this one saying sorry I never received message such and such (the one I threw into the waste basket), you know how it is over here, and could I pretty please keep Jones.

Another four or five days passes and, if they still said no, that message got choice number three.

I would keep kicking this can down the road until I got my thirty days out of Jones at which time, I would pat him on the head, say what a great guy he was, write him a nice Commendation Letter for his records, put him on an airplane and send him on his way.

I was juggling a half a dozen or more Jones's at any one time.

Making Do
—Thailand—

My Grandmother had a saying (actually she had many sayings):

> Use it up
> Wear it out
> Make it do
> Do without

That was my mantra for my first few months in Thailand.

Trying to keep my manning level up was not my only experience as the Interim Commander of Detachment 1.

As the base grew and more and more aircraft, personnel, etc. arrived the local electrical power system (I figured that it was about the same vintage as the telephone lines) creaked, groaned and struggled mightily to keep up with the increased load.

Brownouts were common, but to give them credit, the system never completely failed. If it ever did, we would be out of business and that was not acceptable. Our reconnaissance pilots were risking their lives every day to acquire the photography and we had to hold up our end to see that it was processed, interpreted and distributed to the rest of the Force.

To protect against the day that power might fail I wanted backup generators; however, all my official requests fell on deaf ears, so I sent my scroungers forth. (I had great scroungers.) Sure enough, from somewhere, they came up with six rather ancient generators. They weren't pretty, but they worked.

By the time anyone missed them we had them set firmly in concrete on a pad out behind our buildings. The boys got them working, built a roof over them to protect them from the elements and even erected a telephone pole between the generator pad and our buildings to carry the power lines.

One problem that we didn't foresee was that when the rains came the ground turned to oatmeal and our power pole developed a distinct list to port. When that happened, the powerlines sagged down into the puddles of standing water and walking between the generator pad and our main production building when we were testing the generators could be a shocking experience.

Then there was the time that one section decided to re-arrange their work area. Among their equipment they had four big, heavy safes for the storage of classified material. Each one of these safes was a five-foot-tall, four-drawer, re-enforced steel file cabinet that weighed well over a thousand pounds.

They pushed all four of them together into one corner of the room and they promptly fell through the floor.

That was an exciting experience.

Supplies were a constant worry. We used a lot of "stuff" and being at the end of nowhere in Northeastern Thailand, getting the supplies that we needed to continue operating was a continuing experience.

For example:

To develop the load of film that we received every day we had seven Eastman/Kodak film processers called Versamats. These were the great-grand daddies of every film processor that you see at your local grocery store, Walmart, etc. The film processing chemicals for these machines, the developer and fixer, came in pre-measured packages that we just called cubes. The cubes looked like the boxed wine that you get at the store. We processed so much film that we would use a dozen or more cubes each day, every day, seven days a week.

At one point we hadn't been re-supplied on our regular schedule (actually, we didn't have a regular schedule) and we were down to about a hundred cubes of each. I was crying to the world by message (sent at a higher precedence than "Routine," you better believe) and phone (when I could get through) and wonder of wonders the world responded.

Our parent organization down in Saigon sent us a couple of hundred cubes.

Our old friends on Okinawa sent a couple hundred more.

It seems that reconnaissance organizations all over the world had taken up our cause and had decided to help us out. Every day base supply would call and tell us that they had received more film processing chemicals and would we please come and pick them up because they were running out of space to store them.

Cubes of fixer and developer kept arriving and arriving. I sent out messages saying, "Thanks, we're good now." I made phone calls, but I couldn't turn it off. I felt like Mickey Mouse with the multiplying brooms in "The Sorcerer's Apprentice" from the movie *Fantasia.*

By the time we did get the spigot turned off we figured we had enough fix and developer to last about twenty years.

My scroungers went forth and came back with three big army tents—don't ask, I didn't. We set them up behind the generator pad, stuffed them full with toxic chemical products and went about our business.

As far as I know the stuff is still there. Let the archeologists two thousand years from now figure that one out.

Three months to the day from the time I set foot at Udorn my Commander finally walked through the door and my life as the Interim Commander of Detachment 1 of the 13th Reconnaissance Squadron was over.

I think that definitely counts as an "Experience."

The Student
—Colorado—

When I returned to the states from my tour at Detachment 1 of the 13th Reconnaissance Squadron, I was assigned to the Photo Interpretation Branch of the Armed Forces Air Intelligence Training Center (AFAITC)—as a student.

Why you might ask, as I did, was an officer with over ten years' experience as a photo interpreter being sent to the photo interpretation school? For the answer to that question you have to try to understand how the minds of the people who run the United States Government work.

Good luck with that.

The explanation I got went something like this: when the big build-up in Vietnam occurred a lot of square pegs got pounded into round holes. It is easy for the big brains in Washington to say that we are going to increase our manpower in Vietnam by 200,000 people. It is not so easy to actually do that. It's easy to send a squadron of airplanes from base X to Vietnam. It is not so easy to have all the support facilities, fuel, supplies and personnel in place so that these airplanes can actually do anything once they get there. To get operations up and running in a hurry in Southeast Asia many officers were assigned to jobs that they had little or no training for.

I'm sure that in most cases this worked out OKAY, but as these officers returned to the states, the Air Force was going to correct this deficiency (that they had created) by sending them to school. Probably to be trained to do the same job that they had been doing for the past year—under combat conditions— and might never do again because they had gone back to their regular jobs.

You might ask, "Why should that affect me? I had been to the photo interpretation school."

"Ah yes," the Air Force said, "but you had been to the enlisted photo interpretation school and you are now an officer and you have not been to the OFFICER's photo interpretation school."

I didn't figure that it was worth my while to point out to them that the reason that I hadn't been to the officer's school was that THEY were the ones who said that because I was a trained, experienced photo interpreter it wasn't necessary for me to go to school back when I got commissioned.

But I wasn't really complaining. I was happy to settle into six months of brushing up my skills.

A few years after I had attended, the school had moved from Sheppard Air Force Base in Wichita Falls, Texas to Lowry Air Force Base in Denver, Colorado. We found a very nice three-bedroom, two baths, brick house in the Denver suburb of Aurora. The kids' school was just down the street and there was a terrific little league sports program for the boys. We even acquired a girl baby, Susan, while we were there.

Must have been the water.

I had just been promoted to captain and when I got assigned to a class, I found out that there was a Navy Lieutenant in the class who was way senior to me so I didn't even have to be class leader.

Better and better.

When the class was formed up I didn't let on that I was a photo interpreter and that I had more photo interpretation experience than half the instructors. I planned to just be student X. But I should have known that it couldn't last. I knew too many people on the school staff, many of whom I had worked with or for over the years, and they ratted me out.

The dirty dogs.

I didn't get past the first day. Heck! I didn't get past the first period.

The first period was an orientation and overview of the course presented by a major who was one of the branch chiefs, and was one of the people that I had worked for during my first time in Vietnam. He was also one of the guys who Shanghaied me.

As he launched into his spiel his eyes roamed over the class and found me. It threw him right off stride. I forget his exact words but it was something like:

"What the **##&%@ are you doing here?"

Nineteen pairs of my classmates' eyes lasered in on me as I gave the major my sweetest smile and said, "Hi, Boss."

Of course, explanations had to be made to the

class and as soon as the period ended, I was hauled into the major's office for more explanations. My take was that hey, I'm a student. I explained that I had never been to the officer's school so let's just carry on.

What I didn't know was that with Vietnam sucking up so much manpower the school was critically short of instructors. The next thing I knew I was in the school commander's office and after an interview that lasted about four milli-seconds I was jerked out of class, given a three-day course on how to be an instructor and put to work.

I was an instructor for three years at AFAITC, an instructor for two more years at the British Joint School of Photographic Interpretation, stayed in the Air Force for over twenty years after I left instructing and I still haven't completed the officer's photo interpretation course.

Uncle Vern's Coloring Book
—Colorado—

When they yanked me out of my nice comfortable featherbed as a student, sent me to the three-day instructor's course and put me to work as an instructor I had no idea what it was that I was going to end up teaching. Outside of my long temporary duty in Vietnam a couple of years ago I hadn't done a lot of real photo interpretation work in the last four or five years. When I was at Headquarters SAC, I supervised cartographers and my time in Thailand was spent as a commander and operations officer.

Even when I was in Vietnam and actually working as a photo interpreter, most of my time was spent looking for bad guys along what was laughingly called the Ho Chi Mihn Trail. It was more like a spider's web than a trail and consisted of every form of land and water transportation you can imagine, most of it hidden under triple canopy tropical jungle.

It's kind of hard to see through trees.

The story of the Ho Chi Mihn Trail is best told in the Urban Myth about the North Vietnamese defector who, when he was asked why he defected, said that he had been conscripted into a labor battalion somewhere near Hanoi, then he was handed a big, heavy mortar shell and pointed south. He said he was put on a train and after a hundred miles or so he was herded off the train, walked for a day and a half and then put on a boat.

For the next six months he said he worked his way south, sometimes he was transported by trucks or boats, but it was mostly walking, over mountains, through jungles and swamps, sweltering in the heat, freezing at night, getting body sores from the constant rain and being eaten alive by the bugs, always carrying his big, heavy mortar shell.

When he finally got to the scene of the fighting deep into South Vietnam he was sent up to the front lines, where he then handed his mortar shell to a soldier who promptly shoved it down a mortar tube and fired it off.

He said that when the soldier told him to go get another one, he defected.

Quite right.

To the school hierarchy my previous experience was totally irrelevant. They needed an instructor to teach industrial interpretation and that's where I went. The last time that I had looked at photos of heavy industry was during my student days ten years ago. But, they said, no problem, there was a lesson plan. Just follow the lesson plan.

I hated that. Boring, boring. Puts people to sleep.

In the two weeks that were allocated for the industrial interpretation block I taught the young Lieutenants (boy, were they getting younger) how to tell a steel mill from a power plant and such things.

To aid the classroom work and to give the students a feel for the size of these industrial plants we took two field trips, one to the big Coke, Iron and Steel Mill in Pueblo, Colorado and one to a local electrical power generating plant. I mention this because it occurred to me that the students would benefit from a third field trip to a different kind of industrial plant. I did all the paperwork for an official "industrial" visit, got it all approved and almost every class that I taught went for a visit to the Coors Brewery in Golden, Colorado.

Faye helped me spiff up another teaching aid that I got a lot of mileage out of. Some cleaver instructor long before my time had made line drawings that showed the major components of every industry that the course covered. The names of the component parts were left off for the students to fill in during class. We put all those drawings into a booklet that I handed out to every student at the beginning of the block.

"Uncle Vern's Coloring Book" went over very well. If the student followed along with the instruction and labeled the component parts in his (or hers) booklet it made a nice, unclassified, quick reference guide that the student could take away and use in the field in the unlikely event that they should ever encounter industries again.

223

In fact, the book became a "thing" and many students not only labeled everything but they also colored everything. Several classes had coloring book competitions and the judges were usually me and the class leader. The judging was always done at the end of course class party and the results were sometimes hotly disputed on the entirely unfounded grounds that the judges were not quite sober.

Exchange
—England—

The United States Air Force and the United Kingdom's Royal Air Force have an exchange program where officers from each country are assigned to operational units of the other and live and work with their opposite members for a couple of years. I never knew that this program even existed until I became an instructor at AFAITC and became good friends with the Royal Air Force Flight Lieutenant who was the exchange officer on the staff.

We both liked to play handball and we became a doubles team. We would take on all comers, not always successfully but we usually held our own.

He had two little girls, about seven and five, and as their first Christmas living out here in the colonies drew near, they became increasingly concerned that Father Christmas wouldn't know where they were. So, to set their minds at ease we arranged a phone call to the man himself.

Faye took the call and called Father Christmas in from the toy workshop. I had been well prepared with a checklist that covered everything from their school activities to, of course, what they wanted for Christmas. We had a great chat and when Father Christmas came through on Christmas Day, they were a couple of happy little girls.

As our tours of duty drew to a close my friend asked me if I had ever thought of applying for the exchange job as an instructor at the British Joint School of Photographic Interpretation (JSPI) because if I did, he was sure that I would be accepted.

The fix was in and I got the job.

We (the whole family, Faye, John 12, David 10, Mike 3 and Susan 2) and I were off to England to live with the Brits while I did a two-year tour with the Royal Air Force at JSPI, which was then at Royal Air Force Base Wyton, about a hundred miles north and east of London in an area of England called East Anglia.

I taught the same industrial interpretation subjects that I had back in the states and that included two industrial tours, an oil refinery and a coke, iron and steel plant (I couldn't work in a brewery). The Brit plant managers were a little disconcerted when the Royal Air Force bus pulled up and the class' fearless leader was a Yank.

The Brits took great care of us and we did get base housing. We were the only Americans on base. There were American bases in the area so John and David went to the American schools but when Mike was ready for kindergarten he went to the Brit "Mixed Infant School" and became a proper little "bloke."

226

Faye and I had a blast. We were included in everything that happened on or off the base. We must have visited every castle, manor house and historical site in East Anglia. We went "Punting on the Cam" (poling a flat bottom skiff on the Cam River) in Cambridge. We went to street fairs, carnivals and jousts.

We were at one joust when our oldest son, John, was drafted to be part of the show. They made him a knight's squire, dressed him in a medieval costume and he spent the afternoon handing his principle implements of knightly mass destruction.

When the first moon landing occurred, all our Brit neighbor's kind of drifted over to our house and we all watched the event on our little black and white television. Faye broke out the snacks and sherry and, seeing as we were the only Yanks in sight, we accepted their congratulations on a marvelous achievement.

We learned about cricket—the national game of England. Even today, after all these years, I'm not sure that I understand all the rules. The playing field is a huge circle with a "pitch"—a long, narrow rectangular strip in the middle with wooden wickets at each end. Runs are scored by hitting the ball and running back and forth between the wickets. If a ball is hit and it rolls beyond the outer circle—that counts four runs. If the ball is hit beyond the circle on the fly—that counts six runs. A batter keeps batting until he is out—either by the opposition catching a fly ball he has hit or by knocking the top bar off the wicket. When you are batting you are "in."

So, as I understand it, there are two teams—one team is in and the other team is out. The team that is in stays in until every member of the team that is in has been in and then out. Then the team that was in goes out and stays out until the team that was out comes in and stays in until every member of the team that was out has been in and then out.

Got it?

Seeing as we were a family consisting of various ages, abilities and genders we played the game by slightly different rules. The Brits call it "Pub Cricket."

The playing field is the highways and byways of England. The pitch consists of the pubs encountered along the way. Scoring is provided by the names of the pubs we passed as we traveled. Every pub has a name so to score you just count the legs in the pub's name. For example: The Coach and Horse is a four—The King James counts as two—the Queen's Head, zero, etc. The teams, of course, are in the vehicle—one team has the pubs on the passenger side, the other, pubs on the driver's side.

We always filled our journeys from here to there with pub cricket.

Guns and Waffles
—England—

My Royal Air Force neighbors at RAF Wyton and my fellow instructors at the Joint School of Photographic Interpretation planned a trip to see, what they called, the Royal Tournament and I was invited to come along. They even laid on an Air Force bus with a driver.

I had no idea what it was all about and the guys just decided to leave me in ignorance and let me see for myself.

The bus delivered us to a large indoor stadium (I forget the name) somewhere down near London. The venue turned out to be a military display—actually, a collection of military displays and competitions. There were weapons demonstrations, marching bands from the different services, Gurkhas doing their knife dance, special forces rappelling down from the rafters, etc. All kinds of military stuff.

My favorite event of the evening, and one I will always remember, was the Naval Gun Race.

Seeing as this was England the gun race had a historical background. This is the story of the gun race, as I understand it.

The Gun Race commemorates an incident that happened during the Boar War in South Africa when the Royal Navy was tasked to bring ashore two naval guns and move them inland a few miles to provide artillery support for a ground action. To get to where they had to be the Navy had to move the naval artillery pieces cross-county by manpower alone, no horses. Obstacles along their way included woods, farmer's fields, some undeveloped areas, a couple of stone walls and a ravine. That's the story.

The lights in the stadium went down and when they came back up the entire floor of the stadium had been cleared and the course for the gun race had been set up.

At one end of the stadium were two field guns lined up side by side. These were medium sized two-wheel howitzers mounted on a carriage, the wheels were about chest high, and there was an ammunition caisson attached. A pretty good-sized piece of equipment.

Lined up behind each gun was a team of about twenty sailors.

Looking down the course about twenty yards in front of each gun there was a six-foot wall. Beyond the wall there was a space with simulated obstacles that you had to avoid, and then there was a simulated ravine. The ravine was five or six feet deep and it looked to be about six or seven yards wide. Once past the ravine there was another space with obstacles and then another six-foot wall. Finally, a clear space and then the firing position for the guns. The course covered the entire floor of the arena.

As I said, this was a race.

The starting gun went off and both teams ran their guns up to the wall and in an instant the gun was dismantled—the wheels came off, the gun barrel was separated from the carriage, the caisson was unhooked, everything was in pieces, and every piece was manhandled over the wall.

While this was happening, a small group from each team had raced on ahead to the ravine.

The gun was reassembled on the other side of the wall and sailors pulled the gun through the obstacles to the ravine. By the time they got to the ravine the advance group had already set up a tripod, swung a couple members of their team over the ravine, and they had set up a tripod on the far side and rigged a cable/pulley arrangement connecting the tripods and spanning the gap.

The gun was again disassembled and individual sailors rode the pulley over the ravine carrying the pieces of the gun.

The gun was reassembled on the other side of the ravine and raced on to the next wall. The gun was again dismantled, taken over the wall, reassembled and pulled forward to the firing position.

Bam! Bam! Bam! Three shots were fired.

Elapsed time for the entire operation—less than three minutes, probably closer to two and a half. Wow! Color me impressed.

Of course, not every day was that exciting. On Sunday mornings Faye would see to getting the kids tubbed and scrubbed for church and Sunday School and I would do the breakfast chores. When I cooked

Sunday morning breakfast was almost always waffles. I don't think the kids liked my waffles as much as they liked the good maple syrup that my mother still sent from some of the Montague farms in Vermont.

One Sunday morning while the kids were still eating there came a knock on the kitchen door. It was Simon from next door, age about five, one of Mikes little playmates, asking if Mike could come out to play. I was just telling him that Mike would be out later when Mike yelled from the table, "We're having waffles."

A blank look came over the kid's face and I said, "Did you ever have a waffle?"

He shook his head no.

"Would you like a waffle?"

He shook his head yes, so I sat him up at the table next to Mike and while they chattered away, I got more waffles going. My little waffle iron only made two at a time, but they were soon done and they disappeared as if by magic.

The next Sunday morning while we were going through our routine there was a knock on the door and there was Simon and he wasn't shy at all.

"Can I have a waffle?"

I'm easy, why not? While I was making the waffles, I got to thinking that I probably had a permanent Sunday morning breakfast guest.

The following Sunday I wasn't surprised at the knock on the door but I was surprised to see Simon—and his little sister (can't remember her name). Up to the table they went and the kids chatted away happily while my poor little waffle iron struggled mightily.

When the knock came on the door the next Sunday there was Simon, his sister and two other neighborhood kids, I had to get a couple of chairs from the dining room. So, I now have six kids chattering away at the breakfast table. Faye stuck her head in the door wondering what in the world was going on. I was beginning to wonder where it would all end.

It was with great trepidation that I answered the knock on the door the next Sunday. Would it be four kids, six, the whole neighborhood?

It was...Simon's mother.

She was all apologetic and said that she had just found out that the kids had been coming over here for breakfast on Sunday morning and she felt terrible if they had been a bother. I assured her that all was well, no bother at all, that I enjoyed having them and that I was flattered that they all liked my waffles.

She got a kind of puzzled look on her face and I asked, "Did you ever have a good old Yank waffle? Come on in." I hollered for Faye and the girls sat at the table and chatted while I cranked up the old waffle iron.

She liked the waffles but she didn't think that it was right for the kids to be bothering me and that was the end of the neighborhood waffle sessions.

Dinner at Westminster
—England—

While I doing my exchange tour in England, I even got to take my mother on a tour and dinner at the Houses of Parliament, Westminster Palace, London.

When Sandi was born (We have got to find out what's causing this although I was pretty sure that it was the water) my mother (bless her heart) flew over to England to help out for a few weeks and while she was visiting our local Member of Parliament invited the entire staff of the Joint School of Photographic Interpretation, and their ladies, for a tour and dinner at Westminster.

I asked if I could bring my mother.

Of course.

She received a separate invitation that was engraved to Mrs. Nordman (Senior). She liked that.

The school commander commandeered a Royal Air Force bus and driver and we were off for the two-hour ride into downtown London and the Palace of Westminster.

We got the full tour. I think the regular tour lasts about an hour and a half, we must have been at it for twice that long.

I think that the original palace was started in 1016 and had been added onto over the years. The entire palace was destroyed by fire in 1834 and rebuilt over a period of thirty years from 1840 to 1870. The palace was partially destroyed by bombing during world War II and then repaired. Not to be picky, but I think major repairs will have to be done rather soon.

We entered through Saint Stephen's Gate into the center of the building. To our right was the Victoria Tower, where the Queen enters, and on our left was the Elizabeth Tower, that's the one that houses the Great Clock of Westminster, more commonly known as "Big Ben" (Nobody seems to know why. Probably because it sounds cool, is easy to remember and is not a tongue-twister to say).

We passed through the gate into the Central Lobby and we could look down the long corridor that goes to the House of Lords on our right and the House of Commons on our left. That corridor has all kinds of stuff hanging on the walls and several statues along the way. As we walked down the corridor to the chambers, I think our guide named every one of them.

Westminster has over 1100 rooms, 100 staircases and about three miles of corridors, maybe we didn't hit all of them, but I think we covered most. My little brain couldn't hold all the gee-whiz stuff I heard. The highlights were, of course, the House of Commons on one end of the building and the House of

Lords on the other.

We went into both; I was impressed.

After the tour we were shown into a large sitting room for pre-dinner sherry and then it was downstairs to what we would call the basement and the Brits call the ground floor, and into a dining room. I'm sure that our dining room was just one of many and I would imagine that they are all about the same, a long narrow room with one long table that could seat about forty. The table was made of wood and it looked solid, the chairs too. There were banners hanging from the ceiling and armor and implements of knightly destruction on the walls.

The meal consisted of many courses, soup to start and a cheese board at the end. There were lots of waiters and as soon as you finished one dish it was whisked away and the next course appeared. If you took two sips of wine the glass was refilled.

It was quite an experience.

After dinner we boarded our bus and went to the downtown London, Royal Air Force Club for drinks and chat and then back on the bus and home.

Mom never forgot that one.

Double Whammy
—England—

Ha! The flesh peddlers that work in personnel assignments are not infallible. They really slipped up when I finished my two-year exchange tour with the Royal Air Force at the Joint School of Photo Interpretation at Royal Air Force Base, Wyton and they sent me right where I wanted to go. Just on the other side of the town of Huntingdon from Wyton was an American base, Royal Air Force Base, Alconbury, and that's where we went.

Life was good; we were living in a nice four-bedroom, two bath house in the little English village of Needingworth, the boys were all in school on the American base where they had their friends, sports, band, all that stuff, Susan was in the Brit mixed infant school, I had a job that I was enjoying as chief of a Photo Possessing and Interpretation Facility (PPIF),

239

the baby, Sandra, was busy doing her interpretation of Beelzebub, and Faye was painting and teaching painting classes to both British and American ladies.

Ah, the best laid plans...

The house that we were renting belonged to a Royal Air Force Flight Lieutenant who was doing a two-year posting in Germany which coincided nicely with our two-year assignment at Alconbury. But, for some reason, I never knew why, his tour in Germany was cut short and he came back to England after only fifteen months. Naturally, he wanted his house back.

That put us in a real bind. We had to find another place to live and with only a little more than eight months left, and even with all our British friends helping us look, we couldn't find a landlord who was willing to go for a short-term lease. Our only alternative was to take base housing at Alconbury.

Now you would think that with all my whining over the years that I couldn't get base housing that I would be happy to get base housing, but that was then, this is now. The house that was available wasn't a bad house really, it just wasn't very big. It was a duplex; living room, kitchen, three bedrooms and one—count them—one bathroom and there were now seven of us.

But there was no choice. If we wanted a roof over our heads that was it. We sold off some furniture, put some more in storage and settled in to make the best of it until our assignment was over.

One did not procrastinate in the potty. The boys took most of their showers down the street at the youth center.

Then came whammy number two.

I was selected by Headquarters United States Air Forces in Europe (USAFE) for a temporary duty assignment to test some new equipment for photo interpreters.

The good news was that I would be on the cutting edge of evaluating new equipment and concepts that might change the way we handled aerial photography forever. The manufacturer had put together a test bed and they and the Air Force wanted real operators to come out of the field and wring it out.

The bad news was that the test was planned to be six months long and it was going to be conducted back in the states at Bergstrom Air Force Base, Austin, Texas.

As far as I was concerned the bad news outweighed the good news. That would be six months away from the family. I didn't want to go. My boss was going to lose his PPIF chief for six months so he didn't want me to go. His boss didn't want me to go. Faye and the kids didn't want me to go.

Messages started flying back and forth between my bosses and Headquarters USAFE to try to get me out of it but to no avail. I had been requested by name by the people who were conducting the test (turned out that they were a couple of retired Lieutenant Colonels that I had worked for years ago) and USAFE was going to comply.

I went.

So, I was now in Austin, Texas on temporary duty for six months and Faye and the kids were back in Alconbury, England. When the test was finished, I would go back to England for two months and then we would all go on to a new assignment.

Bummer!

The obvious thing to do would be for Faye and the kids to pack up and come to Texas. But! There is always a but, for non-military folks the system works this way: When you are moved from base to base on a permeant change of station (PCS) Uncle Sam will pick up the tab for moving your family and household goods. If you want to move the family on a temporary assignment it comes out of your pocket. My pockets weren't that deep.

But I didn't just fall off the turnip truck, I had a plan.

I got hold of the folks in personnel assignments and made my pitch. After explaining the situation, I said why not cut my assignment in England short because Alconbury would only have me for two months when the test was over anyway.

They wouldn't go for that. They wouldn't change my rotation date.

Actually, I was pretty sure that my bosses back at Alconbury had already tried that so I didn't think that they would bite on that one so I hit them with the one that I thought would work. I said OKAY how about making my next assignment now instead of waiting until next year then I will have PCS orders and I can move the family.

They went for that one. They knew they had a fish on the line. There are many less than desirable Air Force jobs around the world that the assignments people have a hard time filling and here was a guy who was asking for a favor. The assignments people smiled and gave me my early assignment for—wait for it—Kunsan, South Korea, an unaccompanied one-year tour, can't bring the family.

Another case where I won the battle and lost the war. But they did promise me that I would come back to Bergstrom after Korea.

Faye packed up the house and the gang and headed for Texas.

It was December when the family arrived in

Austin, they took one look and were immediately unhappy with me, something about the weather. England is damp, windy and cold in the winter but ever since I had been in Texas it had been bright and sunny with the temperature in the seventies and a couple of times in the eighties.

The gang came off the airplane in short sleeve shirts and carrying light jackets.

There was four inches of snow on the ground and it was cold and windy. (We lived in Austin for almost five years and that was the only time it ever snowed.)

Then there was the car. Faye sold our old station wagon before she left England and I had shopped around for something that was big enough for all of us. In those days there were no big family vans like we have today but I bought the biggest vehicle I could find—a Grand Torino station wagon.

It worked but Faye really hated that car. She was only a little bit over five feet tall and she was never really comfortable driving it. To make matters worse, despite all my nagging, she had let her Colorado driver's license lapse and she had to take a driver's test, both written and on the road, to get a Texas license. She had to take the test in the big gold machine. She was one unhappy camper.

It was an experience.

We had just come from four years in England. The English drive on the left. Faye had just returned and hadn't done any driving in the states. The examiner got into the car and Faye sailed off down the wrong side of the road.

I thought the poor guy was going to jump out of the car.

My poor sailor was *sooo* embarrassed.

Anyway, she made her apologies and her explanations and they carried on. Faye was a very good driver and he did give her the license.

Kunsan-by-the-Sea
—South Korea—

So, where was this "Kunsan-by-the-Sea" that I was going to be assigned to for a year? Faye, the kids and I went over to the local library to see what we could find out.

You remember libraries, wonderful places, stuffed full of information and knowledge, not like today's internet which only contains slanted opinions, half-truths, out-right lies and pure nonsense. An unending source of truthiness for the feeble minded.

We found that Kunsan-by-the-Sea was located on the coast of the Yellow Sea about a hundred and fifty miles southwest of South Korea's capital city of Seoul. We also found out that while Kunsan was the name of the air base, the town was called Gunsan, (Don't ask me. Everyone just called it Kunsan.) Gunsan didn't look like it was a very big town. It

245

seemed to be primarily a fishing village with some small manufacturing and it wasn't actually on the sea but a little way from the sea on the Geum River.

When I arrived at Kunsan-by-the-Sea I found out that Kunsan-by-the-Sea wasn't actually on the coast of the sea, the Yellow Sea, either, and that you couldn't even see the sea from Kunsan-by-the-Sea, you see.

The air base at Kunsan-by-the-Sea was a few miles inland from the sea and even if you had the desire you couldn't walk to the sea from Kunsan-by-the-Sea because there was enough barbed-wire in-between the sea, the Yellow Sea, and Kunsan-by-the-Sea to fence in Texas.

But, Kunsan-by-the-Sea was close enough to the sea, the Yellow Sea, to get all the nasty weather that the Yellow Sea can generate: hot, humid, rainy, summers and cold, windy, snowy, rainy, nasty winters.

Not exactly the Riviera of Korea.

I arrived at Kunsan in the middle of the night which is not unusual because just about everything that arrived at Kunsan, people or supplies, came in around midnight. The Air Force ran an air re-supply route that originated in Japan and hit all the bases in Korea; midnight was when it got to Kunsan.

The aircraft was a Boeing passenger plane that had been converted to carry supplies as well as people. It was one of those planes with the three engines in the rear. We called it the "three holler." It certainly made some interesting sounds while in flight.

When I stepped off the plane at Kunsan I was met by—no one. I guess they hadn't got the memo. There was a guy with a truck in the area so, at least, I got a ride over to the Bachelors Officers Quarters and found a place to sleep.

Kunsan had a small intelligence division, only seventeen or eighteen people, headed-up by a major which I assumed would be me. Imagine my surprise when I walked through the door and found that there was already a major sitting in the chair. He had been there for two months, had ten months to go on his tour and he was WAY senior to me. (Who wasn't? I had only been promoted a couple of months earlier while I was on the equipment test.)

This guy was as old as Methuselah and he had probably been around when Moses parted the Red Sea, so he was obviously going remain the chief. So, what did that make me? Methuselah had another desk moved into the office and I became kind of an Assistant Chief of Intelligence.

Duties—be quiet and stay out of the way.

Methuselah made a few phone calls and then we trotted our little buns over to base personnel and pointed out the rather glaring fact that they now had two majors assigned to one position.

We were told that that was nonsense, the personnel assignments people would never make a mistake like that, but they would look into it.

A few phone calls later it was resolved—it was my fault.

It seems that between the time Air Force personnel made my assignment all those many months ago and the time that I actually arrived at Kunsan I had gotten promoted.

I didn't mean to.

When the assignment was made, I was a captain and I was sent to Kunsan to fill a captain's slot. Which, by the way, now didn't exist either because one of the lieutenants in the Intelligence Division had been promoted. But the personnel folks said that they would look into it.

They "looked into it" for four months to come to the obvious solution—one of the majors was going to be re-assigned.

Duh!

But it wasn't me. During the four months that personnel was "looking in to it" Methuselah had obviously been quietly working the system and he got the assignment. He got six months lopped off his one-year tour and went back to the states.

I was now the chief, but I had to stay for the full year.

But it wasn't all bad. During the four months that I was the "Assistant Chief of Intelligence" (there was no position for an "Assistant Chief of Intelligence") I learned a lot. Methuselah had been around a long time and knew all the tricks of the trade. But primarily I learned that life at Kunsan-by-the Sea was boring. We trained to be ready if the North Koreans ever did anything. They didn't. So, we trained and trained...boring, boring.

When you are on a remote tour, away from home and family, there isn't much available to occupy your off-duty hours. I went into Kunsan town a couple of times but there wasn't much to see outside of little wooden fishing boats. I think there was one paved street and maybe a half-dozen buildings taller than one story.

In-between the base and Kunsan, there was another little village called Silvertown. You can find a "Silvertown" outside every military installation in the world, a collection of bars, brothels and junk shops. Not my style.

On base, to occupy my off-duty time, there was jogging (I jogged a lot, but I really hate jogging), movies (Hollywood really makes some lousy movies and I saw them all), the library (I read a lot of books), and golf.

There was a little nine-hole course on base. I am not a golfer, but I bought the whole kit, clubs, bag and pull-cart, from a guy who was leaving for fifty bucks. I played every weekend, all weekend, sometimes in the rain, sometimes in the snow, and you can add golf to the long list of things that I am not very good at. I did wear out the wheels on the pull cart.

The only thing to look forward to was that the assignments folks promised me that my next assignment would be back at Bergstrom where My Sailor and the kids were. They did come through on that promise.

Bergstrom is a much larger base than Kunsan so the Chief of Intelligence was a Lieutenant Colonels slot. As a major I was assigned down to one of the squadrons with the same job (PPIF Chief) that I had when I was back in England at Alconbury.

But that was fine. We had bought a nice house before I went to Korea and the kids were all settled into their schools.

When I went up to the Chief of Intelligence's office for a meet and greet there was a brand-new Lieutenant Colonel sitting in the chair.

Guess who?

You got it—Methuselah.

Tom
—South Korea—

*L*ucky for me while I was doing my long, lonely year at Kunsan I found companionship. No! Not the kind of companionship that would have my sailor coming after me with blunt (maybe sharp) objects. No, this was companionship of a different nature.

For those of you old enough to remember, this was the age of the "Pet Rock." Pet Rocks were all the rage back in the states, it seemed like everybody had one. Personally, I found pet rocks boring. I mean, it's a rock. So, I had something much better; I had a pet can of soup. A can of Tomato soup. I called him Tom.

I don't know much about Tom's life before we met. His ancestry must have been Scottish—from Clan Campbell—and I think he had spent some time in Camden, New Jersey. But, regardless of where he came from Tom was superior to a rock in every way. For example:

A rock doesn't move much unless it gets picked up by a glacier or puked out by a mountain. You could tell by the slight dent in his lid that Tom had been around.

A rock isn't very colorful. In fact, it has no color at all, just a dull, boring gray. Tom, on the other hand, was brilliantly arrayed in eight bright colors, red, orange, yellow, gold, green, brown, black and white. A feast to the eyes. I could (and probably did) sit and stare at him for hours.

Unless you are a geologist, what can you learn from a rock? Tom, on the other hand, was highly literate and was well informed in many subjects such as; the culinary arts, law, health, and, most significantly, diet and nutrition. He was even bi-lingual.

Did anyone ever try to take their pet rock for a walk? You would have to carry it everywhere you went. Tom rolled happily along with me when went for a stroll. On the down side, walking didn't do much for Tom's literary offerings and he was hopeless at jogging.

I thought about taking Tom home with me when I went back to the states but I wasn't sure how he would fit in. Thinking about that ravenous horde back in Texas I was afraid that his life might be in danger. Besides, Tom seemed to indicate that he would be more useful helping my replacement through the long, lonely stretches.

I'm not sure how that relationship worked out. When I introduced my replacement to Tom and was expounding on Tom's many virtues, he (the replacement) looked at us kind of funny like and started acting really weird and he put his hands up and backed away from us as though he was afraid of Tom.

At midnight, I climbed on board the three holler and flew away from Kunsan-by-the-Sea. Hopefully, never to see it again.

But sometimes I still think about Tom.

Monarch Butterflies
—Texas—

From Faye's Journal:

Winter is just around the corner, and I KNOW this, because THE event of the year is happening. It seems that in every part of our wonderfully diverse country there is one unmistakable transition point that tells you that autumn is fading and that winter will soon be here.

When I was growing up in Washington just north of Seattle, it was the day that the Big Creek was suddenly full, bank to bank, with spawning salmon headed up-stream.

In New England you know winter is just around the corner when you spend a waning Autumn day in the woods tramping through a glorious palette of woodland colors and the ground is ankle deep in waves of red and gold leaves.

THE moment in Iowa was always a frosty morning of shivering delight as the first fingers of sunlight brushed the whispering corn, and a single avian call rang out and was then answered and echoed into a clarion cacophony as the geese rose, wheeled, turned about to formation height and flew away.

Here in Austin, Texas, one watches as the shortening days turn the sky from a high turquoise to gentle Columbia. At first, you scarcely notice the bits of color moving in the trees and bushes, but then there are more and the tree tops are suddenly spangled with orange. Like jewels and coins of a fabulous treasure they silently and purposefully fly, rarely stopping.

The Monarch Butterflies are migrating to Mexico.

I think, somewhere in our beginnings, man must have migrated too, following his food supply. For, just as the turning tide urges one to go a-sailing, the changing seasons stirs a long forgotten ancestral memory.

Bull Riding
—Texas—

From Faye's Journal:

The big boys, John, eighteen and David, sixteen, wanted to go to the little town of Elgin because some ranch had an arena where you could sit in a grandstand and watch amateurs take a shot at bull riding.

Off we went.

Elgin is about twenty-five miles east of Austin and it was a pleasant drive through gently rolling hills dotted with well-watered farms and ranches. The roadsides and fields were ablaze with Bluebonnets, Indian Paintbrush, Pink Mallow and Yellow Clover. In one area, the Bluebonnets were so rampant that the trees were just green ornaments on an undulating blue carpet.

We easily found the site (Elgin isn't a very big town) which consisted of a tavern with a very large open-air patio overlooking a rodeo type arena.

In a holding pen were the bulls. Somehow, in my sheltered and naïve mind's eye, I envisioned that these "bulls" would be calves, or at the worst, young steers. Well! In this pen were a dozen of the biggest, ugliest, fire breathingest, Brahmas and cross Brahmas you've ever seen.

For example, whilst moving one of these monsters to the chutes, a good sized, buff-colored, mixed Lab went yapping out to help and with one distaining sideways swat, the bull nearly put the dog away.

I should have had a clue when the boys left 'to see if they could help in the chutes' and the rest of us settled down to watch the nuts bring disaster upon themselves.

Imagine my horror and rising panic as first the eldest and then the second of my urban raised sons came into view atop one of those malevolently muscled, belching behemoths.

I was afraid to watch for fear they would get hurt and afraid NOT to watch for the same fear.

John lasted a few wild moments and landed squarely on his dignity, with the bull going away. About the time my heart decided to resume its normal position, and the blood had quit pounding upon my eardrums, out came David. For almost six seconds he really rode that bull, before summersaulting over its head and landing in front of the bull in perfect position to get himself killed.

Damages: a horn grazed collarbone and a hoof bruised arm and breastbone.

I breathed a sigh and thought, "That's out of

their systems and they're all in one piece."

Then a lanky, tobacco chewing, real, live, "cowboy" sauntered over, slapping the dust from his hat on a Levi clad thigh squinting in sun-bronzed tradition, he "allowed as he'd never seen anyone do better their first time on a bull."

Pardner, for a strong, silent cowpoke, you gotta BIG mouth! Now I see visions of trophy belt buckles and hand carved saddles in my sons' eyes.

Auction
—Texas—

While we were living in Austin our local Public Broadcasting Station had a televised auction fundraiser. Local businesses and individuals donated goods and services and bids were taken by phone. It lasted a week and it was fun to watch the items come and go.

The station posted all the items on flip charts mounted on easels scattered around the studio, about a half-dozen items on each easel. As bids were received they would be written next to the item in magic-marker and crossed out as higher bids were received and recorded.

When they figured that they had milked an item for all they could get they would announce that bids would close on all the items on chart "X" in half an hour.

We watched, off and on, during the week and even made a bid on a couple of items. It was the last day of the promotion when we noticed that way down in the lower right-hand corner on one of the charts there was a three bedroom, furnished, condominium in Port Aransas, Texas, for rent for a week.

Wow, we all thought, that would be a great getaway, and, so far, the bid price was only $50. Faye phoned and the next time the camera came around to the chart, there was our bid of $55.

The station then announced that all the items on "our" chart would close in thirty minutes.

The next time the camera came around there was a bid posted of $60.

Bummer! There was someone bidding against us and there was only about fifteen minutes left before the item closed. Faye got on the phone again.

The next time we saw it, there was our $65, but, the next time we saw it, we were crossed out and there was a bid of $70.

Now there was only a couple of minutes left and Faye got on the phone—and couldn't get through.

Oh no!

She tried again, no luck. Again, and made it.

"Was it too late to bid on the item?"

No, not too late.

We were all glued to the TV screen. The announcer was talking about the items on "our" chart and closing them out, when a hand reached in from the lower right-hand corner of the TV, crossed-out the $70 and wrote in our $75.

We were in!

The kids went nuts—you would have thought that we had won the lottery.

Port Aransas
—Texas—

From Faye's Journal:

The big boys (John had graduated from high school and joined the Marines so we let David invite one of his friends so he wouldn't have to spend all of his time with the 'little kids') are off doing their teen-age thing and Vern has taken the rest of the gang, and the "Dragon" off to the beach.

The Dragon is a kite of monumental proportions. It is a fire-breathing dragon's head, about six feet in diameter, with a tail about forty feet long. It takes some doing to get it up, but once it is flying it is truly spectacular.

I am seated in front of the window, looking out on the Port Aransas Ship Canal and watching the passing parade. There are ships and lesser craft of every description; oil tankers that seem to fill the whole channel, working boats, mostly side trawlers, inbound shrimpers carrying clouds of black-headed Laughing Gulls in their wake, charter boats going out for a few hours or a full days fishing and private craft of all description, everything from real yachts to dinghies.

To my joy, there are usually two or three dolphins in the channel, feeding, cavorting or hitching rides on the bow waves of passing ships.

The days have been sunny and bright, the sky dotted with little puffs of cloud that will probably be thunderheads by the time that they reach Austin. The Gulf is bathtub warm with four or five-foot waves which are a delight for jumping, splashing or riding, often among schools of mullet which are, always, just beyond arms reach.

The temperature is about the same as Austin, low to mid-nineties, but, with the sea breeze and lower humidity it feels nicer. You really have to watch the sun or you will find that you are barbequed.

Port Aransas has the look of all seaside villages whose livelihood depends upon a small fishing fleet and summer visitors, with perhaps two exceptions. First, almost everything is built on stilts for the islands are low lying sand reefs, marshy or gorse covered in the middle and a hurricane would have the whole place awash. Secondly, the vegetation is quite tropical, with palm trees, bananas, frangipani and other exotic stuff.

We have been out deep-sea fishing twice and the men folk are going again tomorrow evening. The grand total for our group, to date, is three good-sized Kingfish, a little shark and one Bonito. We dipped one of the Kingfish in batter and pan fried him—and he was marvelous. We also tried a bit of the shark—tasty. It was very mild with a texture similar to chicken.

The rest is in the freezer to take home.

Later that day:

While I was cleaning up after supper Vern took his tackle box, a can of bait and the kids out to the end of the little dock in front of our condo. All the kids needed to fish was a little stick and he would get them rigged up with drop lines so they could catch some kind of little fish that the locals called croakers. It didn't take much imagination to see why they were called that.

After I finished, I wandered out onto the dock to see how the fishing was coming along and the first thing I saw was a herd of children laughing, squealing and running back and forth across the end of the dock.

Then I saw Vern sitting with half a dozen other adults chatting away while this turmoil swirled around them. I joined the group and got the story.

Once Vern had our three rigged up, they immediately started catching croakers. They soon realized that the tide was coming in and that they could catch the croakers on one side of the dock and then run over to the other side and release them. Then the tide would sweep the fish under the dock and they would run back over to the other side and catch another one, maybe the same one, again.

Soon two little kids came out on the dock to see what all the excitement was about and Vern sent them back to the shore to find a stick and he got them rigged up too. After a while other little kids turned up and, of course, they wanted to catch croakers too.

All the noise and excitement drew some of the parents out to the end of the dock and they joined

Vern. While the adults were laughing and chatting away Vern was baiting hooks for about a dozen kids plus our three.

Great fun! We sat out there until it was just too dark to see and the party broke up. I'll bet the same fish got caught a dozen times.

RAF West Raynham
—England—

From Faye's Journal:

We are back in England and I am loving it now that we are over our jet lag.

Our flight from McGuire Air Force Base in New Jersey left at six-thirty in the evening and arrived here in England at three in the morning stateside time, or eight in the morning local time. It was a short night and a hellishly long day, but we managed to keep everyone up and awake until evening. We learned long ago that staying up all day was the best and fastest way to adjust to a new time zone.

There has been some drizzly weather, but it has been quite reasonable. Beautiful mornings, clouding over by afternoon with a steady, fresh, easterly wind, but no real rain.

Vern has been here for three months and he is assigned to the Intelligence Division at the huge American base at Royal Air Force Base Lakenheath but we are living thirty miles north of there at a British missile facility called RAF West Raynham.

As usual, there's a story there.

When Vern arrived, Lakenheath was in the process of converting from three squadrons of older aircraft to four squadrons of much more modern, much more highly sophisticated aircraft. This meant that the base facilities and the number of personnel assigned were going to, at least, double. The Intelligence Division went from nineteen with a major as chief to fifty-nine people with a lieutenant colonel in charge. Vern says that he is one of four majors assigned and is the Officer-In- Charge of the Photo Interpretation/Photo Metrics/Radar Prediction Branch.

When Vern arrived the housing on base was full and off base housing was tight and becoming very expensive. The Brits did everything they could to accommodate us including making available to us Yanks housing at nearby (or not so nearby) British Bases.

Thirty miles north of Lakenheath there was a British Bloodhound Missile Detachment at RAF West Raynham. At this time there were no active flying operations at West Raynham so the base was half empty with several quarters available.

Vern liked it and outside of the commute the only problem that he could see was where the kids would go to school. The American schools were all thirty miles down the road at Lakenheath.

That's when he found out that just five miles from West Raynham there was a NATO standby base at RAF Sculthorpe that was run by the Americans.

Sculthorpe's mission was to play host to various NATO exercises during the year but on a permanent basis there were only about a hundred-people assigned to keep the facilities operational. And, among those facilities there was an elementary school, a two-room school that had about three dozen kids and taught grades one through six and there would be no problem having our two girls attend.

They even volunteered to provide transportation for the girls. Clever devils. They use Susan and Sandra to exercise the little used vehicles in their motor pool. Every morning the girls and I sit by the living room window waiting to see what kind of vehicle shows up at the house. The girls go to school in everything from a dump truck to a limo and almost always come home in something different. Great fun.

Mike is now in junior high school so his school is down at Lakenheath. Every day he joins six or seven kids from Sculthorpe and they go down to Lakenheath by bus. They even rerouted the bus to come by West Raynham and pick Mike up. You can't beat that.

This part of England is about fifty miles, northeast, on the other side of the fens, from where we use to live in Wyton/Alconbury area. Here we have a patchwork quilt of oats, barley, wheat, potatoes and other market crops stitched together with hedgerows and tree lined lanes, knotted at random intersections by small villages. Flint and stone seem to be in common use as building materials, with red tile roofing. Once in a while you see slate or thatch, but not like the villages that we used to wander.

RAF West Raynham is as old, or nearly as old as our exchange base at RAF Wyton. The housing looks the same, two story duplexes and single

269

detached houses, but it is a ghost town. I gather that you don't need many people to run a missile base. We sit atop the highest knoll in splendid isolation and are one of only four families that live on this street.

The quarter itself is lovely. A two story, brick, four bedrooms, one and a half baths, detached house. It is laid out like the Wyton house but nicer. The Brits have worked very hard to get it ready for us, freshly painted, ivory, throughout, a new four burner electric stove with a full-size oven, a good size refrigerator, American washer and dryer and central heating. The heat is an oil-fired unit that sends hot water to wall radiators. Strange and prone to emit horrifying rumbles, but it works.

Downstairs there is a large kitchen, laundry room (which was once the butler's pantry and still has the call box on the wall) dining room, half bath (quite large with a little ell containing coat hooks, so it doubles as a cloakroom) a roomy hall with a telephone nook behind the stairs and a big living room with a fireplace and glass double doors opening onto the back yard.

Upstairs, we have four bedrooms, a bath (tub and sink) and a separate room containing the toilet.

Outside the kitchen door there is a passage way with an old storage bin that was for coal, a tool room and the garage.

Yard! We really have our work cut out for us.

While the quarters were unoccupied the station kept the front lawns mowed, but that was it. The flower beds along the sides of the house are just discernable, mostly from the rare, straggling flower. The back was left to return to nature, which it did. Just before we came, they mowed the back "grass" (?) and attacked the hedges, but there is work to be done.

Six or seven-foot hedges separate our back yard from the farmers' fields beyond and our adjacent neighbors. (at the moment there are no adjacent neighbors) An integral part of all the hedgerows are wild blackberries, the big kind with fierce thorns.

Beyond our back hedge (there is no fence) there are fields of grain, hedgerows and trees as far as the eye can see—three or four miles by my reckoning. The view from the upstairs window is beautiful and a good place for wildlife watching. We've seen rabbits, a pair of collared doves and meadow pipit, which is a little smaller than a robin, dark, streaked brown above, light below with brown spots on it's chest and as it grubs for worms the tail bounces up and down. Also, there are blackbirds, sparrows, starlings, swallows and swifts.

Almost everything I need comes right to the door. The milk is delivered every morning, the local butcher delivers twice a week and the Greengrocers truck comes through the housing area on Mondays, Wednesdays and Fridays. If I need anything else there is a post office/store (mini-mart) on base, about a ten-minute walk.

We are supposed to get our phone hooked up next week and our number will be, Weasenham Saint Peter, 312. Whenever I say it, I have a wild urge to genuflect or say gesundheit or just giggle.

Vern: I will just add a word to Faye's description of RAF West Raynham.

Of all the houses, apartments, condos and duplexes that we lived in (twenty-two, by my count) as we wandered around the world, I think that Faye liked the house at RAF West Raynham the best. The master bedroom spanned the full width of the house with picture windows front and back. She set her studio up on the back side of the house looking out over our back garden and the farmer's fields that stretched as far as the eye could see.

On weekends the kids and I would take the shovels and the wheel barrow and go scrounging through the back yards of the empty houses looking for flowers. All the suitable plants ended up in our back garden so Faye could enjoy them from her "perch."

Star Wars
—England—

I like Science Fiction. I have always liked Science Fiction. I remember when I was a little kid hanging out with Buck Rogers and riding with Flash Gordon in his cheesy looking rocket ship as we went after that arch villain Ming the Merciless.

Okay! So maybe that didn't really happen, but I do remember sneaking my copies of *The War of the Worlds* and *The Time Machine* into bed at night so I could surreptitiously read them under the covers with my flashlight.

This appreciation of fine literature (i.e. SCIFI) carried over to my children. Their mother—not so much.

When the Star Wars franchise first hit the big screen in the 70's we were living at RAF West Raynham, which is north and east of London in a very rural part of England called East Anglia. If you look up East Anglia on Wikipedia it says that the area is covered in Broadlands and Fenlands. True, and it also has lots of quaint little farms, historical sites, manor houses and villages to explore. Wikipedia also says that the climate is mild and dry. In the seven years I lived there the summers may have been mild and dry but the winters were wet, cold and lousy.

Star Wars was playing in London and all of the major cities but that didn't do us any good out here in the wilds of East Anglia, a million light years from anywhere. We all wanted to see it (well, the kids and I did. Faye, again—not so much), but we were resigned to the fact that it would be "someday."

Then in December, wonder of wonders, we heard that Star Wars would be playing at the cinema in our local market town of Kings Lynn, about ten miles away.

Plans were made, and on a cold, raw, snowy, windy Saturday just before Christmas we were off.

We loaded into the "Gutless Wonder," a 1969, right hand drive, Volkswagen van that had been rigged out as a camper. It ran most of the time and we went to a lot of places in it, but all of its "get up and go" had "got up and went," if it ever had any to begin with.

The intrepid travelers for this trip were: Mike, age 12, Susan 10, Sandra 6 and me. Faye could not be persuaded to join this expedition. Snuggled up in her warm, fuzzy robe by the fireplace with a hot "cuppa char" in her hand she thought we were all nuts.

The big wussie.

The rest of us hit the road. The sky was a very dark solid gray overcast with very, very black clouds scudding along beneath spitting out the occasional snow shower. The temperature was right about

274

freezing so the one or two inches of snow that had fallen a couple of days earlier hadn't completely melted away. This left small patches of snow by the side of the road and big patches of ice on the road. The snow that was left was being swirled around by a thirty-knot wind that was howling down straight out of the North Sea.

In other words, a typical December day in northern East Anglia. I was beginning to think that maybe Faye had the right idea.

Onward, and with only a few slips and slides, we made it to Kings Lynn about noon.

Kings Lynn is a smallish town located on the south shore of a large indentation of the British east coast called The Wash. It is an old town whose history goes back to before the Roman occupation. The buildings are a jumble of styles, everything from wood and stone through half-timber to modern. In its latest reiteration, the main drag, the High Street, had been made into a pedestrian way only. With shops on both sides, the town center was about thirty feet wide and a little under a block long. The car park was at one end of the high street and the local cinema on the other.

The only people around on this cold and windy day seemed to be those standing in line for Star Wars tickets. The line stretched from the theater almost to the car park.

We were doomed. It looked like there was no way we would get in but we decided to take our chances and tough out the line.

That is, the kids thought that I should tough out the line while they disappeared into various shops to warm up.

At about twelve-thirty they started selling tickets and the line slowly shuffled forward. It looked like a lot of people had already gone in and sure enough when we were about a half-dozen spaces from the front the manager came out and informed everyone that the theater was full and the next showing would be at five. The line began to dissolve but two groups in front of us held their ground and we did too.

The manager came out and spoke to the first group, a family of four. They went in.

Hope surged.

A few minutes later the manager returned and spoke to the couple in front of us and they went in. We stood there. Some people behind us gave up and left. Time passed. A long time it seemed, but the manager finally reappeared.

"How many?" he asked me.

"Four."

He said he had four seats but they were down in front and would that be all right. You bet. We were in!

I don't know what the theater started out as, Shakespeare maybe. I think a hundred years ago, it had been a music hall for vaudeville and that type of thing. It was just a rectangular building with a stage across the narrow end, auditorium seats and a balcony that started about two thirds of the way back. It had been converted into a cinema by the simple method of mounting a flat screen in a spider web of cables right at the front of the stage. This was all right if you were sitting directly in front of the screen about a quarter of the way back, or further, but as you got closer to the screen you had to look up more and more. Those in the first few rows could get severe neck strain.

As the seating got away from the center toward the edges of the rows the picture became more and more distorted.

Heating consisted of four small steam radiators two on each side of the hall. They wheezed and clanked and made all kinds of noises but the only way you could get warm from one would be to sit on it.

So, there we were, sitting in the furthest right four seats of the front row staring up at the edge of a flat screen with our hats, coats and mittens on and our feet slowly turning into blocks of ice.

The lights dimmed, the music soared, that unique theme that everyone now knows so well rolled through the auditorium. The words scrolled up the screen,

"A long time ago, in a galaxy, far, far, away..." and this huge, magnificent star ship came into view and kept coming and coming and I was hooked.

I've been hooked ever since.

Bobby Burns
—England—

From Faye's Journal:

One of the great things about living on the Royal Air Force Base at West Raynham was being invited to all of the purely British events that took place.

Some of these events took place in the "Officers Mess," a large, rambling, brick structure that was built back in the thirties.

The United States Air Force has what they call Bachelors Officers Quarters (BOQ) where single officers live. They are mostly like motels. The Royal Air Force has Officers Messes and they are like Victorian Era four-star hotels.

If a BOQ is a place to keep your stuff and sleep, an Officers Mess is a home where single officers live and live well. The mess stewards took care of their rooms, their uniforms, provided three meals a day and even handled their mail.

In the building there was also a Pub type bar.

The mess was their home and ladies (unless they were also officers) entered by invitation only. On the days when some of the British ladies and I played racquet ball and we wanted a cool beer afterwards we couldn't just nip into the bar. We had to go around to the back door, get Bob the barman's attention and our beer was handed out to us.

Payment was no problem, we just put it on our husband's bar tab.

The interior of the Mess was very Masculine - dark wood, heavy furniture and all kinds of memorabilia hanging on the walls.

There were two dining rooms: a large one for formal occasions and a much smaller, more intimate one where the residents took their regular meals.

There was also a large library/reading room where they occasionally showed movies. These were regular Hollywood feature length films that came in four or five film reels. The mess stewards would set up a projector and we would sit in the plush, overstuffed chairs with a beer or some other adult beverage in hand and watch the show. When it was time to change reels, it was time for us to hit the bar for a refill.

Last week the movie was *The Towering Inferno*.

The latest "do" at the mess was called Robert Burns Night and we had invited a Major that Vern worked with and his wife to join in the festivities. We had also arranged to have them spend the night in the Mess. There was plenty of room and from what my Scottish neighbors told me no one was driving home after this party.

"Bobby Burns" was hosted by the Scotsmen assigned to RAF West Raynham to pay proper tribute to the Immortal Bard. The dress for the affair was formal military uniform, Mess Dress, for the guys and, of course, evening gowns for the ladies.

We all gathered in the bar until dinner was announced. Anticipation was high and the Scots did not disappoint.

The main dining room of the mess, which was a big room, was cleared out except for just one huge table that was laid out as a big letter U. There were place settings with name tags, but that was about it. The table was without linen and the only light in the room was provided by silver candelabra with scarlet candles, spaced along the center. Also, on the table stood bottles of scotch and pitchers of water, about one bottle of scotch for each four places.

We found our seats and the Church of England Chaplin gave the Selkirk grace:

> "Some 'hae meat and 'canna eat
> And some 'wad eat that want it
> But we 'hae meat and we can eat
> And sae the Lord be Thankit!"

After grace ALL the bottles of scotch were opened, the caps were ceremoniously thrown away and the bottles started going around. I had a moments panic—was I expected to drink neat scotch all evening? One of the stewards appeared at my shoulder, and the Lord be Thankit, wine was provided for the ladies who preferred it.

The first course was cock-a-leekie soup that was served by the Mess's regular stewards all decked out in suitable regalia.

Then, with skirling bagpipes, Hamish

McTavish, aka, the Station's Deputy Commander, looking splendid in his kilts, entered followed by the Senior Steward bearing, upon a silver charger, the Haggis.

The Padre then addressed the Haggis:

> "Fair Fa' your honest sonsie face
> Great Chieftain o' the pudding race..."

The second course was, naturally, the Haggis, 'wi champit tatties and neeps' (mashed potatoes and turnips).

The bottles kept going around.

The third course was a most excellent, prime, Aberdeen-Angus beef, served wi' roastit and champit tatties, wee sprouts from Brussels and wee carrots from Norfolk.

Next item to grace the board was called Atholl Brose. The only way I can describe it is, a hot mead made from oats and honey with cream floating on top. It appeared a strange grayish color, and the taste, while certainly not unpleasant, was one I'm still not sure I liked. Now, isn't that an ambiguous statement?

So, finally we were down to the cheese board and biscuits.

The cheese and water pitchers were cleared away and the bottles of scotch kept making the rounds.

The Chairman toasted the Queen and then said something like:

"Smoke yer pipe wi' sic a lunt." (Lunt means to emit smoke in columns, I looked it up.)

Coffee was served and one of the Scotsmen, who looked splendid in dress Frazer regalia complete with kilt, sporrin, velvet jacket, lace jabot, skeandoo and silver buckled slippers, gave the Immortal Memory—a short speech on the life and works of the bard, including:

> "Fill up your cup with the generous juice
> As generous as your mind
> And drink with one the generous toast
> The bard o' human kind."

I fear my poor attempts to record are but a pale echo of the rich, rolling accents of the evening.

Then we repaired to the bar, where the "generous juice" still flowed and danced to records of Scottish music. It was a merry gathering.

Much to our amusement one of the ladies tucked a mirror into the toe of her shoe to see what was under the kilts.

I never thought I would see a priest in a kilt doing the Highland Fling, but I did. As he was a very rotund gentleman of short stature, he looked a secular, costumed Mr. Pickwick. He was well into his cups, and I heard (on this small post one hears everything) that the stewards were betting whether or not the Padre would make six o'clock mass.

He did.

The next morning our friend John was still snoozing away in their room in the Mess so his wife got up and walked over to our house for coffee and a bickey. Time passed and John still hadn't appeared, so Mary phoned over to the mess and asked the mess stewards to shake him out of bed.

Not going to happen.

The stewards wouldn't ring the room. She was informed by the stewards that the Major was sleeping.

"Wake him up it's time for us to leave."

"Madam, the Major is sleeping."

"Yes, I know that. Wake him up."

"Madam, the Major did not leave a wake-up call."

283

"Look, I'm his wife; go down and wake him up."

"Madam, the Major is sleeping."

"Yes, I know, get him up."

They wouldn't do it. The Major was sleeping and they would not disturb him and that was that. The steam is coming out of Mary's ears. Vern and I are dying. She slammed down the phone and marched out of the house with fire in her eyes. I thought that we had better go with her—just to prevent death and destruction.

She marched into the Mess, glared at the stewards, stormed down the hall, burst into their room and started yelling at her husband.

The poor guy came out of a sound sleep and didn't have a clue why his good lady was reading him the riot act.

You gotta love those mess stewards. If you were one of their charges, they would protect you like a mamma grizzly with only one cub.

On occasion when Vern was on temporary duty, he stayed in various RAF Officers Messes and he had nothing but good words to say about them. It is a very nice way to live. It is like living in an older European hotel with meals and laundry provided. In addition, the mess stewards did lots of little things. If you put your shoes out in the hall at night, they would be all shined up in the morning and every morning, a few minutes before your wake-up call, a steward would silently pad into your room and leave a hot cup of tea on your bed-side table—very nice.

Canal Boat
—England—

From Faye's Journal:

Our week on the horse-drawn canal boat turned out to be a unique adventure.

I was told that there were only four or five horse boats left and the *Pamela* was the only working "bed and breakfast" boat. The others run two or three-hour tours around some of the big cities, like Liverpool.

I liked the Pamela from the first minute I saw her. She was the size of a regular canal boat, about forty feet long and six feet wide, but from there all semblance ended. She was not open to carry goods but closed with sloping sides and a flat roof. The back third of the boat was the owner's living quarters, they had two children about Sandi's age, and the rest of the boat was the B&B section. We had a little sitting room with a small kitchen and two sleeping rooms with four bunks in each one.

Normally, the Pamela did a gentle three or six-day circular route north of where we joined her at Wolverhampton. But, this summer, much of her usual territory was closed to boat traffic for much needed canal repairs so, the owners and operators, Ann and Martin Toms, lovely people, wanted to move the boat down to the Warwick area so they could get a season in.

We had the boat booked for a week so the Toms asked us that instead of the usual B &B cruise would we mind if our trip would be taking the boat from Wolverhampton to Warwick.

What do we know? A boat ride is a boat ride.

We (Vern and me, Mike, Susan, Sandi and David who was home for the summer from college) said, "Sure, no problem," and we were off.

A short word on canals so you will know what we were getting into, we didn't.

The English Canal System was mostly built between 1760 and 1860 as an industrial transportation system, although some passengers were also carried.

The only transportation available at the time was by road and the roads, to say the least, were awful to non-existent. So, a canal boat pulled by a horse, or team of horses over a well-traveled and maintained towpath, was much faster, and cheaper, than horse or ox-drawn wagons slogging over the countryside.

The canal system that the English built was a marvel. It went everywhere, connected everything and flourished until industrial technology came up with the train.

The railroad was, of course, faster and cheaper

and effectively put the canal boats out of business. So, for a hundred years, or so, neglect, disuse, misuse, and lack of maintenance took its toll on the canals.

The English were never anything like a mobile society until the end of World War II. At that time modern thinking took a giant step and the Anglican mind grasped fervently and fanatically upon the private motorcar—much to the decline of British Rail—but that is another story.

With new mobility the canals were rediscovered, not for industrial uses but, as a quiet place for summer vacations. But, when the canal boats reappeared they did so with internal combustion engines, eroding the traditional horse-drawn narrow boat not to mention the canal banks and towpaths. Now, like a glimmer from the end of a tunnel, the British people are becoming aware and concerned enough to speak out and work for waterway preservation. But, I fear, these modern times will never find enough modern money.

So, that's what we were getting into. We were going to be navigating towpaths that probably hadn't seen a horse in a hundred years. The Toms knew; we didn't have a clue.

In fact, Martin made a phone call every evening to some government agency with a report on the condition of the towpaths we had traversed that day.

Our propulsion system was named Gypsy, what I would call a Shire-type. Her color, markings and conformation were Shire, but I reckoned her to be just barely sixteen hands, too small to be a purebred. But who am I to quibble? Her disposition and intelligence were far better qualities than her lineage, or lack of it. Susan and Sandi thought that it was their duty to spoil her. With all the extra grain and apples and brushings

287

three times a day the horse never had it so good.

Anyway, our route was from Wolverhampton through Birmingham, to Warwick. Think of it as oasis to oasis with trackless wilderness in between.

Ann and Martin loved us. We were not just passengers but got into the spirit of the whole experience. Martin walked the towpath with Gypsy, Ann steered the Pamela and the Family Nordman were ready for whatever.

The first day was planned to be Wolverhampton through Birmingham. This was a well-developed area and the only delays that Martin was anticipating were the series of small locks that we had to negotiate.

We came up on the first lock and once we saw how the lock worked, all manual with a hand crank, we said, "Right." Dave and Mike took off down the tow path and had the next lock all set up for Martin and Gypsy, our faithful steed, to pull the Pamela straight in.

Meanwhile Vern and Susan were pacing the Pamela along the tow path. They would close the gate behind us so the lock could fill, we were going up, and open the lock so Gypsy could pull the Pamela out while Dave and Mike were off to the next lock.

What a smooth system. We were through Birmingham by lunch time.

As the days went by, we found that some areas along the canal were foul and decayed, some prosperous, some were tidy farmland and some were incredibly beautiful wilderness. A few town councils have made use of the canal sides with parks, maintaining the tow paths for hikers, bikers and joggers. But most places were sadly neglected. Each day was likely to bring a new and different challenge.

288

One day we found that trees had so overgrown the tow path that Vern and the boys had to range ahead with ax and saw, lopping great limbs and pulling them out of the way so Gypsy could get through.

Once we came to an area that was completely beyond even Gypsy's considerable path foraging ability so Martin had to take Gypsy up a steep bank and around by lane and field to the next bridge and Dave and Mike had to take up the towing. Fortunately, it was just for a few hundred yards.

When the tow paths failed completely, Gypsy happily took to the water. But, on one unforgettable day, we came upon a stretch of canal that hadn't been dredged in a long time so Ann had to steer the boat well away from the bank and we tipped Gypsy in. Fortune smiled, for Gypsy was unscathed, but a bit disgusted with us. Having righted herself and taken a look at the straight high bank, she turned and glared balefully at us before swimming on. It was quite a distance before she could find a place to get out.

There were no tow paths through the several tunnels that we encountered. Without motor power, tunnels were negotiated by whatever power we could provide, poling whenever possible but once by "legging."

We came upon a tunnel that wasn't much bigger than the width and height of the Pamela, much too small to swing a pole. Martin said that if we were willing, we could "leg it." The kids and I didn't have any idea what he was talking about, but Vern did. He said that he had read about it in a Horiatio Hornblower story.

Legging worked this way: Martin fitted wooden planks into slots on both sides of the bow, David lay on one side and Vern on the other with their feet planted on the sides of the tunnel. While Martin walked the horse around to the other end of the tunnel, Vern and David walked along the sides of the tunnel pulling the Pamela through. Long tunnel. The boys were mighty pooped at the end.

I suppose this account sounds like we were exploring the Amazon rather than having a leisurely English holiday, and at times it felt it, but except for the times when the men folk were off dealing with whatever obstacles were thrown in our path by man and nature, we spent the days blissfully watching the English countryside roll by. The top of the Pamela was flat and perfect for sitting or lying on or even putting a deck chair on.

The Martin's two children and Sandi spent all day catching little guppies off the side, putting them into jars, counting them, letting them go and then doing the same thing all over again.

With all our experiences we did finally arrive at Warwick, but of course, our van was back at Wolverhampton. So, while the children and I made ourselves comfortable on the canal side lawn of a friendly pub, Vern took the train back up north to retrieve the car.

Before leaving our holiday, I must add that we were a unique attraction everywhere we went and always drew a crowd. Aside from the attention of hordes of school children on history outings there were the holiday boaters whose voices carried far along the water, yelling, "My God! It's a *horse* drawn boat. Quick, get the camera."

One boat even ran aground in its operators haste to capture us on film.

Lastly and best, wherever we tied up at least

one old Gaffer (bloke for father or grandfather, used affectionately) would appear and almost murmur, "Ah, aye haint seen such like been on fifty year." Or, "Thought not to see a proper boat again." And, "Grandfather had a steam powered Braunston boat. Worked on her as a lad, I did."

Any reply and the offer of a beer or a cigarette brought forth a flood of reminiscences and tales that did more to bring canal life and history to us than all the books we could ever read. We tied up every night by a canal side pub and spent pleasant evenings with good English beer, stories and songs.

Snowbound and Other Experiences
—England—

From Faye's Journal:

I am sitting in my favorite spot in front of our bedroom window. The last of the children are off to school, the sun is well up, but still casting long shadows, spotlighting fields and hedgerows of dewy diamonds. Although the breeze is freshening, the leaves and branches are still gentle in their movements. This morning is quite clear with patches of early mist hugging the horizon and a few wisps of feathery cloud higher up.

Directly in front of me, beyond my hedge of crape myrtle and brambles, are three small fields, then a large field and another big field to my right. The big fields were plowed, harrowed, fertilized and drilled as soon as the grain was cut and the old straw burned. Now, they are lush green carpets, often enjoyed by rabbits. I guess the three smaller fields will lie fallow, at least until spring. Yesterday they were plowed, but not really turned over. In the pale morning light, they resemble salt and pepper corduroy.

I just stopped to watch a bullfinch, sitting in the apple tree, surveying the feeding table. He's the same size as the English Sparrow we all know, but rather gorgeous. He wears a black cap form chin to nape, has a gray back, white rump and from ears and throat to flanks is rosy red—reddish rose would be more accurate. He also has a shorter and heavier bill than the sparrow which gives the bullfinch a rather pugnacious appearance. Although I think the bullfinch a rather handsome creature he is held in low esteem by my neighbors. It seems that bullfinches are overly fond of young fruit buds and a flock of them can wreak havoc in orchards, not to mention your back-garden fruit tree.

Until recently all the cock pheasants had a territory—one bird and his harem per field. Maybe two groups if the field was very large. Now I frequently see two or three cock birds feeding together. I guess that after family raising is over, they don't feel a need to retain and maintain a territory.

Today in East Anglia, the weather is trying to decide what to do. Generally, it is blustery WNW, but occasionally backs a point or two and the sea fog gathers. However, the seagulls are coming in, so Indian Summer is over.

The farmer is working before the weather, and

the sound of his tractor is constant. The big question is: with what will MY fields be sown for next season? Last year, all was winter wheat and barley. This year was a mix, mostly sugar beets and carrots, with a few fields of rape. Some of the rape was cut for stock feed (pigs, I think) but most was long ago turned under. He finished pulling carrots this week, the reason no doubt, for going flat out with all of his machinery. The sugar beet seems a convenient crop, being left in the ground over the winter with no apparent damage to the crop or quality, sometimes until early spring, until the farmer gets around to it, or more likely, the local sugar factory says they'll take it in.

I think I will have to find somewhere other than my bedroom window for writing and painting. I keep stopping to watch a shy little Dunnock hurry along the hedgerow, or take time to observe that darling of gymnasts, the Blue Tit, energetically and acrobatically work his way around a stem of lupine seeds.

Nevermore, in our household, shall Friday the thirteenth be considered a day of ill omen. Indeed, we may campaign to have it recognized as a National Holiday. For it was today, Friday the thirteenth that Vern learned that he had been selected for promotion to Lieutenant Colonel! I might add that I learned this by phone. I haven't seen him in three days as Lakenheath is in the middle of a major exercise called a NATO Tactical Evaluation and he has been sleeping in the shop, when he can sleep. Anyway, as the British blasphemously say "Bloody Marvelous!"

Down to earth and closer to hand I am busy doing sets and costumes for events here. Halloween is nearly upon us, Sandi has a squirrel costume, and Susan and I are working on a Wonder Woman outfit.

Mike wants to be a mummy which will only require the sacrifice of an old sheet.

At the same time, the Children's Theater Workshop is going to do Robin Hood for their Christmas production, and that is only eight weeks away. I can't say enough about the Workshop. What a marvelous activity for the children. The two ladies who run it are very professional and the kids work hard—and they love it. The Workshop recently won the Royal Air Force Theatrical Association's Premier Prize. Well deserved.

Ever since we have been here at West Raynham, I have done the stage sets for each performance. A lot of work, but fun, and I do get a lot of help. For Robin Hood, all the frame work has been constructed, the drops are being sewn together and Wednesday I hope to start sketching. I really would like to have them ready to start painting next week.

Susan's "Maid Marion" costume is cut out, as is Sandi's "Judge of the Archery Contest." Michael's costume is still in the planning stage. As the "Tax Collector" he needs something a bit more elaborate.

And, lest I have idle hands, I have been knitting like anything to keep up with an epidemic outbreak of pregnancies. Only two more baby sweaters to knit—I think I'll make it.

We have been snowbound since Valentine's Day. Vern just managed to get home Friday evening, but others had to abandon their cars and hike home. Actually, by New England standards, our snowstorm was a middling little affair but this country is just not equipped to handle a lot of snow. Most county councils have sanding trucks and a—one—1—"plow." The plow is usually a four-wheel drive vehicle, such as

296

a Land Rover, with a jury-rigged blade. Our five to six feet drifts might as well be mountains.

RAF West Raynham has a small snow blower and yesterday, having finished the working side of the base, they plowed the streets around the married quarters and opened the mile and a half road to our nearest little village of East Rudham and reported that the main roads should be passable with extreme care.

A baker got a load of bread through to the village and a local dairyman loaded a sledge with milk churns and the bread, hitched it up to his tractor and brought it over the fields to the Post Office/Store.

Quite an event. Bring your own milk containers.

Although we had no fresh milk or bread, and eggs and butter were in short supply, no one went hungry. The Post Office/Store had adequate canned goods and we all forbore using any canned milk to save it for families with small infants. I just rationed my emergency box of powdered milk and saved potato water to bake bread.

Ladies Guest Night
—England—

*E*ver since I had been stationed at RAF Lakenheath, we (me and the family) had lived thirty miles north of the base at RAF West Raynham. This gave me a fairly long commute over mostly back country roads every day but it wasn't a problem either for me or the people I worked for until I made the mistake of getting promoted and becoming the Chief of the Intelligence Division.

Now, suddenly, where I lived was a problem. The Powers-That- Be were not happy about me living so far from the base so we had to move down to Lakenheath so I would be closer to the shop.

The whole family, especially Faye, hated to leave West Raynham. We knew that we would miss all our friends, of course, but we would also miss the solitude, looking out over the farmer's fields and seeing the birds and small animals that seemed to be everywhere, especially in our back garden.

West Raynham was peaceful and quiet; Lakenheath was crowded and noisy. Like all quarters the one at Lakenheath had its good points and its bad. The kitchen was much more modern and was nicer to work in but desperately short of cupboard and storage space. The living areas were open and more spacious but the bedrooms were smaller, etc. etc.

However, one kitchen wall was papered; the design being recipes for such English delights as Jugged Hare, Yorkshire Pudding, Lancashire Hot Pot and Bubble and Squeak. We tried them all and they were delicious.

The one big deficiency in our new house was that we couldn't find a suitable place for Faye's studio. We ended up setting her up in a corner of our bedroom but it wasn't anywhere near as nice as her "Perch" up at West Raynham.

Soon after we moved in, we had an open house to meet all the neighbors. Of course, we invited the gang from West Raynham. They not only came in force but they came in a Royal Air Force bus complete with driver so we could really party and they wouldn't have to worry about driving home.

Party we did. The Lakenheath neighbors were wowed.

A few weeks later the West Raynham gang reciprocated and we were invited back up to West Raynham the Officer's Mess for a Ladies Guest Night where we were "Dinned Out" in style.

For months the Mess kitchens had been undergoing a complete renovation and for this event, the first effort with their new facilities, the staff outdid themselves. The menu was ambitious by anyone's standard, but each course was of supreme excellence.

For starters we had a pate Ardennes. This was followed by a fish course of Scampi Thermidor and then the main course of Tornedos Champignon. Yummy.

The sweet was a blackberry and apple syllabub. That's not to mention the cheese board, the wines, coffee and liqueurs.

Dinner music was provided by the Salon Orchestra of the Royal Air Force Central Band. They were so good that at times, instead of chatting to our dinner partners, everyone just listened and applauded.

There was a printed program for their musical selections, but during the first set they discovered that the Yanks, Faye and I, were being dinned out. We were treated to renditions and medleys ranging from the Battle Hymn of the Republic, through Stephen Foster to a rousing rendition of the Orange Blossom Special. Superb.

There were only two after dinner speeches, the Station Commander and me. The Commander had lots of nice things to say especially about Faye's work with the Children's Theater Workshop and he even praised the children for their contributions to station life.

Faye was presented with a large and lovely bouquet of flowers and we were presented with a station plaque. The inscription on the plaque was to Major and MRS. Adding the Mrs. was a most singular honor for the Royal Air Force and that pleased Faye no end.

Finally, we repaired to the anteroom to dance to a live combo until the wee hours of the morning. Fortunately, we had a room booked at the Mess and we only had to toddle down the hall when the evening's festivities were done.

Fun and Games in the Desert
—Egypt—

From England we went back to South Carolina to the same base we had been stationed at over twenty years before when our number two kid, David was born.

Unfortunately, Central South Carolina hadn't changed in our absence. It was still hot and buggy in the summer and the weather was lousy in the winter.

My new job was in Ninth Air Force Headquarters. I must admit I never much liked headquarters jobs. Headquarters are full of headquarters people, desk jockeys and paper pushers. I would much rather be out in an operational unit.

But there I was, the assistant to the Deputy

Chief of Staff—Intelligence (DCS-I) for Ninth Air Force.

It sounds impressive, doesn't it?

Well it was a better title than gofer.

I had three main jobs. The first was office manager—that was easy. We only had about a dozen people assigned to provide current intelligence briefings to the 9AF Commander and the staff.

My second job was considerably more interesting.

Ninth Air Force had about ten operational bases scattered around the southeastern United States, Virginia, North Carolina, South Carolina, Georgia, Florida, one out in Louisiana and every one of them had an Intelligence Division. My job was to keep the Intel Divisions up to speed on current Air Force and Ninth Air Force thinking (such as it was and what there was of it) and to help them stay out of trouble.

I was their sounding board, enabler and mother hen. And, to aid in accomplishing this, my boss wanted me to go out and spend a few days with each unit each year. Don't get me wrong, I did enjoy it and I think I did some good. I met some great people and I was wined and dined in style.

The downside was that this put me on the road away from the family for a week every month. I became very familiar with Hartsfield International Airport in Atlanta, Georgia. One does not travel anywhere in the south without going through Hartsfield. If you want to go next door and visit your neighbor you have to go through Atlanta.

And that brings me to my third job—whatever.

Whatever the boss wanted me to do.

If there was a meeting that the boss didn't feel

like attending, I went. If there was a conference at another base, I usually went. If there was a briefing that the DCS-I was required to give, I usually gave it.

The command structure that now includes the Middle East was just getting off the ground at this time and I was sent to all the organizational meetings. It is now called Central Command but, in the beginning, it was the Rapid Deployment Joint Task force (RDJTF). Believe me, with all the brass in the room at these early organizational meetings my chair was WAY in the back. Lieutenant Colonel that I was I didn't get to sit at the Big Boys table.

And that brings us to Egypt.

One of the RDJTFs first adventures into the Middle East was a joint Army/Air Force exercise with the Egyptian armed forces. Prior to this time Egypt had been more or less a client state of the Soviet Union. Over the years Soviet military forces were present on some Egyptian bases and the Egyptian Army and Air Force had mostly Soviet equipment. But, sometime in the seventies, it seems that the Egyptians and the Soviets had a falling out and the Soviets picked up their marbles and went home. So, I guess we were going to fill the void.

Ninth Air Force was tapped as the Air Force component of the RDJTF and tasked to provide the aircraft and support elements for the Air Force part of this joint exercise.

On the surface this exercise looked like a big bucket of worms and as we dug deeper into the nuts and bolts of the proposed exercise it REALLY looked like a big bucket of worms.

We would be flying out of an Egyptian base called Cairo West which, we were told, was fifty miles out in the desert somewhere west of Cairo.

Sounds lovely.

We were also told that this would be a bare base operation. There were no aircraft maintenance facilities, hangers or personnel living quarters available at Cairo West. They were right too, even the Egyptians who were stationed there didn't have facilities or quarters. Anything that we required to conduct this exercise we would have to bring with us.

I guess the 9AF Commander asked all the active duty subordinate flying units for volunteers. Let's see—you could plan on living in tents out in the desert with the heat, wind and sand, watching your equipment being sand blasted every day and flying with a foreign air force that no one knew anything about.

Nope, no volunteers.

Just when it was getting to the point where the 9AF Commander was going to have to point to someone and tell them to go, the Air National Guard outfit in Albuquerque, New Mexico said that they would do it. I don't know what their motivation was but they sure made a lot of people happy. Of course, 9AF was still on the hook to provide all the support facilities.

In the DCS-I we kind of watched all of this with detached interest. The Air National Guard squadron had their own intelligence shop so nothing would be required of us.

Wishful thinking.

The 9AF Commander then decided that he wanted a representative from each of the headquarters directorates on hand at Cairo West to monitor the exercise. That seemed like a waste of time to me, we could read all the after-action reports.

But who am I?

My boss told me to pick someone from our office, but before I could point to one of our junior officers and say go, another missile came down from above. The 9AF Commander felt that this was an important, high visibility exercise so there was going to be a 9AF Headquarters element present and he expected the directorates to support this by sending more senior officers.

My boss looked at me and smiled.

The more I became involved in the planning for this international turkey, (it had a name by-the-way, Bright Star), the worse it looked. At Cairo West there were no barracks or any other buildings that we could use to billet our troops. At the first meeting with our Army counterparts we asked how many of the big General-Purpose Medium tents they were going to use for their people and if they had extra ones that could they loan to us.

Ah, the Army, ya gotta love 'em.

We, the Air Force, were informed in no uncertain terms that this was training and their soldiers were going to live in their individual shelters out in the desert.

It took a lot of argument to convince them that living in the sand out in the desert wasn't really required for pilots, aircraft maintenance personnel and the like and to get them to agree to bring a couple dozen of the GP Mediums for Air Force use.

They thought we were real wimps.

They would have had a heart attack if they had found out that we were not only going to house our people in the big tents but we were also going to ship all the plywood, two-by-fours and hammers and nails we could get away with so we could build floors for the tents when we got there. We were also bringing all the

307

cots we could lay our hands on.

The Army was going to sleep on the sand. We wanted to get as far from the sand as possible. There are creepy, crawly, bitey things in the sand.

The Egyptians said that they were going to make identification badges for all participants and they insisted that we send them complete rosters listing the names of everyone who would be participating in the exercise.

Impossible! We didn't even know who was going to be participating in the exercise.

There were probably three or four dozen different Air Force organizations who were contributing people to this exercise and if a supply clerk named Smith from base X was nominated today who knew if he was going to be available on the day and another supply clerk named Jones from base Y would be going in his place.

In addition, there didn't seem to be a central organization in Egypt who was coordinating the exercise, so some rosters went to one office and some to another.

Like I said, a real bucket of worms.

The Plans Directorate in 9AF Headquarters was our point of contact with the Egyptians and every time I sent over the DCS-I input it just had one name on it and it never changed—me.

Faye and I had to dig through our storage boxes to find my field gear that I hadn't worn in two years.

The day finally arrived. A C-141 cargo plane showed up and a handful of old majors and lieutenant colonels who were senior enough to be picked to go, and too junior (or too dumb) to get out of it, got on board. The aircraft was already loaded when we boarded. There were pallets and a couple of vehicles tied down in the center of the aircraft and the passengers were sitting in the fabric jump seats along the sides.

Wonderful.

After a long flight that seemed to last forever, we arrived at Cairo West, landed and found—chaos.

We were not the first to arrive, there were three or four C-141's ahead of us, and it looked like the passengers from all those airplanes were milling around in front of what I guessed was the terminal building. There seemed to be a lot of shouting and the waving of arms between the US personnel and the Egyptians.

Both sides seemed to be following the cardinal rule that comes into play when you have a language problem—speak loud and wave arms.

I stayed in the back of this milling mass and I was told that the problem was with the identification badges that the Egyptians had made for everyone. The Egyptians didn't want anyone to leave the flight line without their badge.

OKAY! What's the problem?

The problem was that the badges were not in any kind of retrievable order. They were loosely thrown into cardboard boxes. Sergeant Jones was here and his badge was probably here too, somewhere in one of those boxes. How to get the two of them together was the problem.

The yelling and arm waving continued. C-141's kept landing. The crowd kept growing. I guess the Egyptian's arms got tired before our guys arms did because they suddenly stopped waving them and they left. They just walked out of the building, got into a vehicle and drove off.

The cardboard boxes that held the badges must

have been very valuable because they took them too.

They left the badges; they just dumped them on a table.

So now instead of boxes of badges we had a pyramid of badges.

It was Egypt, after all.

One of our arm wavers told us not to worry about the badges they would get them sorted out overnight and we could come back tomorrow and pick them up. Good thinking. The herd of us picked up our gear and headed off to find our tents.

The engineers were on the ball. They had arrived a few days earlier and our big GP Mediums were all set up but without the wooden floors. There were even unit signs on each tent and there were cots inside. I found the HQ9AF tent just before it got too dark to see.

It was a pretty boring couple of weeks as far as my official Air Force duties were concerned but I managed to keep busy in other ways. I helped the engineers build the floor for our tent—and several others. Then with the leftover plywood we built walkways between the tents and the latrine on one side and the dining hall on the other.

We were improving our living area every day.

The Army hated us.

We were out in the desert but not really that far from Cairo so the Egyptians offered us cultural tours to see the pyramids, the sphinx and such things. That was nice.

But (there is always a but) the Egyptians were obsessed with this roster thing.

If they provided a forty-man bus to go to the pyramids they wanted a roster a couple of days ahead of time with a list of the forty men who were going to be on the bus.

Why?

I have no idea.

Not only that but once the roster was turned in there could be no substitutions and all forty must go. If Jones changed his mind and didn't want to go see the pyramids, no one was going.

I never could figure out the rational, if any, behind that one.

When I flew away from Cairo West, I chalked it all up as an experience, one that I sincerely hoped that I would never repeat.

Egypt II

*A*s you can tell by the title, my wish to never return to the desert was not granted. A year later Bright Star number two went off right on schedule and I found myself right back at my little field desk in the headquarters tent at Cairo West looking around for something to do.

To be fair, with time and experience behind us the second exercise progressed more smoothly than the first. There was more active duty participation from 9AF units, indeed, active duty squadrons were eager to participate. The Egyptians were much more relaxed and their obsession for personnel lists, badges and rosters seemed to have gone away.

We were given much more freedom to move around the country and there was increased contact between the Egyptian and US forces. For example, toward the end of the deployment I was invited, along with the entire headquarters staff, to dinner at the Egyptian Army Officers Club in Giza. This was quite an evening. The club was huge, it even had an indoor rifle range, and it was decked out in true Arabian Nights style. When I stepped out onto one of the balconies on the second floor there was the Great Pyramid seemingly close enough to touch. The dinner was magnificent and for a bunch of Muslims the wine flowed freely.

There was a marked increase in the number of recreational tours that were offered into Cairo and tour destinations were expanded beyond the pyramids and the sphinx. There were even private cars for hire for trips into town, with driver, of course. If you ever have a death wish try driving in Cairo.

My personal favorite of things to see around Cairo was the Sound and Light Show at Gisa which was a narrative of the history of Egypt with the sphinx and the pyramids as the background. The show must be very popular because it made an appearance in one of the James Bond movies.

I went to one of the huge bazaars and purchased silver cartouches for all the girls with their names in hieroglyphics inside. Something different.

One morning we all loaded up into Egyptian army trucks and were driven many miles out into the desert to a bombing range for a joint firepower demonstration. The viewing area looked like it was pretty close, about a half a mile, to the actual target area.

For the High and Mighty a huge tent had been erected that was open on the side facing the range so the H&M didn't have to sit in the sun. The sand inside the tent had been covered with carpets, very nice carpets, so the H&M wouldn't get sand in their toes and there were some very comfy looking chairs set out on the carpets.

The rest of us peons just kind of milled around trying to find a good vantage point.

It was a good show. Aircraft from both countries dropped bombs and fired bullets and they hit the poor helpless desert every time. Among the participants were three B-52's that flew all the way from North Dakota, dropped their bombs and then flew all the way home again, nonstop. Pretty impressive.

I don't know if it ever made it on the air but a crew from 60 Minutes was also present.

But, my most memorable experience from Bright Star II happened quite by accident.

One morning when I wandered into the Headquarters tent there was a gaggle of Air Force and Army Civil Engineers milling about. I found a guy I knew, asked what was going on and was informed that they were getting ready to go out and do a site survey on a couple of bases for possible future US use.

Cool. I asked if they had room for one more. No problem.

I had no idea where they were going or even what a "site survey" consisted of. What do I care? It was a day away from my empty desk.

We walked out onto the flight line and climbed into C-130, Hercules, transport plane and off we went. We flew east, over the Nile south of Cairo and out across the desert heading toward the Red Sea. When we reached the coast, and I presumed our destination, we just started circling. I looked up into the flight deck and I could see that the chief of the engineers, our Egyptian Interpreter and our aircraft commander were in urgent radio conversation with somebody.

The mighty Hercules kept going around and round.

It seems that there was a slight glitch in our travel arrangements, no one had informed the people on the ground that we were coming, they didn't know who we were and they were seriously considering shooting us down.

Personally, I thought that that was a little drastic.

Eventually the folks on the ground were persuaded that we were not a hostile threat and we were allowed to land. We were directed to a parking area in front of the terminal building and when we dropped the ramp and looked out, we found that our airplane was surrounded by the entire Egyptian Army, all of them armed to the teeth and all of those weapons were pointed right at us.

A rather tense round of explanations followed, good thing we had an interpreter with us, and once the Egyptians were convinced that we weren't an invading army and that we were actually there on legitimate business the Third Camel Corps dispersed and the base personnel became quite cordial.

The engineers broke up into small groups, found their counterparts, such as they were, but before they could head off in different directions to survey whatever they were cautioned to stay on the paths.

Do NOT go off of the paths.

What the...?

When we looked around, we could see that every area that was not paved had pathways that were marked out with little rope lines. The Egyptians explained that the previous occupants (presumably the Soviets) had laid mine fields all around the base and when they departed, they had taken the maps of where these mine fields were with them. In addition, it doesn't rain often in this area but when it does the rain can be quite heavy and flash flooding is common. Sometimes the flash floods washed the mines out of their previously unknown locations and into new unknown locations. To keep everyone intact Egyptian sappers had cleared and marked the paths.

Stay on the paths.

We stayed on the paths.

The engineers poked around for a couple of hours, taking pictures, muttering to themselves and writing in their little notebooks. Then they thanked our Egyptian hosts, especially for not shooting us, and we boarded our Herk and flew away.

"Where to next?" I asked.

"Somalia."

Somalia?

Yes, there was an airfield on the north coast that we were interested in.

We flew south right down the middle of the Red Sea with Egypt on our right and the Arabian Peninsula on our left, out across the Gulf of Aden and we landed, without the previous excitement experienced at our Egyptian base, in Berbera, Somalia.

The reason for our uneventful landing was that Berbera was a working civilian airfield. Not necessarily a busy one, however. While we were there, I didn't see any takeoffs or landings but I could see a couple of C-47's parked on the tarmac and what looked like a 1930's vintage tri-motor.

That was the civilian side. The other side of the field looked like it was deserted and I was told that that was the military side. We parked on the military side and we were met by a couple of people in uniform. I guess they were Somalian Army although in a country with a hundred militias it is hard to tell. These guys had a truck and a couple of our engineers went with them off towards the town. The rest split up into their little groups and started poking around.

I kind of wandered off by myself and at first, I thought that I had stumbled onto the set of an old B movie science fiction production. You know the scene where the heroes, survivors, whatever come upon the deserted, abandoned town or military installation. The buildings were intact but empty except for sand that had blown in on the floor and crude wooden furniture some of which was turned over. The doors were off their hinges and the windows were open (or broken) with the curtains blowing in the wind.

Spooky, but not a mutant or a zombie in sight.

On past the little buildings there was a row of aircraft parking revetments. These were just horseshoe shaped earth berms that planes would be parked in. There were no airplanes present but there were munitions, bombs and bullets. Lots of bombs and bullets. The first revetment that I looked into had piles and piles of ammunition. These were big bullets each one was about a foot long and three inches in diameter and there were hundreds of them just lying around out in the open. I am not a munitions expert but I thought that they were 23mm.

The Soviets are very fond of 23mm.

I wandered on.

The next revetment did not have big bullets. Nope, just bombs. Lots of bombs, big bombs and bigger bombs. There were piles of the smaller size and some of those piles had fallen over. The larger ones were mostly individually packed in wooden crates but some of those stacks had fallen over too and some of the crates had broken open leaving a scattering of big bombs lying around.

You could, and in later years they probably did, make a million roadside bombs out of this stuff.

That was as far as I went and I headed back toward the central area. Seeing as I was an unofficial passenger and only one or two of the guys even knew who I was or that I was even along, I didn't want to be left behind.

As I started back, I happened to look up behind the aircraft revetments and I saw a radar antenna with a small van next to it. On closer examination I figured it was part of a surface to air missile radar. Old stuff but interesting.

I reported what I had found to the engineers but they didn't seem very interested. It might have gotten written down in one of the note books.

We took off and had an uneventful flight back up the Red sea to our base at Cairo West.

Now, that was an experience.

Reprieve
—South Carolina—

*M*uch to my surprise I was really enjoying my headquarters assignment. I had a good boss that I liked and respected and he kept me busy with meaningful jobs. When I went to Ninth Air Force, I was afraid that I would be chained to a desk pushing paper around but the job turned out to be anything but that. I worked for the Deputy Chief of Staff—Intelligence. I was his personal fire brigade. If there was a problem anywhere within the Ninth Air Force intelligence community old Uncle Vern was sent to take care of it. I loved it.

But (there is still always a but) like all good things it couldn't last. My boss was going to retire and I would be getting a new boss who had already been nominated. Unfortunately, I knew this guy and I didn't like him and he didn't like me. Now I get along with just about everyone but from the first time we met a couple of years ago we just rubbed each other the wrong way.

At the moment we were in separate organizations so our mutual disregard for each other didn't rise to the surface but now he was going to be my boss. The future didn't look very rosy.

Then, out of the blue, the phone rang.

The caller was a Colonel who was the assistant to the Deputy Chief of Staff—Intelligence at Headquarters Tactical Air Command. Ninth Air Force was a subordinate command of TAC so she was my counterpart at the next highest headquarters. I didn't hear from her too often and usually it was to coordinate something before we brought it to our bosses' attention. She was one very sharp lady and it was to my advantage to follow her advice on whatever project we were working on.

But that's not what the phone call was about this time.

She cut right to the chase, "What do you know about the Army's High Technology Test Bed?"

"Never heard of it."

She went on to explain that the Army Chief of Staff was frustrated with the slow pace of the existing Research and Development organizations and he was putting together a little think tank to explore alternative operating strategies and to see if other services or countries or even the civilian community had off the shelf equipment that could benefit the Army.

To this end he had created the HTTB and he had invited the other services, and other countries, to send experts to join in their endeavors.

The Air Force had agreed to support the HTTB

with a liaison team of five officers and one of the specialties that they wanted was someone who knew the nuts and bolts of Air Force Tactical Reconnaissance.

She said that the job would probably be a three-year assignment and it was strictly voluntary.

"Wow!" I said, "That's a lot to take in at one time. Where is this HTTB going to be located?"

"Fort Lewis, Washington."

Fort Lewis, Washington, I almost fell out of my chair. How many times over the years had I tried to get stationed in Washington? Fort Lewis is on the southern shore of Puget Sound about fifty miles south of Seattle. And, here this assignment just fell into my lap.

I didn't even take this one home to the sailor for discussion. I said "YES!" on the spot.

It got better. The Powers-That-Be wanted me out at Fort Lewis ASAP. I was gone from Ninth Air Force before my boss retired and before my nemesis took over the shop.

Am I lucky or what?

I had to go to Washington by way of Virginia for briefings at Headquarters Tactical Air Command with both the Intelligence and Operations Directorates.

My first meeting was with the Lady Colonel who ushered me in to meet the Deputy Chief of Staff—Intelligence for Tactical Air Command. I was pleasantly surprised to see a newly minted Brigadier General sitting in the chair who had been a classmate of mine many years ago in Officers Candidate School.

It is good to have friends in high places.

They admitted that they didn't know much more about the HTTB than I did and that it was the Operations Directorate who were in charge of the liaison team. They reassured me that if I needed anything, support, assistance or information just call. I did—many times.

Then I was off to the Deputy Chief of Staff for Operations for a meet and greet and here I got a much colder reception. Not to me personally, fortunately, but, I think, to idea that the five warm bodies were going to come out of TAC's hide.

I had a private meeting with a Major General and he had only one instruction for me—do not commit the Air Force to anything. Not that there was much chance of that. TAC was sending a full Colonel to Fort Lewis to be the team chief and, I guess, to make sure that us young whippersnappers didn't do anything dumb. (As it turned out I was older than he was.)

I also found out that TAC had several liaison teams assigned to various places around the world and for administrative purposes we were lumped together in an umbrella organization called the 4525 Combat Applications Squadron. (I have a plaque).

With happy hearts the family and I were off to the Great Pacific Northwest.

Life with the Army
—Washington—

ort Lewis was a very large base that was divided by Interstate 5. The main base, that had about 90% of the facilities, was on the south side of I-5. The north side, called North Fort, consisted of older buildings, warehouses, storage areas and the like and that's where the High Technology Test Bed (HTTB) had set up their operations.

Our Air Force Liaison Team was given office space in an old, wooden barracks building that had probably been there when Lewis and Clark paddled down the Columbia River and discovered the Space Needle.

There were also liaison officers from the Marines and the British and French Armies.

We began to 'Liase.' But, exactly how does one 'Liase?'

We were surrounded by a gang of Army eager beavers who had more nutty ideas than a tree full of squirrels. It seemed to me that we spent our time telling them what the Air Force had and why the Army couldn't have it. I began to understand what the General back at Headquarters Tactical Air Command was talking about.

Our office area soon became a hang out. We kept the coffee pot going all the time, there were tables and chairs scattered around, our wives would send in cookies and it seemed that there were usually donuts every morning. The Army guys would wander in and we would just sit around and talk. Some of our best, and worst, ideas came out of these bull sessions.

I was never sure if our efforts in behalf of the HTTB were productive or not, but they were certainly interesting. We were asked a lot of questions and we quickly found out that we didn't know a lot of answers.

One day we were asked if our Air Force Airborne Warning and Control System (AWACS) could see things moving on the ground. The AWACS are big airplanes that were originally modified Boeing 707s. They had a big radar dish attached on top that could see everything that's flying, but whether the AWACS could see things moving on the ground, I had no idea. Not my area. But no one else knew either.

We told the Army guys that we didn't think it could see things on the ground, but we would find out. We did a lot of that.

In this case, the manufacturer, Boeing, was just up the road in Seattle. We phoned, made an appointment and headed on up. Boeing was very gracious. They gave us a briefing on the AWACS system, a tour of one of the AWACS airplanes that was in for rehab and lunch.

After lunch we got down to the question of whether AWACS could see things on the ground. The answer was theoretically, yes, but they didn't think it would work very well and if the radar system was reconfigured to spot and track targets on the ground it wouldn't be able to track aircraft in the air.

These guys were way over my head but I gathered that it was up or down, take your pick and the Air Force had spent BIG bucks for up.

When this was reported back to the HTTB they asked if the Air Force would be willing to spare an aircraft for Boeing to play with.

In my opinion there was zero chance of that happening, but I kept my mouth shut.

Our Colonel was very tactful and said that he doubted that the Air Force could spare an airplane (there were only about thirty of them and they were committed all over the world) but he would go check. He went down to Oklahoma, where the AWACS live, and the answer, as expected, was not only no, but Hell No.

The fact that there wasn't anything immediately available to do the job didn't mean that it was a bad idea. Smelling a contract, Boeing thought that it was a good idea. I don't know if the official Research and Development program originated at the HTTB, Boeing or somewhere else, but time warp to the future and the idea of an airborne platform that could track ground targets found its way into the system and in later years one was developed and fielded that did just that.

Meanwhile, I fell into the clutches of a couple of really smart Army Intelligence Officers (this time that was NOT an oxymoron). Their primary goal was to figure out ways to get information on what was going on in his immediate area of responsibility to a front-line commander in a timely manner. In our many brainstorming sessions the smart majors told me what the Army had for battle field reconnaissance and I told them what the Air Force had.

These guys were computer nerds before there were computer nerds. We (that's using "we" loosely) put all our information on existing reconnaissance assets together in a spread-sheet that showed exactly what part of a potential battlefield each reconnaissance asset covered and how long it took for the information to get to the commander who needed it.

We covered everything from the eyeballs of the ground commanders foot patrols to high-altitude fast-moving reconnaissance jets. This was thirty- five, forty years ago and satellites were not yet crowding the space lanes.

The results were not encouraging. There was a lot of information floating around on what was going on just beyond the FEBA (Forward Edge of the Battle Area) but the machinery wasn't available to get that information to the guys who would be in the fight in a timely manner.

We put all that we had learned into a briefing and presented it to the HTTB staff. They thought that it was just the type of problem that the HTTB was set up to solve so with a little polishing (OKAY, a lot of polishing), HTTB sent us and our briefing up the Chain of Command to our next higher Headquarters, I Corps. I Corps put its stamp of approval on it and sent us on to the Pentagon.

We spent a week in the Pentagon and presented the briefing to anyone who wanted to listen right up to the Army Chief of Staff. Seeing as the HTTB was the Chief of Staff's baby, he was very pleased. His marching orders were simple—get on with it and solve the problem.

Okay. Now what? The Army Intelligence guys knew what they wanted—a surveillance platform that would be under the control of the front-line commander with sensors that could data-link right into his command post to give him real time information.

When you put that into a sentence it sure sounded simple and straight forward, but when it came to putting those few words into practice, we found that we had a few small problems. Looking at our list of wants—sensor platform, sensors, data-link and ground station—we not only didn't have any of those things, but we didn't know if anyone did or if they even existed.

We started making phone calls without much success until one of the guys remembered that he knew someone who worked at the Jet Propulsion Laboratory (JPL). The phone call to JPL led to an invitation and we soon found ourselves in Pasadena, California talking to some REALLY smart people and in the space of an hour we had crossed three of our wants off our list.

JPL said that they had been working on airborne sensors, both optical and infra-red, that could data-link to a computer on the ground.

Could they build a mobile ground station that could receive the signal and move around with the Army?

Sure.

What they put together was very sophisticated; a five by five by five metal container with antennas sticking out of it that had a table, chair and computer inside. For power it had its own little generator.

For mobility they stuck the metal box on the back of a pick-up truck.

We now had everything we needed except something that flew that we could put JPL's sensors on. We asked both the Air Force and the Army for anything airborne that we could play with and when they turned us down, we went out and bought our own airplanes.

A company called Rutan Aviation in Mojave, California manufactured and sold kit-built airplanes, buy the kit and build your own little airplane.

We bought two of them. I forget what type they were, but several years ago I saw one on the cover of a National Geographic Magazine. The story was about a guy who lived in Maine and flew down to Boston every day to go to work.

The kits were shipped up to Fort Lewis and the Army Aviation folks at Gray Field on Fort Lewis got interested in the project, put them together for us and agreed to fly them. The HTTB got us into an Army exercise at Fort Bliss, Texas. JPL showed up with their sensors and the pick-up truck, installed the sensors in our little airplane, parked the truck as near to the command post as they would let us and we were in business.

Despite its limitations, (i.e. we didn't have a real drone, the data-link was strictly line of sight and the ground station wasn't really in the command post), it proved the concept. The Army was impressed and the drone era was underway.

Just three years later a joint Army, Navy, Marine Corps project produced their first drone, the RQ2, rightly named "Pioneer."

We called our project "Mercury Green." I don't remember why.

On the operations side, the HTTB was thinking about light, fast Army units that could get around the enemy's front-line forces and raise hell in the rear echelon areas. 'Strike Deep' they called it.

Out of their many ideas there was one that I remember very vividly. The Fast Attack Vehicle (FAV).

OKAY! It was a dune buggy, but it was painted olive green and they were fast.

The idea was that a couple of guys in an FAV armed with shoulder fired anti-tank missiles could get into the rear of the enemy's heavy armored formations, kill a couple of tanks and run like hell. (There is a FAV in the Army Museum at Fort Lewis.)

I didn't have anything to do with this particular project and the only reason that I remember it so well was that one day one of the young soldiers asked me if I wanted to take a ride with him in his FAV.

I guess I will never learn. I was certainly old enough to know better, but I said, "Sure."

Off we went. As long as we were on the paved roads of Fort Lewis that were patrolled by the Military Police my Private kept to the speed limit, but once we got off road and started driving through the woods in the maneuver area it was pedal to the metal.

We took off at Warp 8 down a woodland path that a goat would have a hard time following, zooming through the trees, bouncing over every bump, tree root and rock in the Pacific Northwest. Even strapped in as tight as I was, I was bouncing around like a rubber ball.

Seeing the trees whiz by me was like the Star Wars movie where they rode the gravity defying flying scooters at a zillion miles an hour through the Forest of Endor.

My suicidal Private was having the time of his

331

live. The Army had given him this wonderful toy to play with and he was enjoying every minute of it.

I didn't do that again...ever.

That was life at the High Technology Test Bed. You never knew what experience the next day would bring.

Live Oak
—Shape, Belgium—

J was going to retire.
I really was.

I had over thirty years of service, we were finally stationed right where we wanted to be in the Great Pacific Northwest, we bought a house and I was already shopping around for a job. Then, those sneaky devils at Air Force Personnel called and made me an offer that I couldn't refuse.

The phone conversation went something like this:

"Have you considered your next assignment?" they asked.

"What next assignment? I've got over thirty years in."

"Well," they said, "there are always assignments open on international staffs for senior officers."

I wasn't all that senior, and translated from bureau-speak what the flesh peddlers meant was that the Air Force was committed to filling positions that are outside the normal Air Force career progression channels and they would rather fill them with old guys who are not going to be promoted rather than with young up and comers.

Okay! I'm easy.

"What's the deal?" I said.

Actually, there were several assignments available, but the one that made my eyes pop was the position of Senior Intelligence Officer on a multi-national planning staff at Supreme Headquarters Allied Powers Europe (SHAPE) which is located just south of Brussels, Belgium, for four years.

Wow! Talk about a plum assignment.

It took Faye about a milli-second to agree that four years in Belgium was a fine idea, so all retirement plans were scrapped, we rented out the house and we were off. Faye said that we were like a couple of old circus ponies—we hear the music and we start prancing.

I started calling around to try to find out something about the job. All that Air Force Personnel could tell me was the location, that the name of this particular planning group was "Live Oak"—whatever that meant—and that I would be the Senior Intelligence Officer. So, I started asking my buddies, who were scattered in various places around the world, what this Live Oak business was. Nobody knew 'nuttin.' Most had never heard of Live Oak and the ones that had said that it was highly classified. Whatever it was that these guys did it was the best kept secret since "Who shot JR."

I never did find out anything until I actually got

to SHAPE and signed into Live Oak and, yup, it was highly classified—like BBRTST (Burn Before Reading Then Self-Terminate). This job was so secret that I was not permitted to know what I was doing. A state of affairs that I fitted right into.

It was different. Live Oak was supported by, but separate from SHAPE with its own building that was located right next to the SHAPE headquarters building. Live Oak even had its own communications and operations centers.

Live Oak was staffed by representative from four countries: The United States, The United Kingdom, France and West Germany.

There were only about ninety people of all ranks assigned and included in that number were: three generals—One British Army Major General, an American Army Brigadier General (his wife and Faye had been classmates in high school) and a French Air Force Brigadier General, nine full colonels—four American, two French, two English and one German, and twelve lieutenant colonels. You might say we were a little rank heavy.

The three generals were all heads of their respective national delegations and the British Major General was also Chief of Staff.

Seven of the colonels were planners, one was chief of the operations center (my boss) and the German colonel was head of the German delegation.

Nine of the lieutenant colonels were planners of one kind or another. For the other three, a British Royal Signals Lieutenant Colonel was chief of the communication center—which accounted for over a quarter of all the enlisted personnel assigned, an American Air Force Lieutenant Colonel had the administration section and I was the Senior

Intelligence Officer, in charge of the whole, complete, entire Intelligence Section. My domain consisted of me and a Royal Air Force Squadron leader.

When Faye and I arrived at SHAPE, we looked around a little bit at off base housing, but in the end, we opted for a quarter on base and that worked out OKAY. Sandi could walk to school and I could walk to work, but if we had known how much entertaining we were going to be doing over the next four years we might have gone for something bigger off-base.

But the assignment was great and we were right in the middle of Europe. We had the opportunity to visit lots of neat places both officially and on our own.

From Faye's Journal:

Belgium is green, reminiscent of England but without the hedgerows and it is intensively farmed. The houses tend to be tall and narrow, gray stucco or red brick with red tile roofs.

Domaine (housing) offered us a quarter on base which I looked at and accepted. It's a two-story town house on the end of a row of four. It has three bedrooms and one and a half baths. From the front door you enter a large entry hall. Immediately to your right is the half bath, a large coat cupboard and the stairs to the second floor. On your left is a door to the living/dining room and straight ahead beyond the stairs is the door to the kitchen.

The kitchen is a reasonable size and has an American made stove and   refrigerator. It is light and airy and the single large window looks out into our back garden. From the kitchen there are doors to the dining room and laundry.

The laundry, in addition to the washer and

dryer, has a fair-sized storage cupboard. There are doors from the laundry to the garage and the back garden.

All the walls are painted white and I think that they are solid cement which will make picture hanging a challenge. Speaking of pictures, the master bedroom has a huge picture window facing the street which, I think, will make a perfect place for my "studio."

Keys. Every door and window have a handle - there are no round knobs in Europe—and every door, the kitchen cupboard included, has a key. I plan to leave all the interior keys in the locks because I am already carrying around the keys to the mailbox, front door, back door, garage and car. If I attached the whole lot to a belt, I could easily imagine myself as a medieval chatelaine.

Neighbors. In our row of four we have an English couple (two sons away at school) next door and another American family next to them. At the end of the row there is a very young Turkish couple. She is very young, I think that they were married just before coming to Belgium, and I would guess she is from a very rural community and had never been off the farm. (Goat ranch?) I am told that when they first arrived, she was very upset because she couldn't keep a couple of goats in the back yard and spent some time looking for the well. Water coming out of a hole in the wall—quite a novelty.

For neighborhood entertainment we have an Italian colonel and his wife living across the street. Don't get me wrong, we all love them. They are both Rolly, Polly Mr. and Mrs. Fezziwig characters and as nice as they can be but they argue constantly, loudly and publicly. The neighbors can't miss it as the volume starts to rise. The climax is usually predictable. The

337

"discussion," complete with the waving of arms, will spill out onto the front porch and the colonel will head for the car. With a final burst of Italian, he will drive away only to return a minute later with some rejoinder that he just thought of. Ten minutes later all is quiet as if nothing happened.

Language. Belgium is a bi-lingual country, Flemish in the north and French in the south where we live. Everybody tries to learn basic French, and all seem to learn basic English, so we get along. I find French very difficult and when I am out shopping I still communicate by sign language and charades. When I really get bogged down, I switch to German and the Belgians think that I am a rare thing—a bi-lingual American. I am amazed at how much of the German comes back. I'll be racking my brain for a word and the German just pops out.

History 101
—Belgium—

When I first arrived at Live Oak in the mid 1980's the Soviet Union was already starting to unravel and over the next three or four years the shroud of secrecy that surrounded Live Oak started to lift and our operation became more public.

Stick with me and all about Live Oak will be revealed.

At the end of World War II, the Allied Powers agreed that post-war Germany would be occupied by the four principle victorious nations, The United States, The United Kingdom, France and The Soviet Union. Each of the four nations would administer their individual "Zones of Occupation." Lines were drawn on the map and The Soviet Union (let's just say Russia) was assigned the part of Germany roughly from the Elbe River east and the United States, the United Kingdom and France divided up the rest.

The Allies also decided that Berlin, the capital of Germany, would also be occupied by the four powers so Berlin was divided along the same geographic lines, the Russians to the east and the Allies to the west.

However, Berlin lies over a hundred miles inside the Russian Zone of Occupation and the big brains who thought up this division made no provision as to exactly how the western powers were going to service their garrisons stationed in Berlin.

Chaos reigned.

The Allies needed to move men and material in and out of Berlin and the Soviets didn't want them using their roads and railroads. The Soviets also objected to the Allies using their airspace to fly in and out of Berlin. And, to make matters worse, the Russians clamped down on all east/west contact with what Winston Churchill named "The Iron Curtain."

Well, we did drive convoys and trains to Berlin and the Russians grudgingly let us but there were many confrontations.

And we did fly to Berlin although there were close calls and a few crashes. But air travel was worked out by the establishment of the Berlin Air Corridors.

But tensions remained high and in 1947 the Russians shut down all Allied road and rail traffic to Berlin. But for some reason they didn't shut down air travel.

The Allies responded with the now famous Berlin Airlift and for almost a year, until the Russians lifted the blockade, everything that the city of Berlin needed, from food to fuel, was flown in. This was no easy task. Hundreds of airplanes and thousands of aircrews had to be mobilized, staging bases had to be developed, air traffic control procedures had to be worked out, on and on. Men and machines were lost.

At the time there were many people, both military and civilian, who thought that the Berlin Airlift had been the wrong response and that when the Russians shut down Allied access to Berlin, we should have confronted them militarily.

Twelve years later they almost got their chance.

In 1959 the Cold War was on. East and West snarled at each other all over the world but especially along the border between East Germany and West Germany, the Inner German Border. West Germany, with Allied assistance, was becoming a viable democracy with a thriving economy and living conditions were rapidly improving. West Germany was also taking steps to integrate West Berlin into West Germany both economically and politically. I guess that the Russians didn't like that and when West Germany announced that they were going to tie the economies and currencies of West Germany and West Berlin together the Russians threatened another blockade.

The Supreme Commander Allied Powers Europe looked at the developing situation, thought about the Berlin Airlift and asked for alternative solutions. He directed that senior officers from the three victorious Allied nations of World War II be appointed to a planning staff whose charter was to come up with alternatives to an airlift and Live Oak was born. (As far as I was ever able to determine the term Live Oak has no particular meaning, it was just picked off of a list of names.)

The planning staff was formed and plans for military actions and political initiatives were developed and submitted to the Supreme Commander.

Then two things happened, first the Russians

never carried out their threat to shut down Allied access to Berlin and second, for some reason the planning staff wasn't disbanded when the threat was over.

Live Oak lived on, making plans, nominating forces to execute these plans, exercising the plans and traveling to the defense ministries of the United States, the United Kingdom and France to brief and gain approval for the plans.

When I arrived, Live Oak had been in business for over twenty-five years and the only major change to their operation was that West Germany had been added to the planning staff. Berlin was still occupied by the four powers, the Allies still moved men and material back and forth from West Germany to West Berlin by road, rail and air through East Germany, the Berlin Wall, which had been built in 1961, was still dividing Berlin into West and East and the Iron Curtain still stretched from the Baltic to the Adriatic.

On the plus side neither the Russians nor the East Germans had interrupted, interfered with or threatened our access to Berlin in over twenty years. The two Germany's had reached commerce and trade agreements in the early seventies so civilian goods flowed freely back and forth over the border.

But Live Oak lived on.

We, the staff officers in Live Oak, slaved away at the task of making plans and watching Berlin 24/7.

Well, not actually. We didn't work on the weekends. So, we slaved away 24/5.

Exercise they tell me is good for the mind and body so Live Oak had every Wednesday afternoon off for "sport." All were encouraged to use Wednesday afternoon to engage in some kind of rigorous athletic activity.

We had a bowling league.

So, when you factor in Wednesday afternoons, we slaved away planning and watching Berlin 24/4 1/2.

Of course, Live Oak Staff Officers didn't work 24 hours a day. No, like all sensible staff agencies we worked nine to five.

So that would make our duty hours and days 8/4 on the non-sport days and three hours on Wednesday.

Staff Officers have to eat to fuel the mind and body so we had two hours off for lunch.

So, we are now down to slaving away 6/4 plus the three hours on Wednesday. For those of you who may be mathematically challenged that's twenty-seven hours a week.

If the truth be known, not many of the Live Oak staff actually reported for duty at nine in the morning. Most everyone kind of drifted in between nine and nine-thirty and anyone found at his desk after four in the afternoon was considered to be some kind of workaholic fanatic.

I could see why the assignment to Live Oak was the best kept secret in the Air Force.

Brussels
—Belgium—

*O*nce we had the house squared away, we were all itching to go exploring and the girls wanted to go to Brussels. I had my reservations because it sounded like another church crawl to see some relic or another.

I have seen churches. In our seven years in England, Faye wanted to see them all and we probably did. Somehow it seemed that even the smallest of villages had at least one church that my sailor found architecturally interesting and it also seemed that all of these churches had "Relics."

Now I don't mean to sound skeptical, but in my travels, I have seen enough saintly bones to populate New York City and enough pieces of the true cross to make a forest.

While we were England, Faye also got us into

Brass Rubbing and I spent many hours crawling around cold church floors making impressions of dead guys.

But this was Belgium and today we were off to Brussels. It is only about thirty miles to Brussels and for some reason, we decided to take the train. I don't know why we decided to take the train but I was pretty sure that we wouldn't do it again.

We drove into Mons, our nearest big town, and parked at the station. That was the easy part. Finding the train that was heading in the right direction was challenging as all the signs and station announcements were in French, which might as well have been Ancient Greek (or modern Greek for that matter), and suddenly none of the natives spoke English or even knew where Brussels was.

Finally, we got tickets and got on a train. It probably wasn't the right train because before we got to Brussels, we had to change to another train which looked remarkably like the first train and was headed in the same direction.

In due time we arrived at the Gare Centrale in Brussels, which, thankfully, was right downtown and I was pleasantly surprised when we wended our way on cobbled streets past former high muck-a-muck mansions that are now museums and colleges—not to a church, but to the Royal Palace.

When the King and his family are not in residence the state rooms were open to the public—for free. The only restrictions were, you must check cameras and bags at the door and they wouldn't let ladies wear spiked high heels. One look at those beautiful floors and I could see why.

We bought a guide book that was printed in English and German, and were delighted to find that the rooms were numbered, (#3—white drawing room, #8—throne room, etc.) and important pieces of furniture and paintings were also numbered. Best of all, the numbers matched those in the guide book.

That was a treat. In my travels I have discovered that most guide books are written by professors of ancient languages who have never been in, or even seen, the buildings that they are attempting to describe.

The throne room was magnificent. It was all white with gilt everywhere, trimmed in deep red, with, (I think I counted) eleven glittering chandeliers and seventeen matching wall sconces. Underfoot there was the most beautiful inlaid, parquet floor I have ever seen.

After we wandered the around palace for a while we headed toward the Grand Platz, the main market square, and on the way, we stopped to get our French Fries. There are two things that the Belgians do really well: French Fries and beer.

When we came into the Platz (pronounced Place, though we never did) we were surprised to see a bandstand, crowds of people and everywhere—jugglers. We had hit some kind of juggler's festival. There were jugglers wandering around on foot, jugglers on stilts and even a couple on unicycles.

We found a seat in an outdoor café, ordered a beer, studied the architecture, listened to the band (who made up what they lacked in skill with enthusiasm) and watched the entertainment.

Faye said that most of the buildings around the square were once guild houses, carpenters, masons, etc. so each building was decorated with carvings and plasterwork unique to that particular guild and it seemed that all the buildings were all covered in gold leaf. Pretty spectacular. It was fun trying to identify the individual guilds.

But most of our attention was on the jugglers.

A young fellow wearing bright green baggy trousers, a purple shirt and a large, red, false nose decided to put on his show in front of our café.

We ordered a second glass of beer.

His crowd gathering technique was one of consummate skill. Hiding the clown nose, he would stroll past his "victim," turn behind them, don the nose and then as he followed them, he would imitate their every action. It was all done in good taste and good humor, and in less time than it takes to tell, an amused and happy crowd was collected.

Then the entertainer went into his juggling act, which was pretty good, too.

After passing the hat, there was time for the crowd to disperse before the crowd gathering show began again.

We learned later that once street entertainers had been a common sight in Brussels and that it had kind of died out. The town council had invited the jugglers in to put on this big show in hopes that the entertainers would find it lucrative enough to regularly ply their trade in the market places.

Wouldn't hurt the tourist trade either.

In a letter from Faye's folks they said that they recalled that the Mannekin Pis was not far from the Grand Platz. They had a good memory. From one corner of the Platz it was only a couple of blocks to the statue.

I guess everyone knows the story. The little prince got lost and the kingdom was frantically searching. The king decreed that wherever he was found and whatever he was doing a statue would be erected. When he was found, there he was doing what little boys do whenever they have to do it.

Over the years many individuals and groups have made clothes for the little boy and the statue is often dressed in one of the costumes (a soldier the day we were there). The building on the corner next to the statue is now a museum that houses all the clothes. We took a look. Mannekin Pis has hundreds of suits, national costumes, top hat and tails, sports attire, military uniforms, you name it.

A great day and our train back home was a direct shot to Mons, no changes. I never did figure that one out. Next time I'm driving.

Berlin
—East Germany—

From Faye's Journal:

*L*ast Sunday Vern and I drove to Berlin with some English friends—in a British staff car. Don't ask. Now I have a souvenir I think I will frame and show off to my grandchildren, a military travel document with Russian stamps on it.

When you drive to Berlin you have to cross the Iron Curtain and drive through East Germany and it is quite a procedure. You take the West German autobahn to the border between east and west—the Inner German Border—to the town of Helmstad and present your authority to travel at the Allied border crossing checkpoint. You have probably heard of "Checkpoint Charlie," which is actually in Berlin, this was "Checkpoint Alpha."

Here the American Military Police check your

paperwork, give you a slide show briefing of the three autobahn route turnings that you have to take to get to Berlin, give you another briefing on what to do if you have trouble on route and note your starting time. At the speed limit it takes about two hours to get to Berlin and if you don't check in within four hours they send someone to find out why.

After leaving the Allied checkpoint, the first barrier is the East German gate. This gate is always open and we just drive through without stopping because; 1. We don't recognize East German authority and, 2. Even this long after World War II, Berlin and the access routes to Berlin are still occupied territory.

Then you drive up to the Russian checkpoint and stop, as directed by your (my) first real live Russian soldier. He turned out to be a grim visage boy of nineteen or twenty, who had a crease in his jacket and bit his fingernails (though not in our presence).

The routine here was, Vern got out of the car, handed the soldier our travel documents who read through them at least three times, and when satisfied handed the papers back and pointed to a little hut.

Vern went to Berlin often and he told me later that if he thought that the Russians were taking too long playing with the documents he would just start wandering around, looking behind the buildings and up at the guard towers. This made the guards nervous and they would usually follow behind and give the papers back.

The nut was going to get himself shot.

Vern took the documents into what looked like an old train station in a little town and he described it as a small, austere room with a wall on one side in which there was a window that was so dirty that you couldn't see through it with a slot at the bottom.

352

Rather like a bank teller's cage. You shove the papers through the slot at the bottom and a great hairy hand appears to whisk them away, you see the lights from the copy machine flashing and eventually everything is returned with a new collection of stamps.

There is also a table that is covered with propaganda pamphlets in every language from Arabic to Swahili. You are, of course, encouraged to take one and read up on the joys of communism. On one of his many trips to Berlin Vern, the nut, scooped them all up, carried the armload out to the car and dumped them into the trunk.

Vern came out and again handed our papers to the soldier, who read everything again and finally saluted indicating that we could go.

Whilst Vern was in the hut, the soldier strolled deliberately all around the car jotting things down in a little notebook.

After that the drive was a letdown. The road was terrible with potholes and vegetation growing in at the edges, and this was supposed to be an autobahn. What a difference from the modern roads in West Germany. There was nothing to see but fields of potatoes, red cabbage and field corn. Occasionally there were people in the fields and they always waved. We always wave back, especially to the children because the Russians tell the kids that we are monsters who eat babies for breakfast, and it makes the Russians mad when our guys grin and wave.

When you reach Berlin, you do the whole checkpoint routine in reverse and enter West Berlin through "Checkpoint Bravo." Vern told me that there are more than two dozen checkpoints at various locations all around the city and most of them are used for only one purpose like bringing in coal or taking out trash.

The next day, while the guys worked, we ladies did some sightseeing. West Berlin has to be one of the most sophisticated, liveliest, gayest cities in the world, but it is a paradox. It is also the saddest. The WALL is an awful, sobering place. West Berlin is truly a tiny island defying the tide.

The main drag, the Kurfurstendamm, called the Ku'damm, is a shopper's paradise. There is one department store, called the KaDaWe, that is better than Macys. The place is huge, six stories high and every floor has a different specialty. For example: The sixth floor is nothing but food. If they don't have it, it's not edible. There are tiny lunch counters tucked away in odd corners which makes the sixth floor a popular place at lunch time. I chose a little counter that seemed to be the least crowded. This turned out to be a place that served nothing but potatoes (with "fixens"), all kinds of potatoes, cooked in all kinds of ways. For about two dollars I had a kind of casserole of shredded potatoes, ham and cheese, and, a glass of beer. Yummy!

On another floor we stopped in the sewing notions. There was an area as big as our house selling nothing but buttons, all kinds, sizes, shapes, colors, you name it.

In places on other floors there were great bins of feathers, huge piles of furs, a large wall of tiny drawers with a bead or sequin glued on to illustrate the contents. They even had my Bing and Gerundial seagull dishes that we had gotten from Denmark. What a place.

As this was a working visit for the guys we could only stay in Berlin for a couple of days. I will be back.

Amsterdam
—Netherlands—

Bright and early on an April Saturday morning we were off on a bus tour of Amsterdam with some stops along the way. I like bus tours, leave the driving to someone else. This wasn't our first trip to Holland as we had previously been to the gardens at Keukenhof and the miniature city of Madurodam.

It is a long ride from SHAPE to Keukenhof but Faye said that it was worth it. To each his, or her, own, I guess. Keukenhof was just one really big flower garden. Don't get me wrong, I like flowers and at everyplace we ever lived we had at least one flower garden, but they only flourished because my Sailor has a green thumb. She was management I was strictly labor because I have a black thumb. I can kill an artificial plant.

Faye described Keukenhof this way:

355

"Keukenhof is a huge park, wooded, watered and planted. There was a lake, streams, walkways, fountains and grass. The landscaping is exquisite. It seems that everywhere you look there are drifts of flowers - Daffodils, Narcissus, Tulips, Iris, you name it. If it grows from a bulb you will find it at Keukenhof, beautifully displayed, in profusion and all labeled. A nearly two thousand acres treat for the eyes and nose."

While we were visiting Keukenhof I noticed that the children on the tour weren't nearly as thrilled with the flowers as their parents were and I thought, 'Well they will like Madurodam.' They did and so did we.

Madurodam is a city in miniature that is built to 1/25 scale. It has everything that you would expect to find in a major city, large buildings, traffic, airport, seaport, train station, etc.

Each of the major buildings and transportation hubs on display is an exact copy of a real place somewhere in the Netherlands and everything works. Planes taxi about the airport, ships ply the harbor and waterways, trains stop at stations and factories hum. The churches even have stained glass windows, carved gargoyles and spires.

I think that the kids enjoyed the novelty of the size, suddenly becoming Gulliver. The adults soon get caught up in the craftmanship and the mechanics.

The miniature city is a composite of the Netherlands and the excellent English language guidebook that we bought, at an exorbitant price, had a history of the important buildings along with what their function was and where they came from. I guess you could say that seeing Madurodam is seeing the Netherlands in a nutshell.

But today we were off to Amsterdam.

356

We left SHAPE at seven AM on a clear but cold day. We picked spring for our trip because we thought that the weather would be nice. Unfortunately, spring hadn't sprung yet and we were glad that we'd brought along scarves and gloves.

The trip to Amsterdam usually only takes two to three hours but this one took five as we had stops along the way.

My first impression of the Netherlands was that it was wet and flat. Water, water everywhere, ditches and canals stretching out over the fields in every direction. Anything that is over a couple of stories tall can be seen for miles. It's rather startling to look out across a farmer's field and see a big ship apparently swimming along through the green grass.

Everything, from houses, towns and farms looked well kept and tidy. The people that we met were welcoming and friendly and I think that everyone over the age of three had at least two bicycles.

Before long windmills started to appear. Lots of windmills. Not just a few relics of a time gone by that were left for show, but real working mills that can grind grain and pump water. Old mills have been restored and they are also installing the new high-tech windmills that have sails that look like airplane propellers.

I like the old ones with the huge canvas sails, massive wooden gears and wheels noisily grinding against each other. They seemed alive.

We crossed three rivers, one being the Rhine, which were squeezed into permanent channels by levees. The Rhine must have once had a flood plain two or three miles wide. I guess that's why they had all the windmills.

Our first stop was at a diamond factory where

they showed us how they make very expensive sparkles out of bits of what looks like dirty glass. Everywhere we looked there were piles of pricy stones both set and loose. We saw some finished emerald and diamond and ruby and diamond creations that were really sparkly.

But we were Just looking, no buying, not at those prices. There were no gift packets for the tourists either. They had lots and lots of rocks just lying around, seems like they could have given the tourists at least one.

The next stop along the way was a place that made wooden shoes. I guess I expected to see little old men carving blocks of wood, but there was no hand crafting here. These shoes were turned out in minutes by a big golopola-golopola machine. (Well, that's what it sounded like.)

They set a form the size and shape they want into the machine—these looked like the wooden forms once found in shoemaker's shops—then they shoved in rectangular block of very wet willow. The machine grumbled and chomped thunderously at the block of wood, chips were spewed out in a spectacularly satisfying fashion, and voila, you have the outside shape of a wooden shoe. By putting on another block of wood and reversing the gears so the machine ran backwards it made a mirror image, instead of a true image, and you had a pair.

Another machine did the same to hollow out the insides. And, all those wet, aromatic chips that were thrown out all over the place were bagged up and sold as fuel for smoking meat, fish and eels.

Just before lunch we toured a little cheese factory, and of course, our favorite part was the tasting. Unlike the stingy diamond factory, these guys gave out samples. We sampled a lot. We even tried a cheese flavored with nettles. Faye told me that nettles were once used to dye wool a color that she called 'hospital green' and if you were hungry enough, nettles could be boiled and eaten.

Nettles in cheese? It wasn't bad, but it would never be my favorite. Thinking about lunch, we bought a chunk of cheese flavored with onion and garlic.

For lunch we stopped at the fishing village of Volendam on the Zuider Zee. The Zuider Zee was once an arm of the North Sea which was diked shut, the salt water pumped out and fresh water pumped in. It is BIG, you can't see the opposite shore and the day that we were there it was choked with chunks of ice up to two feet thick. From this "sea" the Dutch take, in great quantities, eels and a small fish that looks rather like a roach.

We parked near a large fish factory with a smokehouse that was located right at quayside. The factory had their own push carts out roaming up and down the street selling seafood, (fresh, cured or cooked) and served on buns.

Now, I have eaten some strange things in my travels: haggis, grasshoppers, and Indian Curry that was so hot it would vulcanize your eyeballs. I have caught, cooked, served and eaten many a fish in its whole state but, there is something disconcerting about ordering a fish *sandwich* and getting it with the critters' head and tail hanging out of the bread roll.

With the offending parts quickly shared with clamoring flocks of very appreciative black-headed seagulls, and our cheese for dessert, it was a tasty feast.

Leaving Volendam, the two-lane road runs along the top of the dike. This is a BIG dike. On one side, just a few feet below the road, was the Zuider Zee and WAY down on the other side are the houses, farms and towns. In many places the water level is way higher than the rooftops. We didn't think that we would be happy living there.

We rolled into Amsterdam around noon and were told to be back at the bus by four.

To maximize our sightseeing time and to get in out of the cold we took a boat ride in a nice, warm, glass enclosed canal boat around the canals of old Amsterdam. Amsterdam has lots of canals. When the Romans showed up a couple thousand years ago and conquered the cluster of mud huts that existed at the time, their first project was fortification. It's pretty hard to fortify a swamp as wooden palisades rot and stone walls tend to sink. Backed onto the Amstel River the Romans dug a semi-circular canal, drained the swamp and as the town expanded it was enclosed by another canal and another, etc.

The Netherlands is a small country and a full third of its existing land area has been reclaimed from the sea. Land was, and is, very expensive, so the buildings we saw along the canals tended to be narrow and tall. Fortunately for them, they are built wall to wall because the older ones, some dating from the 16th and 17th centuries and built on wooden pilings, tend to tip and lean in the most alarming manner as they slowly settle into the ooze and stand only with the help of slightly sturdier neighbors.

The tall skinny houses are all painted different colors and decorated with statues and plasterwork around the windows and doors.

We were also amazed and fascinated by the number and variety of houseboats that sit bow to stern along every canal bank. We were told that every one of them is built on the old hull of a real boat and registered as a working boat. By a vagary of Dutch law, any boat waiting for a load has the use of city services for free and does not have to pay taxes. No wonder there is a long waiting list for canal space.

The style of these houseboats ranged from squalid, through whimsical to opulent. We saw one that resembled an ark with the deck space completely screened and loaded with cats. The boat is owned by an elderly lady who feels that it is her mission in life to care for strays. From the number of kittens, I wonder if anyone ever informed the dear old soul about the birds and the bees and other related matters.

In the whimsical there was one that sported on its roof a Mannikin Pis, fully functional and watering the canal.

When the tour guide wasn't calling our attention to the wonders of canal side life, we happily watched the other residents—waterfowl—a variety of swans, geese, ducks and grebes.

After the canal boat ride, we wandered around the old main square for our own exploration. Making our way through jam-packed walking streets we opted for a salad supper at a restaurant with a window table.

Faye wrote in her journal:

Between my parents and Vern, I've had a very sheltered life, for which I am not ungrateful. I never saw, or imagined, anything like the parade that passed before us in Amsterdam. I was fascinated by the show of costumes and hairdos; posh, weird, exotic and chaotic. Even as chilly as it was there was plenty of bare skin.

After dinner, Vern and I took a stroll through the seedier part of town. Much to my shocked surprise there was open drug dealing, right in front of God and everybody. If I notice it, it's really blatant. At every corner there was the sweet whiff of hemp. I learned that a 'hash house' is not a cheap restaurant and the term 'red light district' took on a whole new meaning. These establishments really do have a red bulb over the door and they also have 'store windows' lit by red fluorescent lights, wherein the scantily clad 'merchandise' displays itself.

Well! I suppose drugs and prostitution can be found in any city, but I've never before encountered a town where one didn't have to look, or know where to look, to find it.

As dusk began to fall, we made our way back to the coach and we gratefully settled into our seats and slept all the way home.

Leningrad
—Russia—

*B*ack in the old Cold War days when we were stationed at Supreme Headquarters Allied Powers Europe (SHAPE) in Belgium. Faye got an opportunity to take a seven-day trip to Russia visiting Leningrad and Moscow. I wish I could have gone but in those days, it was just not possible.

From Faye's journal:

Day 1, Saturday, April 11.

Belgium to Leningrad on a Russian airplane. All the books said Russians were patient and, boy, did we practice that virtue. The bus from SHAPE arrived at the Brussels airport at eleven thirty, and we gathered at check-in 'B.' We waited until one o'clock while the travel people sorted out a guy who had cancelled yesterday but then changed his mind.

I guess once you cancel you are cancelled. He was not allowed to come.

At ten minutes after two we were still waiting for ground transportation to our plane. Two thirty was our scheduled take off time, but that time passed while we were boarding. Then we waited some more while a German student from another tour group, whose pocket had been picked and her passport taken, was soothed, deplaned and her luggage removed.

This took a crew of six nearly two hours.

From the outside, our plane looked like a Boeing copy but inside was another story. We sat in "first-class" so we only saw the front section. A plane-wide galley, curtained at both ends, separated the two sections.

In our section there were three seats on each side of a central isle. The seats were small and the rows were so close together that MY knees nearly touched the one in front. We wondered how we would get in and out until we discovered that the seats flipped up and the backs flipped down at a touch.

And this was first class.

I think that the only difference between the classes was that we were up front and had curtains.

The dinner trays that they used must have been purchased in the West because they were obviously made for more spacious seating. They nearly cut everyone in two. The overhead luggage store was open racks, no bins, and there was no provision for oxygen should the plane become depressurized.

Very reassuring!!

We finally took off at ten after four.

I am sure that it was only due to international law about flying over water that we had a life jacket demonstration. I say this because the life jackets were stored in the overhead rack in heavily lashed canvas bags. Not very accessible.

One hour after takeoff we were over Copenhagen and we finally got lunch—a meat and salad box fixed by Sabena, not bad, very tasty. We were offered tea, coffee, apple juice, wine or mineral water. The bottled water tasted like rusty pipes.

The cabin crew and pilots also got fed. A tray of empty water glasses went forward into the cockpit with the lunch boxes. When the tray was picked up it also held two empty vodka bottles.

We flew right up the Baltic Sea. The jumbled areas of pack ice below made lovely patterns on the water that looked like marble.

Nearing Leningrad I could see areas of marshland and birch forest. There were also large barren patches but I couldn't tell if they were large farms, small towns or what. It looked like every deforested place had a group of small houses, other buildings and huge apartment blocks.

We landed in Leningrad at a quarter to nine, local time, and sat in the airplane for forty-five minutes waiting for transport to take us to the terminal. We could have walked it in about five minutes.

Customs! Passport control was slow, but it moved along. It was like a grocery store checkout line. Then we went into a larger room, about the size of two classrooms, into which three planeloads of people were crammed. At one end of the room there was one small conveyor belt loop for luggage. Once you found your bags, the next obstacle was to exit through a single security doorway.

On the other side of the door there were four

baggage and declarations inspectors. The bags went through another x-ray and a bored, surly agent checked me.

Finally, we stepped out into another small waiting room.

Here we met Marina, our Intourist guide. She would be our shepherd until we boarded a plane in Moscow for the return flight to Belgium. Marina was young (mid-twenties), spoke excellent English, was always smartly dressed ("I buy all my clothes on the Black Market"), and a master of subtle propaganda.

Our hotel was the Pribaltiskaya, at #14 Korabestroiteley. (Shipbuilders Street) The hotel was on the western end of Vasilevskiy Island, overlooking the Gulf of Finland. The Pribaltiskaya was one of Russia's largest and pleasantest hotels with two thousand four hundred beds, a swimming pool, sauna, and a bowling alley.

It was about a 50-minute drive to the hotel from the airport.

As it was after midnight when we finally got to the hotel and I thought we might have to resort to our emergency rations for supper. But no, they opened a snack bar and after another, mercifully short, wait we were given a salad plate (not very fresh), some roast beef and soupy mashed potatoes covered in gravy— and the nasty mineral water.

We finally got our rooms and got to bed about one-thirty. My last conscious thought was, "God, we've got to do that airport scene twice more."

Day 2, Sunday, April 12.

Breakfast at nine o'clock consisted of two kinds of bread, an off white that was tasty and a rye that was sour. There was also butter, jam, sweet rolls and a metal dish that contained two, very solid, poached eggs. We also had apple juice and a very potable coffee.

A little after ten we started the morning tour which was a bus ride around Leningrad with photo opportunities. From the bus, the land looked as if there wasn't any grass, just mud. There was grass, but it was squashed flat and dirty from heavy winter snows.

The city that Peter the Great laid out had grandeur without being grand; it was majestic, but not magic. The classical style "old city" was painted, each building a different color, trimmed with white, terra cotta, ochre, green or turquoise—and a lot, like East Berlin, was a façade. Looking through archways and alleys into courtyards and back streets, you could see a crumbling, untidy world.

It also seemed like every building was once somebody's former palace and was now a state or local ministry or a museum.

We were told not to take pictures of people in uniform, but it was kind of hard not to as uniforms were everywhere. Most had plain red epaulets with the letters "CA" on them, which I took to mean Russian Army. I saw lots of black uniforms with flat hats that had ribbons hanging down the back and long coats piped in gold—Navy.

We returned to the hotel for lunch. Throughout the tour we almost always returned to our hotel for lunch. Our lunch was a relish tray with luncheon meats, cheese, cured fish and a vegetable soup (which was always good). This was followed by a meat and potato entrée.

Dinner was the same relish tray, an entrée and dessert.

All of our meals were substantial, nourishing and standard. While we were not treated to gourmet cuisine, the horror stories about the food were just stories. Our greatest lack in the food line was a drink of plain water and anything fresh, like veggies or a salad.

After lunch we went to the Piskerovshy Memorial Cemetery which commemorates the half million people, military and civilian, who died during the World War II siege of Leningrad. There were small twin buildings that tell the story with photographs and mementoes and an elevated terrace with an eternal flame that overlooks a long avenue of roses and mass graves. The roses were still covered with little wooden "houses" for winter protection.

The avenue lead to a large statue of Mother Russia holding an oak bough. To the Russians, the oak tree symbolizes grief. Here there were many flowers, usually a single stem, often placed by children, around the flame and on the graves.

While watching the Russian people at the Piskerovshy Memorial, I realized that they have a different way of thinking about history. It lives and they really care. Every joy or sorrow of their long history as a people might as well have happened last year.

That evening sixteen of us went to the circus. One ring and intimate. A super show. Only photography without a flash was allowed. They had trained camels, seals, horses, COWS and an alpaca. Clowns did bits and skits while equipment for the next act was rigged. The clowns were good! I guess laughter transcends all language. It was well worth the thirteen-dollar admission price.

Day 3, Monday, April 13.
Today's breakfast was almost a repeat of yesterday except that two sausages that tasted like hot dogs replaced the eggs. Then we were off to the Michael Palace which is now the Russian Museum.

The former Michael Palace is the centerpiece of the "Square of Arts," an architectural complex built around a small park. In the park, a line of trees and slender strips of floral bordered lawn provide the illusion of privacy for the wide, paved, bench lined paths leading to the central statue of Pushkin reciting poetry.

The Michael Palace was built in 1819 for Grand Duke Michael, the youngest son of Tsar Paul. In 1896, Tsar Nicholas II turned it into a museum. The palace had a large courtyard and attractive iron railings. The central portico and eight Corinthian columns were covered in scaffolding, as were parts of many buildings throughout Leningrad. The first rooms contained an impressive collection of icons. The 18th and 19th century rooms were the best: paintings of seascapes by Aivozovsky and Repins huge canvas of "The Volga Boatmen." The few Impressionist paintings were lackluster and everything after that was Socialist Realism.

The afternoon tour was to the Peter and Paul Fortress; built by Peter the Great in 1703, it's where Leningrad (Saint Petersburg) began. The city came later. Peter built the fortress because he wanted to protect this access to the sea that he had just taken from the Swedes.

Within the fortress complex, Italians built the Cathedral and the tall spire. The Rococo interior looked very 'Western.' The walls and columns looked like they were pink and green marble, but they were actually painted wood. Russians seem to be very fond of gilding. I haven't seen so much gold leaf since I wandered into the Buddhist Temple in Seattle.

All of the Romanovs, except the last, Nicholas II and his family, are buried here. In fact, the transept and north isle are filled with meter high vaults. The earliest are plain white marble and progress to awesome examples of the stone carver's art in highly polished azurite and malachite.

Today I started noticing the "Little Remarks" Marina slipped into her briefings. At the Russian Museum she said, "What the Western artists took five hundred years to develop, Russian artists did in two." True, but not at the same time, sweetie.

The biggest difference in our history books came at the Cathedral when one of the kids on our tour wanted to know where Anastasia was buried. What a bombshell. Marina said they were disposed during the Revolution, "retired" to Ekaterina Palace, and, when they eventually died, the State buried them elsewhere.

Well, I don't think Marina believed us either when we told her that the whole family had been murdered and dumped.

After dinner we went to a performance of Cossack Dancing. The theater was an addition to another Intourist hotel, and there was no box office, Intourist sells the tickets. The costumes were colorful and the dancers were well trained and exuberant. Every dance was highly choreographed. It was hard to tell if they were based on real folk dances or just what the Russians thought we wanted to see.

Day 4, Tuesday, April 14.
Most of our group went on an optional tour to

another former palace. The guidebook said that it was in the "if you've seen one you've seen 'em all category." I decided to join the minority and go downtown to find a bookshop that was reported to have posters. None of us were brave enough to go exploring on our own, but after much gentle haranguing by Marina and increasingly stubborn resistance from us, five rebels took off.

The hotel had two telephones on the counter, black and red, and Marina picked up the red phone as we went out the door.

We opted to try the subway, (Metro). The escalators in the Metro were awesome. Hordes of people were engulfed, whizzed up or down and spewed out at terrific speed—and only about one in twenty stumbled when hauled up short at the end.

We found the bookstore, which hadn't opened yet, and also discovered that we had acquired two tails. Of course, they could have been products of our own over active imaginations, but not likely. One was so obviously following us he could well have been just a curious citizen. The other was a woman that one or the other of us would glimpse off and on—down in the subway, back on the street, in the department store.

While waiting for the bookstore to open went into a department store. The department store we found can only be described as an experience. Rather like an indoor departmental flea market. It was a very large establishment, but after a while you noticed repeats in the displayed merchandise, and many items did not have a price, an indication that they were not in stock. I saw nothing of exceptional quality, but the prices were premium.

From time to time there would be a scurrying and at different places in the store a line would form. I elbowed my way into one line long enough to see what the excitement was about: soap, toothpaste and nylons.

We did get to the bookstore and after buying posters I took a local bus back to the hotel. I had my hotel card out to ask the driver if I was on the right bus, but he was enclosed in a glass cage.

Not one person looked directly at me although I saw eyes slide in my direction, and no one spoke. But one lady, as she left the bus, gave my hotel card a quick tap and without turning her head, murmured, "You are correct."

I also couldn't figure out where or how to pay the five-kopek fare until a babushka tugged at my sleeve and pointed to a box mounted on the wall that looked like a square flower sifter. You put the money in the top, turn the crank and tear off the ticket at the bottom

The bus sounded like my old coffeepot just before it died, and the motor stalled every time we came to a full stop, but I did get to the hotel in time for lunch.

The afternoon program was visits to St. Isaac Cathedral, Palace Square and the Hermitage.

The Hermitage. What can I say? An art lover's paradise! We went through room after room at a steady clip for three hours, pausing briefly for glimpses of one or two important pieces in each room. I doubt that we could have seen it all, even if we had spent every moment of our time in Leningrad at the Hermitage. To reinforce the memory, I bought a thirty-dollar book.

From the third floor of the Hermitage we had an unexpected photo opportunity, a view of all the troops in Leningrad practicing for the May Day parade.

Our bags were packed before breakfast so the hotel could transfer them to the airport. Hand luggage went on the bus with us. We had a morning tour before our flight to Moscow. We went about ten miles southeast of Leningrad to the town of Pushkin to see the Catherine Palace.

The whole town of Pushkin is really a large complex of palaces, parks and digs of the nobility and I was told that it was the Czars official summer residence. The whole place was all but destroyed during World War II and only the state apartments were nearing final restoration. Talk about Baroque! The façade was something! And, when restoration is completed, the flash of gilded Atlantis figures, capitals, window surrounds, vases, etc., will be blinding. The columns were painted white and the rest was sky blue. It was a dazzler!

Inside, there was so much ornate gilding that my eyes kept looking for something peaceful to rest on. The floors were made of beautifully inlaid wood with no two designs alike. Also, almost every room had a huge, from the floor nearly to the ceiling, blue and white tile stove. Unlike English royalty of the same era, the Russians tried not to freeze in the winter.

We had lunch at another Intourist hotel and then we were off to the airport. They said it was not the same airport that we had come in at, but I could see the International Terminal across the field. Incidentally, this internal flight was the only time we used a jetway.

We again sat in the forward area, that's first

class on US carriers but that's where the resemblance stops. They didn't serve anything; no Pepsi and peanuts, no caviar and vodka, nuthin.'

All in all, delays were minimal, and we were only one hour late getting into Moscow.

Moscow

—*Russia*—

From Faye's Journal:

On our flight from Leningrad to Moscow we learned that due to various 'congresses' that were in town and the preparations that were being made for May Day, the Kremlin and Red Square were closed to tourists. As 90% of what we wanted to see in Moscow was there, this news created unhappy talk.

Once we landed In Moscow it was back on a bus to take us to the Cosmos Hotel.

First impressions: Moscow was BIG, crowded, seemed to have endless apartment blocks and it looked dirty and drab.

Maybe Moscow will look better in the morning light.

Day 6, Thursday, April 16.

I opened the curtains of room 2454 of the Cosmos Hotel to see the early morning sun washing a panorama of Muscovite apartments. I was delighted to see a park across the street that had a little red and white church decorated with blue domes. Unfortunately, when I had the opportunity of a closer inspection, I found that it was derelict and vandalized.

To my right, in a generally southerly direction, I could see 'rush hour' traffic on the Prospect Mira, a long queue at the round Metro building, a gleaming 295-foot monument to Russian space exploration and the 550 plus acres and sixty pavilions of the Economic Achievement Exhibition.

We took the closure of the Kremlin and Red Square as gracefully as we could. Intourist scheduled another museum to replace it. Our next disappointment was when our guides went to get us tickets for the Bolshoi Ballet. No can do—too many Heavies in town. Grumpily, we agreed to go see another circus.

I overheard Marina tell Svetlana, our Moscow guide, that we couldn't get circus tickets either—and when that gets announced!

The thing is, Intourist knew that all this activity was going to be happening in Moscow before we ever left Belgium and they could probably have reversed the towns, Moscow first and then Leningrad, and kept everyone happy—if they had wanted to.

Ah well! On to other things, but first a word about souvenir pins. It seemed that the thing to do when touring Russia is to collect pins and it seemed that the best place to get them was from little kids.

In Leningrad it was hard to find a kid who swapped pins for gum. Not so in Moscow. This morning when we were leaving the hotel for a city bus tour, we ran our first gauntlet of a dozen or more kids holding out their hands and chanting, "Goom, goom." If you stop, put a hand in your pocket or say, "pin," you're mobbed. I noted that one boy always hung back and acted as a lookout so maybe they would be in trouble if the police caught them.

In less time than it takes to tell I had another ten pins, and I could have had lots more but I only had two packs of gum with me.

Bus tour. Moscow is pretty much like any other big, old city. What's not new is falling apart. Svetlana's commentary as we drove around was mostly, "on your left, or right, is the Ministry of this or that." Come to think of it, the only thing that distinguished the uninspired architecture of the ministerial buildings from the surrounding blocks of flats were the carvings above the entrance which, I guess, indicated what it was the ministry of and all the government buildings had a flagpole.

Privately owned vehicles were more in evidence here in Moscow than in Leningrad, but there was still not a lot of traffic. The main drags seem to be mostly three lanes. Actually, they were only two lanes because the only traffic using the center lane was the occasional, official looking, big, black Zil.

Sometimes drivers were very irate, yelling and gesticulating like Italians. Road Rage Russian style.

There were a lot of buses and you could tell who's who by their paint jobs; the big red and white buses were tourists, orange buses and yellow trams were for the general public, blue and white were military and they usually had curtains over the windows so you couldn't see who or what was inside.

The city was ringed with new housing estates

each containing up to a hundred, identical, twenty story prefabricated apartment buildings.

I was told that there were four railway stations in Moscow, each serving a different region of the country. I think the station on the Prospect Mira near our hotel was the North station because I saw a schedule pasted on the wall that said PURA—Riga.

Police were everywhere and we often saw them checking someone's papers, even pedestrians. Once, I saw a woman standing between two uniformed men, weeping. Fun town.

One stop for a photo opportunity was at the Lomonosov University which sits atop the Lenin Hills. To get there we crossed the Moskva River on the two-tiered Crimea Bridge. Impressive. The top deck of the bridge is for regular traffic and the bottom is for the Metro.

In front of the main university building there was a red granite terrace that offered a super panoramic view of the Moskva River, the Kremlin, Kremlin Wall and downtown Moscow.

Looking in the other direction, up into the hills, we could see a ski jump. Svetlana said that it was open all year round, and covered with a plastic carpet during the summer. I can't imagine going ski jumping for a days' recreation.

I am no longer positive about the names of things. When our Russian handlers are asked a specific question, an answer is always given. But it seems that no two people give the same answer. I haven't decided if this is because they don't know the answer and don't want to appear dumb, or if it's some innate security quirk.

Our last stop was the Novodevichy Convent. This is where Peter the Great's first wife and his troublesome sister, Sophia, were sent when they became too annoying. I guess it's good to be Czar.

In this Convent's Smolensky Cathedral Boris Godunov was elected Czar in 1589.

A crenellated wall with twelve battle towers enclosed the Convent and Cathedral. Besides being a Convent for ladies of noble birth it was also a major stronghold on the road from Moscow to Smolensk and Lithuania.

The Cathedral was about the only place where Intourist turned us loose—for twenty minutes—the guides didn't go in, and we soon discovered why.

Smolensky Cathedral, dedicated to "Our Lady of Smolensk," lies within the walls of the Novodevichy Convent. It is a state museum, and is also one of the few 'working churches' in Russia. So, priests and parishioners have to put up with herds of tourists. We barged in, not realizing that it was still a church or that Mass was in progress. Good timing, what? With horror and rising anger, I realized that the Russian state was using us to hassle the religious—and that the short time limit that we had been given would insure a second disruption when we left.

We went back to the Cosmos for lunch and after we ate, we were bused to the Economic Achievement Exhibition, even though it was just across the Prospect Mira from the Cosmos Hotel. I could see it from my hotel window.

The 550 plus acres of the Exhibition contained sixty pavilions arranged around a broad, central avenue. Each pavilion was in a different Soviet style, and dedicated to some facet of Soviet life—agriculture, industry, science, etc. As most of the exhibits were not due to open until May first, we saw mostly work crews putting up facades.

The Memorial Museum of Space was open. There were mock-ups of all kinds of space vehicles with wall charts to tell you what it was, where it went and what it did. The "NASA control panel" looked rather primitive. There were two "Hall of Fame" astronaut (cosmonaut) photo boards and the dog, Laika (?), was stuffed and sat in a mock-up of his little compartment.

Two exhibits amused us; one was a wheeled contraption, I assumed that it was supposed to be a lunar rover, that looked like a flying bathtub, and the other was a set of space long johns that were on a department store dummy and displayed in a glass case. They were made of a strange looking waffled fabric with string ties and had an array of hoses and strategic zippers.

We were allowed to walk through the park back to the hotel on our own. As the afternoon held mild sunshine, I stopped and sat down on a bench to jot down a few notes and observe the only "average citizens" who didn't seem afraid. On an opposite bench were an elderly lady and a small child. I don't know if the child was male or female because all the little ones that I saw were so bundled up in layers of sweaters, hats and snowsuits, they looked like rosy-cheeked cabbages. Anyway, the little one soon toddled over to see what I was up to. I had a roll of Lifesavers in my pocket, so I took one for myself, gave "grandma" a questioning look, received an affirmative nod, and gave the roll to the kid. I got a smile and what I hope was a garbled thank you.

I noticed that grandma's eyes had rested more than once on my retractable Paper Mate, so, when I got ready to leave, I stopped by her bench and gave her the pen. From her reaction you would have thought I was Santa Claus.

It was on this walk back to the hotel that I got to check out the little church that I saw from my window. Very sad.

Day 7, Friday, April 17.
Today was mostly walking, starting with a train and station hopping tour of the Metro. The Metro stations were beautiful. A ride only costs five kopeks, the same as any bus, train or trolley. Distance and transfers are unlimited so for five kopeks (a couple of pennies) you could spend the whole day riding and looking at stations. All were impressive and each had a different, graffiti-free décor.

The Metro may be pretty, but it is also a practical people mover. When rail lines cross, they cross on different levels and these levels are all connected by escalators. The escalators are FAST and swallow people and spew them out at tremendous speed. Getting on and off takes some fancy footwork.

Trains only stop for forty-five seconds, but if you miss one another train arrives every three or four minutes.

Lunch was at another Intourist hotel, about three blocks from Red Square. Marina and Svetlana announced that because the Kremlin and Red Square were still closed to tourists, a bus would take us to yet another museum—a Museum of Soviet Military Uniforms.

No! No! No!

Revolution was in the air. This was Russia, after all.

We knew that there was a big Berioska (foreign currency) Store on the OTHER end of Red Square and since this was our last chance to purchase souvenirs, we, with or without guides, were going *through*!

Svetlana took some of our group to the museum but the majority of us marched across Red Square, harried and chivvied along by a very nervous Marina every time we stopped to snap a photo.

On this, our last night, we were given a special dinner with wine and ice-cold vodka, which you were supposed to toss back neat. Then you quickly eat something to keep from keeling over when your tum thaws out the booze. After a few belts you forgot that the "steak" that you had just consumed whinnied instead of moo-ed and sat back to enjoy the floorshow.

A floorshow with dancing girls and costumed "Indian Maidens" who showed a lot of skin. How decadent can you get?

Day 8, Saturday, April 18.

And so, goodbye to Russia. We were all glad we went, for the glimpse, but happy to leave.

After a sad airplane meal of rubbery, hairy chicken we were back over Belgium. It looked very green and beautiful.

We could hardly wait to get a meal and a drink—a meal of fresh, green, crispy salad, and a drink, a glass of cold clear water.

Canoeing the Lesse
—Belgium—

*L*ive Oak, all of Live Oak, went on an "outing." For our Wednesday afternoon "sport" we were going canoeing. Of course, we took the whole day.

In a caravan of a couple of dozen cars, or more, we drove from SHAPE to the town of Dinant, Belgium which sits at the conjunction of the Lesse and Meuse Rivers, about fifteen miles from the French border.

Dinant is a town of some nine thousand people, founded in the sixth century. A fortress town with a stormy history because it sits astride the main north/south corridor through the Ardennes and the Meuse River valley. The citadel that once commanded the river is now a museum.

Once we arrived in Dinant we gathered at a lovely, old, three story, half-timbered riverside inn, parked our cars and boarded a bus for a half-hour, winding, hilly ride to point twenty-one kilometers up the Lesse River (let's see, twenty-four kilometers is fifteen miles, so roughly thirteen miles). This was our starting point for a twenty-mile canoe trip down the Lesse River.

Here we rented one or two-man "canoes" which were kind of a molded plastic cross between a canoe and a kayak. They were either kayos or canaks. I think real canoes would have been easier to handle. We also rented life jackets and a bucket with a water-tight lid for anything that you didn't want to get wet or lost, such as, car keys or lunch. And, we were off.

The river was high (we were told later that it was much higher than normal) and moving along at a pretty good clip so Faye and I decided to go together in a two-person rig. We soon got the hang of it and found that if we could stay out of the main channel, we would not be whisked along quite so fast. In fact, by staying along the banks we could plod along at a leisurely pace.

I was a beautiful day, warm and sunny and there was a lot to see as we drifted along. We started in the hills with woods on both sides of the river that at this point was only about twenty yards wide. As we went along the woods gave way to meadows and then pastures. We could see some cows but none seemed to be close to the river. There were probably fences that we couldn't see.

At one point there was a tree down in the water and to get around it we had to edge out into the main channel. It was a struggle to fight our way out of the current and get along with our drifting. Everyone else must have gone racing with the current because we were the only boat in sight.

However, there were some unexpectedly tricky

bits, most notably two barrages that spanned the whole river. The first was the most difficult and it was made harder because as we approached, we couldn't see over it so we didn't know how high the barrage was or what was on the other side.

The river was quite a bit wider at this point and there was a sort of chute on one side that most of our gang seemed to be taking so we lined up for that. That turned out to be a good choice because as we found out the barrage was about ten feet high. The chute was like a kid's slide going into a swimming pool. The water at the bottom was rolling and swirling into unpredictable eddies but we didn't have time to think about it as we shot down the chute. The plan, I guess, was to go down the chute and when you hit the churning water at the bottom go straight through to the smoother water away from the barrage.

Not as easy as it sounds.

Down the chute we went and for a moment I thought we were going to make it, but then a back current smacked us on the side and over we went.

Once we were a few yards from the barrage the water was not very swift and only about waist deep so all you can get damaged is your dignity. There were a couple of convenient sandbanks where we could beach to tip the water from our craft and share pitiful excuses as to why we dumped with other hapless folk.

Fortunately for our dignity we were not alone on the riverbank dumping water out of our canoe. It looked to be about 50/50, half made it and half didn't.

The second barrage was just a little way past the first. This one was only a couple of feet high and with the river as high as it was, we just kind of flopped over it.

Once we got going again, we found that a little

further down the river the Live Oak NCO's had organized a bar-b-que on the riverbank so we all pulled in and dried out in the sun while we had a burger and a beer. Very nice.

After a pleasant lunch on the riverbank we climbed back into our sturdy craft and proceeded on down the river. As we got closer to the junction of the Lesse with the Meuse, the Lesse slowed down and spread out creating a multitude of small islands and sand bars. There were ducks and other waterfowl all around us and we just kind of drifted along letting the current take us where it would.

Eventually we reached the end, joined the Meuse River and turned right for just a few yards to the Dinant Inn where we had left our cars.

We had been told to bring a change of clothes as there were changing rooms and hot showers in the inn's cellar. Feeling much perkier and less bedraggled after a hot shower and wearing dry clothes we repaired to a terrace table overlooking the Meuse for a glass of beer and to watch the rest of the troops paddle in.

The consensus was that, although we were a bit sore, the outing had been "a blast."

Poce sur Cisse
—France—

From Faye's Journal:

Early on a July morning I started driving south toward Chateau Poce, France for my week-long painting holiday. I had been told by the Frenchmen in our art group that it was only a four or five-hour drive but I figured that that was by French standards. I was right, it took me six.

The only difficult part of the trip was finding my way through Paris to the Perifique Sud. After going around in circles for a while, I was lucky enough to spot two gendarmes. So, I parked, illegally, at a taxi stand and waited for the police. As they approached, I hauled out my maps and put on my most winning smile. What could they do? The poor lads could only respond with Gallic courtesy and send me on my way, on the right road.

Paris is not only the center of France, it is also the divider of France. South of the city, the weather gets better and warmer. The green fields of root crops that we see up where we live just over the border in Belgium give way to the gold of wheat and sunflowers. There is also sunshine.

The village of Poce sur Cisse (po-say-sur-cease) is about five miles from the town of Amboise sur Loire and is nestled in one of the many little valleys that cut through the limestone hills spawning streams that join the Loire River.

The Chateau Poce is adjacent to the village. The Chateau's large wrought iron gates are flanked by cottages of warm, yellowed stone. From the gate, the drive up to the main building passes through a small park. The drive then swings around a circular flower bed, and ends on a flagstone terrace.

Off to the right as I drove up, I could see the old stable buildings and a mill that was built over the River Cisse.

The cream and rose turreted Chateau backs and snuggles into a limestone bluff with a commanding view out over the park in front and to the left looks down over terraced rose gardens, wide lawns planted with venerable trees collected from around the world and over the River Cisse. The river is partially blocked at this point by a weir to create a small lake and water garden. A beautiful setting.

The limestone bluff is also studded with hand-hewn caves that are used for garages, growing mushrooms and for the making and storing of wine. This is France, after all.

The common rooms in the chateau were huge, loaded with antique furniture and the walls were covered with very large portraits of what I assumed were past residents. The bedrooms were more of the same, bathroom down the hall. Our studio was in a salon on the first floor looking out over the park.

We went to work.

We rose daily at seven and breakfasted at eight on croissants, jam and coffee.

From nine to twelve-thirty we painted or sketched either in the park in front of the Chateau, out on location in good weather, or in the salon when it stormed. When we were out on location, we painted in the neighboring village of St. Ouen les Vignes (san-twan-lay-veen-ya) or we drove a little way down the valley to the town of Amboise which is on the much larger Loire River.

We also visited local wine caves and Castle Amboise which, I was told, was Leonardo da Vinci's last home.

Luncheon and dinner were taken at a restaurant called Le Voyageurs which was in St. Ouen les Vignes.

The afternoon painting sessions were from two-thirty to six. We were off to dinner about seven and we seldom returned to the Chateau until nine-thirty or ten.

The French weather was a challenge, stormy, with sunny breaks. More than once the weather for a morning or afternoon painting session would seem fair and we would lug easel, chair, canvas, paints, etc. out to a chosen spot, get set up only to be chased by thunder and splattering rain back into the Chateau.

Of course, after changing into dry clothes and getting all set up again indoors in the salon the sun would come out.

I decided that painting from nature was good

exercise but not very productive. In my opinion the best option was to use the sunshine for sketching. You only needed to take a few pencils, a sketchpad and an umbrella.

One afternoon we had a real storm. We were in the park in front of the Chateau when we noticed black clouds boiling over the top of the bluff. We beat a hasty retreat indoors as the tops of the large Cedar of Lebanon trees in the park started agitating like they were stuck in a washing machine.

Then it started raining, a heavy rain full of wind driven leaves. For nearly an hour the leaves whirled and swirled and filled every exposed exterior nook and cranny of the Chateau. As I watched the leaves blow around, I was reminded of the time when I was a young girl and was fascinated, sitting at a wintery window, watching blowing snowflakes and trying to follow just one from sky to ground.

That evening when we went to dinner at Le Voyageurs, we saw many tree limbs, and even whole trees, blown down and in one area it looked like a trail or path had been cut through the woods. The downed trees looked as though they had been twisted off, as you might wring a handful of broom straw. Rather awesome, and we surmised that our "gale" might have spawned a little tornado.

The week sped by and I learned that professional painting is hard work, especially on location. For me, the greatest benefit of my painting holiday was the companionship and fresh ideas that came from a group of people whose only common denominator was a love of painting. So often we spend all our painting hours alone.

I came home exhausted, but with renewed enthusiasm for my paint box.

Going in Style
—France—

From Faye's Journal:

We just got back from Paris where we had been a part of the planning staff's official visit to the French Ministry of Defense. Or, Visite d'état Major Live Oak.

Just like Americans, all the nationalities involved in Live Oak are jealous of their independence, so the joint plans that Live Oak comes up with have to be cleared through each country's diplomatic and defense agencies. It's not as though there are going to be any objections, these trips are strictly for show and seeing as each host delegation wants to put its best foot forward, spaces on these visits are highly sought after. Especially by the ladies, because while the guys are "working" there is always a separate program for the ladies.

All of the official visits are arranged by the host nation involved, in this case, France, including how many people from each national delegation can attend, and the guest list starts at the top. With all the Generals and Colonels at Live Oak we are pretty far down on the pecking order and we were only invited on this trip because our senior Air Force Colonel and his wife had to cancel (an electrical problem in their rented chateau and they feared that their house might burn down) and another Colonel declined. (His wife said that she couldn't possibly pack in one day.)

Ha! Give me a shot at one of these trips and I can pack in five minutes.

So, early on a Wednesday morning we were off. It's only a couple hours drive to Paris so we arrived well before noon and left our car at a French Army compound in the city center.

At noon we checked into the Hotel Tourville and had a bite of lunch. The hotel was arranged by the French and it was all right, the rooms were on the small side but each had its own bath. The most exciting part of the Tourville was the elevator. The elevator was a one-person job (two if you were really friendly) so it took a while to shuttle all the people and their bags up to the rooms.

At quarter to two the guys left for a visit to the French Army Museum, "Musee de l'Armee," and Napoleon's tomb. I thought that Napoleon was planted in the cold, cold ground out on an island in the South Atlantic. Apparently, he was but the French had him dug up and brought back to France.

At two, we ladies were taken on a shopping trip that was hosted by the Live Oak French delegations' wives who acted as guides. That was great fun.

By five we were all, guys and gals, back at the hotel and getting ready for a seven o'clock cocktail party that was hosted by a French Navy Vice Admiral who, if I understood correctly, was Major General des Armies. We were bussed to and from the cocktail party which, in my opinion, was a pretty stuffy affair.

The rest of the evening was free so we just strolled the streets around the hotel stopping here and there for a glass of wine and to people watch.

This was just a warm up exercise for the schedule to follow.

The next morning the guys left at nine-thirty for a day of briefings, working meetings, etc. I like the French and English, they start work at a decent hour of the morning, not at the crack of dawn like some countries I could name.

The ladies also left the hotel at nine-thirty for a tour of the workshops and museum of Hermes. I liked this place. Hermes started life as luxury harness makers to the high and mighty and they still do a lot of leather goods. One group that I saw while we were on the tour was working on luggage and travel cases embossed with the Royal Saudi coat of arms.

The Hermes museum was all antiques, and about horses. Fabulous.

Hermes is the kind of place where the doorman probably wouldn't have let me in had I not been with an authorized group. It is also a place where most of us couldn't afford to shop. For parting gifts, they gave us each a catalog and a bottle of perfume. The catalog is not going to do me much good.

At 1 PM we had lunch at Bofingers Brasserie, which I guess is quite famous, it looked posh, and after lunch we were taken on a tour of the Paris Opera House, the "Opera des Paris." Located on the Place de l'Opera. It took fourteen years to build (1861-75), seats 1979 people and is arguably the most famous opera house in the world. What an opulent place with very elaborate multi-colored friezes, columns and lavish statuary - Baroque but elegant.

As we approached, we had a quick look at the main façade that is on the southside of the building overlooking the Place de l'Opera. The façade has a row of Greek statues along the top and ground to roof columns in front with giant size busts of the major composers in-between.

This place was built when seeing the show was not as important as being seen. It was the setting for the original *The Phantom of the Opera*.

Inside we zoomed around through all kinds of "gee-whiz" stuff and then I had a "moment."

We were taken into a smaller room that had ballet practice bars and mirrors lining the walls.

Instant déjà vu.

I'm thinking, "I know this room. Impossible, as I've never been here before; but I've seen this room somewhere."

Just then the guide said that this room was where the dancers would come after a performance to chat with their admirers and meet gentleman friends.

Then he said, "Over in this corner is where Degas would sit and sketch."

Bingo! I had been here with Degas in his paintings.

At five we were all back at the hotel to get ready for dinner which this evening was the Bateau Mouche dinner trip on the River Seine through Paris. This was a cruise on the Seine in a glass topped tour boat. As we cruised along, we were served a huge dinner that included lobster, steak and lots of wine. Quite an experience.

The dinner trip started just at dusk and as we cruised along it was fascinating watching the city turn from day to night and become "the City of Light."

We shared our dining and cruising experience with large group of Japanese tourists. We were mostly incomprehensible to each other but we had a great time trying, with the required waving of arms, and of course, toasts, lots of toasts.

The next day the guys were off for another day of meetings and briefings with some really high muck-a-mucks that, I think Vern said, included the Chief of the French Air Force and the Director, European Sector, Ministry of Foreign Affairs.

At nine-thirty the ladies were bussed to the outskirts of Paris to Compiegne for coffee at the home of a former French Live Oak Deputy Chief of Staff. After coffee we had a tour of the Chateau Compiegne. You and I would probably consider Chateau Compiegne a palace but the next day we toured Versailles and by that standard this little hunting chateau was "roughing it."

We had luncheon at the Chateau and after lunch we went back into Paris for a private tour of the Yves Saint Laurent factory—the one that makes cosmetics and perfume. At the end of the tour they gave each of us a travel case with skin care products and a sampler box of four perfumes. Very nice.

Somewhere along the way we got behind time and the rush hour traffic in Paris didn't help. We finally got back to the hotel at quarter to seven and we were scheduled to leave at seven for a dinner party.

The bus was there and the guys were all there, ready to go. Now, you can make trains go three hundred miles an hour and you can put boots on the moon but there is no way in heaven or on earth you can get two dozen women ready for a dinner party in fifteen minutes.

We were late.

The next day was Saturday and the official visit was officially over but we all decided we would go to Versailles before we headed home.

What can I say? I have never seen such magnificent splendor. And what a tragedy that anyone could, or would, create a Versailles while their people lived in squalor and died of starvation. But Versailles is glorious and deserves many visits.

I was overwhelmed by room after room of gee-whiz stuff but I was particularly struck by the Hall of Mirrors, I guess everyone is. The room is 230 feet long and was empty when we were there. I was told that among other items that can go into the room is a silver throne. The hall looks out onto the gardens and the seventeen huge mirrors that line the interior wall are designed to reflect the gardens as seen through the windows.

The ceiling was completely covered with huge paintings, thirty scenes of the life and times of Louis XIV.

I could have spent all day in the queen's apartments, the Petit Apartment de la Reine, a suite of rooms that have been restored to the condition that they were in when Marie Antoinette occupied them in 1789. The rooms are furnished in Louis XVI style with some earlier pieces. I was told that some pieces like the fireplace mantel, a center table and the mantel clock were Rococo.

What I remember most vividly was a simple story:

It seems that one of the many Louis', when a

young child, became angry when he was told that he had to finish his lessons before he could go riding. Taking his pen-knife Louis scratched his name on the table top. The gouges are there to be seen, but the tale as to how they got there was considered fiction until about fifteen years ago when someone found among Louis's mother's private papers a sheet of childish writing that said; "I must not write on tables. I must not write on tables."—fifty times.

Young Louis's "punishment lines" are now on view atop the scratched table.

We had lunch in Versailles at the Garrison Officers Mess, then disbanded to make our separate ways back to Belgium.

The whole trip was "laid-on" and we were treated like royalty everywhere we went.

Definitely an experience.

\

Paderborn
—West Germany—

The girls were home on vacation for the summer, Susan from college and Sandi from high school, and we decided that a holiday was in order. After kicking around a few choices we settled on Berlin. I thought that rather than drive or fly I would see if I could arrange us passage on the "British Duty Train" (more on that later). I also suggested that rather than try to get to Berlin all in one day we could stop about halfway at the city of Paderborn in West Germany for a night.

It took a little while, but eventually all the permissions to travel to Berlin were obtained and all the reservations were made. I really lucked out. Not only did I get us on the Duty Train but I also got a couple of rooms in the USAF Officer's Transit Quarters at Tempelhof Airport in Berlin so we didn't have to spend mega-bucks (marks) at a downtown hotel.

Bright and early on a Saturday morning we were off. It was about a five-hour drive to Paderborn and we took our time along the way. We got to Paderborn a little after noon and checked into the Hotel Hellmann. Actually, the hotel was in a suburb of Paderborn called Schloss Neuhaus. The Hellmann had been recommended by the Germans in Live Oak and it was a modern looking building that was nestled amongst a maze of half-timbered, wattle and daub dwellings that dated back to the late seventeenth century.

After checking into the hotel, we went into downtown Paderborn which is an old walled city dating back to Roman times. I read that the city was upgraded in the eighth century when Charlemagne built a castle near the Pader Springs.

Shortly after that, in 799, Pope Leo II was bounced out of the Popeship, fled his enemies and somehow made it to Paderborn. There he met Charlemagne and they cut a deal. Charlemagne restored Leo as Pope and Leo crowned Charlemagne as Holy Roman Emperor. Such a deal.

The city center is now a walking mall with narrow cobbled lanes holding together the carpentry of centuries - old, restored and modern. Typical tourists, we bought hot, sweet waffles dusted with powdered sugar from a street vendor and walked the streets doing a lot of rubber-necking.

Of course, we visited the Dom (Cathedral) zu Paderborn. I must admit, it was pretty impressive. The present structure mostly dates from the thirteenth century with restorations that were made after World War II. There must have been a lot of restoration because as far as I know Paderborn was pretty much flattened during the war.

As near as I could make out from the really lousy information booklet that was available, the present Dom is the fifth or sixth church to stand on the site. The first was built by Charlemagne in 777. Some of the others burned down and one was torn down by a bishop who wanted to build something bigger and better.

One of the most eye-catching, and really ugly, things inside the church was a huge Baroque memorial. It was made mostly of black stone, a big black lump that reached almost to the roof, with statues and allegorical carvings done in different colors all over it.

This monstrosity was dedicated to the memory of Bishop Dietrich von Furstenberg, who was also responsible for building the church next to our hotel in Schloss Neuhaus. Faye said that maybe we shouldn't think of it as just a massive monument to a man's vanity. The folks of the time probably thought it mighty, beautiful and fitting. No accounting for taste.

What I did think was beautiful were the wrought-iron gates that sealed off the western choir and side chapels. These gates were huge and were covered with Biblical scenes: The Garden of Eden, The Last Supper, etc. and were all done in perspective. I've never seen their like and would have taken photos but I noticed that other visitors were telling beads, lighting candles and visiting the confessionals. I'm sure that flash-bulbs wouldn't have been appreciated.

During dinner back at the Hotel Hellmann, we noticed a group of young adults at the bar enjoying a convivial mug. Another fellow came in and the whole group downed glasses, filed into a back room and closed the door. Just as we were wondering if this was a meeting of the local terrorist group there came a sound from the back; rumble, rumble, crash. In shocked surprise we all exclaimed, "They've got a bowling alley back there!"

They sure did. One alley, with funny shaped pins. They were shorter and wider than regular pins but they were not candle pins. Hard to describe. The alley was very narrow, only about twenty-five or thirty feet long and opened like a "Y" about ten feet before the pins. The lane was cambered so the melon-sized ball, without finger holes, made unexpected curves. The alley had an automatic pinsetter too. The pins had strings attached to the top and it was amusing to watch them dangle and dance like puppets as they re-set.

I bought a round for the players and we laughed and cheered until they were finished and then we tried our hand. Our scores weren't very high but it was great fun.

The Hotel Hellmann is also hard by the church—Furstenberg's revenge. We stayed Saturday night and early Sunday morning we were awakened by a cacophony of bells. What a racket. We quickly noticed that the Germans didn't ring changes that float out musically over the countryside like they do in England. The German Catholics made up for musicality with industrious enthusiasm. Aren't bells supposed to be a joyful noise? The bells of Schloss Neuhaus will certainly get God's attention even if they risk offending his ear.

After breakfast we drove the last hundred miles to the Inner German Border (the border between West Germany and East Germany) at Helmstad, left our car with the British, turned over all our travel documents, were driven to the train station and assigned a compartment on the British Duty Train.

We were off to Berlin.

Berlin II
—East Germany—

*T*he British Duty Train through East Germany—where to begin? At the beginning, I guess.

As I mentioned earlier, at the end of World War II, Germany was occupied by the four victorious allied nations: The United States, The United Kingdom, France and The USSR (Russia). Berlin was also to be occupied by the four powers; however, Berlin is very inconveniently located a hundred miles inside the Soviet Zone. Many problems arose over what access the Allies would have to their garrisons in Berlin and exactly how Western personnel and supplies would move through the Soviet Zone to Berlin. Over the years this boiled down to the three Berlin Air Corridors, and one road and one rail line from the Inner German Border at Helmstedt, West Germany to Berlin.

Airplanes and cars can pretty much go as they please without running into something, but rather nasty things can happen if trains aren't carefully regulated, so specific times were assigned for the allied trains to travel on the East German rail lines. The allies call their trains 'Duty Trains.'

I'm not familiar with the American or French Duty Trains; I never rode on them. I was told that the American train had bare-bones coaches, boarded-up windows (God forbid that we should catch a glimpse of the Godless commies), box lunches and travelled at night.

The British, on the other hand, have much more experience in the realm of international relations and see no reason to miss tea or otherwise make themselves uncomfortable if it is not absolutely necessary.

I agree, you don't have to practice bleeding.

When dealing with the lesser peoples of the world (which, to the British, is everyone who is not British) the Brits do it with style—with panache.

The British Duty Train traveled from and back to Berlin every day of the year except Christmas and it traveled during daylight hours. The train had British Rail first-class coaches and a superb dining car. It even had a name—The Berliner.

It even had its own wine label.

On the Berliner you could enjoy an excellent meal and a glass of wine while rolling through the East German countryside looking out the window at the comrades.

The Berliner left Berlin every morning at eight and arrived at Helmstedt on the Inner German Border about noon. Then it went on into West Germany for another ten miles to the town of Braunschweig where it spent the afternoon, returning to Berlin at 4PM.

We boarded at Helmstedt where the West German engine was changed for an East German locomotive.

At the next station, Marienborn, which was just inside East Germany, the British Train Commander, a British Army Captain, the Train Conducting Warrant Officer, Royal Corps of Transport, and an Interpreter marched up the station platform carrying a briefcase that contained the travel documents of everyone one the train. They halted in front of the Russian delegation, salutes were exchanged and then they all went inside the station where the Russians checked all the passports and travel orders before allowing the train to proceed.

While this was going on, another group of East German soldiers checked all around the outside of the train (they are not allowed inside), the engine and undercarriages. I had no idea what they were looking for. I'd never heard of someone trying to sneak INTO a communist country.

Then we were on our way. From Marienborn the train passes through the town of Eilsenben to the city of Magdeburg. As we went through Magdeburg you could see the Cathedral with its twin spires and to the south a prison that was believed to hold political prisoners.

From Magdeburg the assigned route passes over the Elbe River and then to the Gusen area. In this area Soviet and East German tanks and armored vehicles can sometimes be seen on maneuvers. A little further on at Kirchmoser there is a large Soviet tank repair workshop.

The next large town was Brandenburg which claimed to have the oldest shunting hump in Germany and one of the oldest in the world.

Then on to the town of Werder which has an engine shed where the Kaiser's personal engine was once housed. From Werder the train crosses over the River Havel and enters Potsdam.

At Potsdam the engine is detached and searched, an East German Train Guard joins the train and the train enters the "Corridor" at Griebnitzsee. The train passes through "The Wall" and look out towers and posts with armed East German soldiers can be seen to the north and south.

So, after a pleasant four-hour ride through the East German countryside that was capped with a great meal, we arrived at Charlottenburg Station in the British Sector of West Berlin. We caught a ride over to the United States Air Force Transit Quarters at Tempelhof Air Base in the American Sector and tucked in for the night.

Located right smack in the middle of Berlin, the buildings (or building, I guess it's all one) of Tempelhof were a massive marvel. Unlike most airfields Tempelhof is round. The original building constructed in 1927 was built to handle zeppelins and was the first airport terminal in the world to have an underground railway. A reconstruction project that was started in 1934 replaced the old terminal and the current semi-circular building extends for more than a mile around the northern edge of the almost circular airfield. With its huge columns and facades of shell limestone the terminal building is a knockout and built to impress.

Tempelhof was a great central location to explore the city, starting right at our front door with the Berlin Airlift Memorial on Platz der Luftbrucke (airbridge). The memorial displays the names of the thirty-nine British and thirty-one American airmen who lost their lives during the Berlin Airlift.

Then we were off to the WALL. Not far, and we got the obligatory photos of the girls posing next to and leaning on the wall.

Our next stop, and again not far, was Checkpoint Charlie. We visited the museum that shows many of the escape attempts, both successful and unsuccessful.

There is a viewing platform at Checkpoint Charlie where you could look over the wall into East Berlin. What a contrast between West and East. West Berlin was a vibrant, pulsating, modern city while the East seemed gray, slow, plodding. I was reminded of the movie The Wizard of Oz, black and white on one side, technicolor on the other.

I did take the family on an organized military tour of East Berlin because it was the safest way for us to go. There were civilian tours but you never knew if someone was going to do something stupid.

On some of my trips to Berlin I had taken what we call 'Flag Tours' of East Berlin. A Flag Tour was just a drive around East Berlin in an American Military Staff Car—just to prove that we could.

If a trip to East Berlin didn't make you a grateful and patriotic citizen of the U S of A, nothing would. It had to be seen to be believed. The tour I took the girls on went mainly to the shopping area around Alexander Platz and the Brandenburg Gate. Alexander Platz and the main streets immediately around it looked posh and prosperous, but it was all a façade. A Potemkin Village. The store windows were full of merchandise and decorated, but inside the shelves were nearly bare.

In my drives around East Berlin I found that

once you get a couple of blocks behind, or away from, the tourist streets, all was drab and shabby.

I did buy an East German knockoff of Swiss Army Knife for a buck. (24 East marks, which was 4 West marks = 1 buck)

To think, East Berlin had the highest standard of living of any place behind the Iron Curtain—including Moscow.

The week flew by. We had no plan but went where our whims took us. One day we did the main shopping drag, the Kurfurstendamm and went to the huge KaDaWe department store.

What is it with ladies and shopping?

The female of the species must have an extra gene spliced into their DNA that says 'shop.' If a guy wants a new shirt, he goes to the store buys a shirt and goes home.

Ladies march to a different drummer.

If a lady wants an item of clothing, or nothing at all, it seems that she will visit every store within a twenty-mile radius and try on every item found therein. And, if the ladies are in groups of two or more the time consumed in this exercise can be multiplied by the square of the number of ladies involved.

My girls love me and knowing my love for shopping I was deposited at a very pleasant outdoor table in front of a friendly tavern with a cold beer in my hand while my girls disappeared down the Ku'damm.

But, there is always a but, my girls had an ulterior motive as every now and then one or the other of them would reappear and leave me a bag or package to guard.

I wonder how many shopkeeper's sons and daughters I sent to university that day. I could have opened my own shop right where I sat.

We visited the Kaiser Wilhelm Memorial Church which had been destroyed during WWII. The old bombed out church has been left as a memorial and a new steel and glass version has been built next to it.

Another day took us to Charlottenburg Palace and the Egyptizes Museum to see, among other things, a bust of Queen Nefertiti. The story is that this particular bust is the master bust that was in the sculptor's studio at Amarna from which all other busts of Queen Nefertiti were copied.

And that's a lot of busts.

Apparently when Tutankhamun abandoned Amarna the bust of Nefertiti and other models, no longer considered requisite, were left behind. I don't know how it ended up in Germany.

We saw the Brandenburg Gate from both sides (West Berlin and East Berlin) and we even went to the Zoo.

All to soon our week was gone and we were back on the Berliner, rolling through East Germany, enjoying an early lunch in the dining car, heading for West Germany, Belgium and home.

Going in Style
—West Germany—

From Faye's Journal:

Monday was mostly gray, punctuated by short, sharp showers and we were in Bonn, West Germany for the Live Oak official visit.

Our cars were parked in the German Ministry of Defense compound and a bus had transferred us into downtown Bonn to the Stern Hotel. The Stern occupies the northwestern side of the main Market Platz just two doors south of the Rathaus (town hall) which commands the north. The hotel's imposing façade, that once comprised dining rooms and a lobby, is now given over to shops and a restaurant, but upstairs the comfortable rooms and bathrooms are still of generous proportions.

In the center of the large, cobbled Market Platz

is the former public water supply which is now just a fountain. The fountain is a small cenotaph with four catch basins and the basins are decorated with gilded snakes. Today one tends to shudder at the thought of snakes but they have symbolized medicine and healing from time immemorial and their presence on the fountain proclaimed the water potable to our unlettered ancestors.

We found that every day was a market day and the lower half of the square was filled with stalls selling fruits and vegetables.

On pleasant days many restaurants and pubs (the Stern included) set up tables outside on the Platz. It was nice to sit outdoors in the evening, have a beer and watch the world go by.

Nearby there is the even larger Beethoven Platz which hosts the Munster Church and a large statue of Ludwig.

They call this area "Old Bonn" and it includes the Market Platz, Beethoven Platz, a small flower market and all the streets between and around. This makes a delightful, mostly cobbled, walking precinct. It must make a person feel very civilized to live within such a carefully maintained history and to be able to stroll, sup or just sit in such congenial surroundings.

We ladies lunched at a Bavarian style restaurant and following lunch we were taken on a bus tour of the city and then we had a private tour of Beethoven's birthplace, which is only a couple of blocks from the Stern Hotel.

The house stands, pale pink, shuttered in apple green and festooned with window boxes of trailing geraniums, off the street in a grassy courtyard. At one end of the garden there is a bronze statue of Beethoven that was made by one of Rodin's students.

The room where Ludwig was born is on the second floor and is reached by a narrow, winding, wooden staircase. The room was bare except for a marble bust set on a pedestal that raised the sculpture to Beethoven's adult height. It looked to be about five feet seven or eight to me.

A larger room next door contained personal mementos of Beethoven such as ear trumpets, a grand piano and a viola. There were also two casts of his face, one taken when he was forty-two and the other after his death.

In the small rooms downstairs, there were a few pieces of furniture, some original scores and the keyboard from the church pipe organ that Beethoven played when he was ten years old.

Tuesday, we went to the nearby diplomatic enclave of Bad Gotesberg and, after being treated to champagne and a private showing of a pearl exhibition, we hiked the two miles of wooded hilltops overlooking the Rhine River to the ruins of Rolandsbogen.

Here's the story:

According to legend, Roland was in love with the princess who lived across the river at Drachenfels. It seems that they spent a lot of time on opposing terraces sighing, waving and blowing kisses.

But Roland had to go off knight erranting, questing, slaying dragons and all that sort of stuff. To remind his lady love of himself and his faithfulness Roland built a large stone arch on his terrace for her to look at.

Time passed and Roland was still roving. The lady received reports of Roland's demise and in a fit of melancholia, and figuring that she was now likely to remain a spinster, took the veil and entered the cloistered community, which still exists, on the small island below Roland's castle.

Return the conquering hero. He learns that he now has to find a new girlfriend and puts on a truly immature, emotional display, knocking over most of his memorial arch, and throwing himself over the cliff.

We took a large tour boat back downriver to Bonn. It was a short ride, but very nice and in the evening, all spruced up, the entire Live Oak delegation walked next door to the Rathaus for a reception hosted by the Lord Mayor.

The Rathaus is a pleasant, Rococo building with a pink and gray façade, now ornamented with scaffolding and netting. Like much of Bonn, the Rathaus is getting new paint and gilding for next years' two thousandth anniversary.

There was great excitement early the next morning when some of the construction material around the Rathaus caught on fire. All sorts of excitement, noise, shouting, bells, fire engines and hullabaloo right in front of our hotel and Vern and I slept through the whole thing.

Wednesday dawned warm and sunny and the ladies made an early start to visit the cathedral in Cologne. What a gigantic edifice, its size is overwhelming. I can understand why it took them over six hundred years to get it finished.

Our tour guide was not all that fluent in English, but I think I got the story.

In 1164 Frederick Barbarossa returned from Milan with relics of the three Wise Men. Freddie gave these to the archbishop of Cologne who created a shrine in the existing church. Pilgrims flocked into town to see "The Shrine of the Magi" and by 1248 the church and the city fathers determined that a newer, bigger cathedral was needed.

Work got underway and they finished the chancel in the 1300's and were working on the towers by the mid 1400's. Then, for some reason, they seemed to say, "The heck with it," and nothing, or practically nothing was done for four hundred years.

Up until 1840 all the old paintings of the cathedral show a half-finished front with a wooden crane sticking out of the roof. It wasn't until the mid-1800's when Neo-Gothic fever swept the architectural world that Cologne finally finished building the church.

Outside, the apse is a multitude of pinnacles and turrets.

In the south transept doorway there are bronze doors with one side depicting Celestial Jerusalem and the other, Cologne in flames. The façade is Gothic, with stepped windows and slim, soaring gables and spires.

Cologne Cathedral is such a jaw-dropper that I found myself gawking in wonderment rather than concentrating on the guided commentary. I remember that in the north aisle there are five magnificent stained-glass windows from the fifteenth century showing the lives of the Virgin and Saint Peter. All of these windows were taken out and stored during World War II, and a good thing too, seeing as Cologne and the cathedral were hit hard during the war.

In the north transept there is a statue of the Virgin and Child from the 'Beautiful Madonna's' period, and in the south transept there is a large, Flemish polytych called the "Altarpiece of the Five Moors." Just off the ambulatory, hanging in a chapel, I saw a unique cross that I think could have dated back to the tenth century. The Magi's Shrine, which I would call a reliquary, is a glorious example of the goldsmith's art, even if you don't believe in old bones. The shrine stands in a glass case behind the high altar.

Next to the cathedral is the Roman-Germanic Museum. This very large, modern museum was constructed around a Roman floor, called the Dionysus Mosaic, which remains in situ, on the lower level.

Over the centuries many Roman artifacts have been discovered in and around Cologne: public monuments, tombs, villas, the port, the drainage system and a variety of art works. Today, all of these items, including private collections, are displayed in the museum and are grouped by theme. A whole day would not have been enough to absorb it all. Everything was interesting. The jewels and ornaments of gold and cloisonné are an archeological treasure, but the showcases of glassware, both precious and every day, really keep you leaving nose prints on the windows. Wow!

That evening we had tickets to the Laubenpieperfest (folk festival), hosted by the city-state of Berlin. Each of the West German states, and city-states, represented in the Bundestag host a festival sometime during the year and getting an invitation to one is something special.

The event turned out to be a block long, crowded, free carnival with several bands providing music and numerous stalls dispensing free food, beer and souvenirs. We munched our way from one end to the other, rubbing elbows, shoulders, hips and a great portion of the remaining anatomy with the crème de la crème of the political and diplomatic communities that are represented in Bonn, collecting beer stains, as well as steins, an umbrella, potholders and key chains.

When we'd had our fill, both figuratively and literally, we walked up the Adenaurallee and through the Hofgarten back to our hotel on the Market Platz and spent a pleasant hour sitting at a table outside, with a glass of Pils, watching the passing parade.

Thursday. After a morning at the Bundestag, talking to Members of Parliament and sitting in on a parliamentary session (all in German, of course, I didn't get much out of that) we lunched at a restaurant in Rheinaue Park, then joined the menfolk for a guided tour of Bonn's Munster Church that included an organ recital. The acoustics were good and the musical selections, ranging from baroque to modern, demonstrated the full range of the instrument.

The exterior of the Munster church is Romanesque and elegant, a typical trefoil plan with flying buttresses supporting the nave. Inside, the nave is transitional Gothic, but all the furnishings are Baroque. At the lower end of the nave there is a bronze statue of Saint Helen and, under the raised chancel, an eleventh century crypt. The best bit was a lovely Romanesque cloister on the south side of the church with arcades on three sides and a fountain in the center.

After the organ recital, we went by bus out into the countryside to the town of Altenhar in the Ahr River Valley for wine tasting and dinner.

Over the Ahrgebirge Hills we rolled, between fruitful fields and through villages with streets so narrow that everyone drew in their breath to help the bus squeeze through, until, lipping the crest, the road dropped down between slatey cliffs upon whose every cleft hung rows of Burgundian vines. Down and down, through the vineyards to the River Ahr. The Ahr River would be merely a good-sized trout stream in some parts of the world, but whatever its size, it is beautiful, path-lined, gliding and riffling through meadows and trees.

Because the Ahr Valley is more canyon than valley the grape vines are sheltered from the wind and kept from extreme cold by the warmth of the heat retaining rocks. Naturally, we stopped for a little wine tasting. The wine produced here has a deep rich red color, but it is thin and much too dry and tart for most palates, especially mine.

Some white wines are produced and they'll pucker your cheeks.

Somewhat fortified, in spite of the chilly, dank cellar where we did the wine tasting, we proceeded up the valley to the village of Altenhar for a specially prepared dinner.

Altenhar lies between two closed river bends and is overlooked by the ruins of the castle of Burg Are which is lighted at night. On one corner of the town's one intersection sits the Schaferkarre, a half-timbered, seventeenth century inn that was restored, not remodeled, in 1979. On one corner gable there is a glockenspiel that was played, just for us, as we approached. Nice touch.

Once inside, we were escorted up a spiral, wooden staircase to a large private dining room whose interior was all carved wood with an open beam ceiling. Hard to describe, but very medieval.

I might mention that the regular dinner menu consists of local foods that are prepared from recipes from "olden times," but that was not for us. What followed for our group was a gourmet treat of gourmand proportions that Vern and I rated Five Pointy Fingers, out of a possible five. FYI, that's very good.

Already reassured by ambiance and aroma, we tucked into a starter of creamy onion soup, served piping hot, with knobs of melting butter swimming on top.

When the first course had been cleared our host, Herr Schafer, presented the entrée, a whole haunch of pork that had been marinated in wine and spices for ten days, and roasted all afternoon over a slow fire. The pig was carried in on a spit by two cooks, despitted and carved.

Mercy! It was fantastic.

Accompanying the roast pork were dishes of potatoes, cut like cottage fries, but roasted in an oven and a creamed cabbage that was delicious.

Throughout the meal, like an old-fashioned bucket brigade, earthenware pitchers of Ahr wine flowed steadily along the table.

I cannot remember a more scrumptious meal.

Along about coffee time Vern excused himself to visit the toilet and when he returned he reported that it was one fancy facility with gold faucets and urinal rims decorated with flowers. Whether from need or curiosity, all of us soon found occasion for a trip.

I will describe the lady's room. The ceiling was painted pale green with white plasterwork and overhead there was a crystal chandelier. The white, tiled walls and the floor were randomly decorated with a stylized, red, crane bill flower motif. The ceramic frames around the mirrors and the washbasins and toilets were all edged with the same floral design. The taps and all other metal work were gold colored including the decorative paper holders in the booths. Pretty fancy.

Between the wine and the meal, I don't think

anyone was awake on our bus ride back to Bonn and the Stern Hotel.

Thus, endeth our official tour of Bonn. The next morning the bus took us back to the German Ministry of Defense parking lot and our cars. Home again.

Into the Sunset
—Belgium—

"And now the end is near and so I face the final curtain." So, the song goes, or something like that.

My four years at Live Oak, SHAPE, Belgium and my military career (such as it was) were drawing to a close. The retirement paperwork had been submitted and the administrative wheels were churning. Like everything else that is associated with a bureaucracy, I found that hoops must be jumped through, i's dotted and t's crossed before I could actually retire and this was made even more difficult because I was stationed overseas.

One thing that I needed before I could retire was a Retirement Physical. I must admit I never really understood why that was necessary. What would happen if I flunked? Would I have to stay on active duty if I was deemed not healthy enough to be a civilian?

Of course, I couldn't just utilize the excellent medical facilities that were right there on SHAPE to get this physical. No, it had to be done in an American military facility and the closest one was in Germany. So, on a bright and sunny spring day Faye, our youngest daughter, Sandi, and I headed for Ramstein Air Base for a few days.

Sandi was seventeen and a senior in the International High School at SHAPE. The high school years had been quite an experience for her. Her classmates were American, Italian, German, etc., just about all the NATO countries.

Among other things, the International High School had sports teams that competed with American Department of Defense high schools in Europe. It seemed to me that all the high schools were about the same size but for various reasons the teams that SHAPE fielded were so powerful that they just overwhelmed the opposition.

Imagine a high school soccer team full of Dutch, English, German and Italian players.

I remember having a chat with the football (American Football) coach and he told me that by halftime the score was usually so lopsided in SHAPE's favor that most of his seniors had never played in the second half of a ball game.

For a couple of years, I helped out by coaching the "B" squad of the girls' volleyball team. The school had a coach but she was overwhelmed by having about forty girls turn out to play. Sandi blew the whistle on me that I had played some volleyball and the coach asked me to help. Of course, I said "Sure."

We divided the team into A and B squads. She

took the first team, the seniors and juniors, the six footers and anyone that had any experience. That left me with the freshmen and sophomores, the midgets and all the girls who had never played before. Not a spiker in the bunch.

I figured that it would be a waste of time to teach this group of Munchkins power volleyball so we worked on ball handling and defense. We also didn't waste time on blocking. My midgets wouldn't have been able to block on a tennis court.

The first few games were pretty rough and we got plowed under pretty good but my girls were a determined bunch that practiced hard and learned. By the middle of the season they were holding their own and even winning games.

As the season drew to a close my little girls were driving other teams crazy. It seemed that no matter how many times they banged the ball over the net my Munchkins would dig it out and it would come floating back over the net to their side.

The girls had a great time and they always rubbed my bald head for luck before they went on the court.

Sandi and her classmates traveled all over Europe on cultural and history tours and when they graduated, they did it in style, in Saint Waudru's Cathedral in Mons, Belgium.

Back to my physical.

I got Faye and Sandi settled into the transit quarters at Ramstein and dutifully reported to the big Army Regional Hospital at Landsthul, Germany.

Yup! The same hospital where our oldest son, John, had been born thirty- three years earlier.

After many practitioners of the medical profession poked and prodded me for half a day, they decided that except for being overweight I wasn't in too bad shape for a guy in his fifties.

Ha! Overweight! Doctors, what do they know? The correct medical term is "under tall."

Seeing as we were in the neighborhood, we drove around the Sembach area (the Air Base was long gone) trying to remember all the places that we used to visit when we lived there all those many years ago.

Of course, we went to Otterberg. It was bigger but it really hadn't changed a lot. The cobble stone Hauptstrasse that the Tipsy Troubadours had wandered was still there but the store fronts were all modern. The church and monastery still looked the same.

We showed Sandi the house where we used to live and she said that it looked like a dump. Well, that might have been a little harsh, but admittedly it hadn't changed in over thirty years. Oma and Opa were long gone so we didn't stop in.

Back at Ramstein we wandered into the Officer's Club Gift Shop and Faye was quite taken with a Black Forest cuckoo clock that had been made in a secret forest glen by Gnomes. Anyway, she seemed to really like it and while I kept her busy at the bar, Sandi nipped around, bought it and stashed it away in the trunk of the car.

Faye wrote in her journal:

I had a lovely birthday. I was surprised with a cake at the bowling alley and Vern and Sandi gave me a Black Forest Cuckoo Clock that I had admired when we were in Germany. It plays the *Happy Wanderer* on the hour and *Edelweiss* on the half. I won't unpack it until we get back home to Gig Harbor.

426

Me again:

The packing and sorting were the usual; what to keep and take with us, what to throw away and what to put into the garage sale.

I shouldn't have said that.

In SHAPE housing you were NOT supposed to have garage sales. A couple of times a year SHAPE would allow everyone to bring all their stuff up to the Bon Marche shopping center parking lot for a big flea market.

In my opinion hauling stuff up to the parking lot was a pain in the lower regions. Just for the record, we DID NOT have a garage sale. Our garage was just open, was full of stuff and we put out the word that some of it was for sale.

I could have gotten big bucks for my gas-powered, American made, lawn mower but I gave it to my French Army buddy in Live Oak.

Faye wrote in her journal:

The Spring Art Exhibition is over and I sold ten of fifteen entries. Of the five unsold, one was not for sale, and another Vern likes, so I deliberately overpriced it. Now I have packed away my studio. That, more than anything, has brought the realization that this move, and its import, is truly upon us. I have just addressed over a hundred invitations to our retirement ceremony and now spare moments must be directed toward sorting and packing.

A glance at our engagement calendar only confirms the observation. We have been giving a series of dinner parties, mostly to say goodbye to old friends, but partly to repay past invitations. The menu and

427

format have settled into a routine. Vern barbeques, the steaks and veggies from the grill always winning acclaim.

Of course, a real outdoor barbeque—in Belgium—in the spring—would be a chancy affair, weather wise, so we hedge our bets. Vern opens the garage door and sets the grill up there, with chairs and beer and wine available for kibitzers.

We eat inside. European guests (we usually invite four couples) come prepared for any crazy American eventuality, and the expressions of amazement (or relief) when they see a fully laid out table are fun to watch. I think Vern has half convinced them that they will spend a cold evening, outside, squatting around a campfire.

On the morning of the dinner party, I put the steaks to marinate, bake two apple pies and while away the hours polishing the bronze ware and crystal, laying the table and checking the level in the port and sherry decanters.

Vern takes care of the steaks and prepares the veggies for grilling when he gets home.

About noon I go to the Bon Marche and buy fresh crevettes (une flute de pain) and my favorite truffled chocolates to serve with the coffee. Home again, I make the sauce for the shrimp cocktail first course, slice the flute of bread and pop it into a zip-lock bag for future reference (how did we manage before zip-locks?), mentally preview the evening to make doubly sure that all is ready, go take a long, leisurely bath and dress.

Voila! Nothing to do but keep the family from eating all the peanuts before the guests arrive and the fun begins.

Two weeks ago, the guest list included the

French General assigned to Live Oak who is the head of the French Delegation to the planning staff, and his wife. I had met them a couple of times, but I didn't know them very well.

My evil twin whispered in my ear and I deliberately served a CALIFORNIA wine with the steaks.

One uplifted nose and gimlet-eyed glance said it all, he was NOT going to like this.

One sip—surprise - another, and he said, "You know, this wine is very acceptable."

High praise.

The highlight of the evening came when the general was relating an escapade from his cadet days (he was quite a raconteur) that involved a cannon, and the seed was sown as the table talk turned to the imminent departure and retirement of our British General, a former artillery man and our Chief of Staff.

As Sherlock would say, "The game was afoot.

One week later, at the stroke of noon, as the Live Oak Chief of Staff prepared to leave his office, the base and the military for the last time, his transport arrived. The expected staff car had been replaced by a piece of wheeled field artillery, bearing a saddle for comfort and equipped with his golf bag and a pannier of provisions—cheese, bread, wine, etc.

Once he was properly mounted the men of Live Oak towed him through the gate with the rest of us lining the road and cheering him on. Once through the gate, he joined his wife in a limo for the remainder of their journey to the channel.

We shall miss them.

I do not think our departure will involve gun carriages, unless it be Napoleon style, that is at the barrel end—more likely tar and feathers, and rails.

Leaving is bittersweet. There have been so many farewells, I'm ready for a happy hello.

Me again:

From my perspective it was a very nice retirement ceremony, all our friends, co-workers and Faye's art buddies came and it was conducted by no less than the Chief of Staff of SHAPE, a four-star United States Air Force General.

He didn't know me from left field, but he knew Faye from the Arts League and all the work that she had done to support the Officers Wives Club. From his speech you would have thought that he and I had been buds forever.

When it came I my turn to reply I was struck dumb. It wasn't that I was uncomfortable speaking in front of large groups, after all I had been an instructor for five years. I had given hundreds of briefings both to the High and Mighty and to the Low and not so Mighty. I had been a guest speaker at banquets a few times and I had certainly given many a farewell speech when Faye and I had been posted from one base to another.

But this time it was different, there was no next posting, this was IT. I stood there looking out at my friends and co-workers and I was at loss for words.

The years started scrolling before my eyes. All the places that Faye and I had been, all the things that we had experienced. Of course, ninety-nine percent of those experiences would have no relevance to this audience. All that we had in common was the time we shared at Live Oak.

Military life is a series of snapshots. You share an experience with a group of people for period of time

430

and then you go off to share another, totally different, experience with another group.

But I thought about all those things; The Marines and Parris Island, school and meeting Faye, re-enlisting and getting married, singing Christmas Carols in a German village and snakes, Officers Candidate School, Vietnam and Thailand, The Royal Air Force Exchange Tour, dining at Westminster and Korea, West Raynham and Lakenheath, Egypt and the High-Tech Test Bed, and finally Live Oak.

It was all a kaleidoscope in my mind.

No, I couldn't tell them all that so I kept it short and sweet with the standard "thanks it's been good to know ya" speech and sat down.

So, after being a Navy Brat and then wearing Uncle Sam's suit for thirty-five years, five months and five days, that's what my DD-214 (service record) said, it was over.

The General pinned a medal on me, patted me on the head and sent us on our way.

As usual, I was without a plan. I was now retired, a civilian, and all I knew was that I was facing two big questions:

What was I going to do?

What was I going to wear?

www.ingramcontent.com/pod-product-compliance
Lightning Source LLC
Chambersburg PA
CBHW071700120626
46550CB00001B/53